Restructuring Higher Education

Restructuring Higher Education

What Works and What Doesn't in Reorganizing Governing Systems

Terrence J. MacTaggart

and Associates

with Cynthia L. Crist

Jossey-Bass Publishers • San Francisco

Substantial discounts on bulk quantities of Jossey-Bass books are available to corporations, professional associations, and other organizations. For details and discount information, contact the special sales department at Jossey-Bass Inc., Publishers (415) 433–1740; Fax (800) 605–2665.

For sales outside the United States, please contact your local Simon & Schuster International office.

 Manufactured in the United States of America on Lyons Falls Pathfinder Tradebook. This paper is acid-free and 100 percent totally chlorine-free.

Library of Congress Cataloging-in-Publication Data

MacTaggart, Terrence J., date.
    Restructuring higher education : what works and what doesn't in reorganizing governing systems / Terrence J. MacTaggart and associates. — 1st ed.
       p. cm. — (The Jossey-Bass higher and adult education series)
    Includes bibliographical references and index.
    ISBN 0–7879–0193–8
    1. Public universities and colleges—United States—Administration—Case studies. 2. Higher education and state—United States—Case studies. 3. Educational change—United States—Case studies. I. Title. II. Series.
LB2341.M254   1996
378.1′07′0973—dc20
                                  95–40654

FIRST EDITION
HB Printing   10 9 8 7 6 5 4 3 2 1

The Jossey-Bass
Higher and Adult Education Series

Contents

Preface

This book is about changing the way public higher education is governed, why and how these changes come about, and their consequences. *Governance restructuring, reorganization,* or simply *restructuring*—these terms are used interchangeably in this volume—refers to shifts in authority among the various individuals, agencies, administrations, and boards that collectively oversee the way public, and sometimes private, higher education is led, funded, and managed.

The book focuses on restructuring in five states: North Dakota, Massachusetts, Alaska, Minnesota, and Maryland. Its purpose is not to record the bare history of complex organizational change in these states but to wrench from these stories lessons that can be applied by people responsible for leading change in other parts of the country. Each author was asked to grapple with questions covering three aspects of restructuring: the context and background leading to restructuring, the change process itself, and its outcomes.

We felt that readers needed to know the answers to questions like these: What combination of political, economic, and social events underpinned the change? By what processes was the change brought about, and how did the change process influence the results? Is the higher education enterprise better or worse off as a result of the change? Will the public be better served under the new order of things? Is the new structure stable, or does more dislocation loom in the near future?

The answers to these questions are important to all Americans. If the power and prosperity of nations rest—as Robert Reich (1992), Lester Thurow (1992), Peter Drucker (1994), and so many others argue—on the intellectual capacities of its citizens, the way our country manages the development of its collective intellectual resources is of the first priority. Much of the task of enhancing the nation's intellectual capital falls to the public colleges, universities, and systems. If they are well led and managed, if the taxpayers have faith in their value and are willing to support them, if the combination of tuition and financial aid is sufficient to allow very large numbers of students to profit from them, our collective future may be bright. If changing the structure by which public higher education achieves its goals results in improvements—say, lower costs or still greater responsiveness to societal need or more harmonious and effective interactions among interests within higher education—the future may be brighter still. But if these changes suffer from inept leadership, a desire to reposition rather than improve, or thoughtless or merely politically expedient solutions, the result will be reduced effectiveness and diminished public confidence, and our society will be worse off.

Audience

Though it is no exaggeration to say that the issues described in the book will affect the quality of life of all Americans, professionals in higher education and state government will find it especially pertinent. Administrators, board members, faculty involved in governance and collective bargaining, legislators, legislative and executive staffs, public policy analysts, and students of higher education and of change in public organizations will find some helpful and some disturbing ideas in this book.

Professionals and interested citizens across the country will find this material relevant because few states are exempt from serious discussion of governance restructuring. There are now proposals to eliminate the New York Board of Regents, a body with over two hundred years of governing experience. The governor of New Jersey, Christine Todd Whitman, has gained national acclaim for her bold efforts to reinvent government in the Garden State, including the elimination of the once powerful Board of Higher Education. The governor in Illinois has proposed eliminating several of that state's governing boards, replacing them with local campus boards and increasing the power of the coordinating board. In 1990, Nebraska voters amended the state's constitution to give far greater authority to a coordinating commission. Montana, facing unusually severe reductions in state tax revenue, combined four baccalaureate institutions and five technical colleges under its two comprehensive universities. The appetite for reinvention and downsizing by the new majority in Congress and in many state legislatures promises still more organizational change in higher education across the nation.

Organization of the Book

This book is divided into three parts: Context for Change, Five Case Studies, and Lessons of Restructuring. In the first chapter, I argue that the failure of higher education to reform itself in a highly visible way has opened the door to further state intrusion in the form of governance restructuring. I acknowledge that the public sometimes holds contradictory expectations, such as generous admissions policies and high retention rates. It is also true that some legislators prefer sound bites to constructive dialogue. Still, the failure of higher education to address some of its most visible problems—such as the quality of undergraduate and teacher education, the rising cost of attendance, and stagnant productivity—makes it more likely that governors and state legislatures will change the way higher education is governed in order to secure the reforms they desire.

Richard Novak, in Chapter Two, summarizes the historical trend toward consolidation and centralization from the 1950s onward, then analyzes the advantages and disadvantages of that movement. Reduced public confidence in higher education, fiscal problems, and a fascination with reinventing government, he argues, drive restructuring. Change is the order of the day, but the direction of change is unclear. Efforts to centralize authority in an executive office or a new board are juxtaposed across the country with initiatives to restore as much power as possible to the campus. Novak concludes with thoughtful alternatives to restructuring, including systematic ways to develop governing boards.

Part Two documents the restructuring as it occurred in each of the five states: two in the Midwest (North Dakota and Minnesota), one in the Far North (Alaska), and two on the eastern seaboard (Massachusetts and Maryland). Their experiences offer considerable variation. For example, the faculties in Minnesota and Massachusetts are unionized. In Alaska, faculty at the community college, but not the university, work under collective bargaining agreements, an incongruity that greatly exacerbated restructuring in that state.

Each of the restructured systems includes a range of institutions. The research universities in Fairbanks, College Park, and Grand Forks find themselves in the same system as four-year comprehensives and, in the case of North Dakota and Alaska, with two-year colleges as well. They vary dramatically in size. Minnesota's new system will rival the State University of New York (SUNY) in the number of institutions with sixty-four, although institutional consolidations may in the future reduce that number to perhaps thirty-four. The merger of the University of Maryland system with the state colleges collected some eleven institutions under one board. By contrast, Alaska hosts a small system of three universities, albeit each with several additional campuses under its wing. It has a full-time-equivalent enrollment of about fifteen thousand. North Dakota, a state with a declining population of approximately six hundred thousand, supports eleven institutions with a total system enrollment of about thirty-five thousand.

The cases studies begin with North Dakota because restructuring in this small Great Plains state has been a success in many ways. It illustrates the advantages of a concentration of authority with a participatory approach to decision making. In their unpretentious way, the Regents of North Dakota and the chancellor's staff have used their new authority to implement a serious reform agenda. Costs have been reduced by combining administrations of two small campuses. Functions that have been administered centrally in some states are outplaced to the college or university best suited to offering them. The principles of total quality management have provided the credo for much of the change. The relative success of North Dakota derives in large part from its purposeful, highly participatory approach.

"All politics is local," a phrase favored by Tip O'Neill, helps explain why Massachusetts continues to struggle toward stability after two major governance changes. The presidential ambitions of Michael Dukakis, the politicization of the board, conflict between the governor and the legislature, and the habit too common among higher education officials of leaving when the going got tough contributed to an ineffective and unstable governance system. This chronicle of statewide organizational change in 1980 and again a decade later points out the need for responsible leadership from the campus to the statehouse if such change is to have worthwhile results.

The case of Alaska, where restructuring has become a way of life, reminds us that massive organizational change courts disaster just as it promises reform. The latest of several restructurings was conceived in the midst of an economic collapse triggered by a sharp decline in the price of North Slope crude oil. The story of restructuring in Alaska reads like a study of how *not* to induce successful change. Lack of vision, poor communication, and a naive disregard for the power and enforceable rights of labor unions resulted in a system that remains unstable. Although certain important groups (students of traditional age, for example) probably benefited in some ways from the change and some money was saved, at least temporarily, the system remains troubled by instability exacerbated by the merger process itself.

In the Minnesota chapter, I describe the emotional responses to a massive restructuring of that state's higher education systems. The change, which created a new board and a new administration to oversee what had been three independent systems of community colleges, technical colleges, and state universities, altered literally hundreds of lives and careers. Though there were winners and losers aplenty, the most common desire among the people interviewed was a wish to be creatively engaged in the new order of things. This applied to those with long careers before them as well as to people nearing retirement. The chief lesson of the Minnesota experience is that leaders of restructuring should involve as many people as possible in the change process but should also be alert to the need to manage the destructive attitudes and actions stimulated by the changes in loyalty and power.

The Maryland chapter is the longest in the book. Because Maryland has the longest experience with restructuring, authors Robert Berdahl and Frank Schmidtlein are able to analyze both the political process that produced the new system and its progress over six subsequent years. Based on detailed interviews with a number of key players from the governor's office to the campuses, Berdahl and Schmidtlein remind us that once an initiative as politically complex as restructuring higher education begins its journey through the legislature, the outcome becomes very difficult to predict. They point out some of the intriguing accidents of history and personality that resulted in a structure quite different from that intended by the legislature or the governor. Although few people interviewed feel that the restructuring has resulted in marked improvement, the authors report a widespread feeling of "all passion spent": leaders and others have accommodated themselves to the new way of doing business and believe that further change would only be disruptive.

The third and final part presents more general lessons from the struggles of each of the states. Reviewing both the claims for less centralization of authority in systems and the views of observers who see value in continuing to locate lobbying, labor relations, and financial oversight, among other functions, in some formal, centralized system, Aims McGuinness argues that systems will prevail. The need for stability in the midst of political volatility, increasing demands from consumers for consistency in quality and access, and the pressures for cost containment combine to rationalize the need for systems. However, he goes on to propose a reinvented system that profits from the lessons of restructuring described in this book and elsewhere. This carefully architected structure of policies and relationships is intended to increase higher education's responsiveness to society's agenda, to create rewards for demonstrable improvements in educational quality, and to push responsibility down to the campus and local level.

Whereas the penultimate chapter focuses on changing the structure to yield improvement, the concluding one emphasizes the actions that policy makers and executives must take and the character they must display if restructuring is to be successful. The general lesson for policy makers—governors, legislators, key staff persons, and regulatory agency heads—is that restructuring is only one remedy for problems in higher education, and often not the best. Focused legislation, transfer of authority among existing regulatory agencies, and clear statements of expectations are all alternatives worth considering.

Executives charged with carrying out change must take advantage of the crises that propel restructuring but must coolly analyze the political and policy scene before setting out their vision for the change. Managing change successfully requires the involvement of as many people as possible, yet it also demands that the leader be surrounded by a team of savvy professionals to help lead in what is a very lonely and difficult task. The chapter concludes that a more important work than designing the organizational structure is to create and nurture a climate within the new organization that will be hospitable to risk and innovation.

The fact that we exist in relationship to our environment and that this relationship colors our opinion holds true for the authors in this volume. Douglas Treadway, author of the North Dakota chapter, led much of the restructuring and reform in that state for three years. Pat Crosson served as a faculty member while Massachusetts restructured. Pat O'Rourke's role as the chief executive of the University of Alaska, Fairbanks, provided him with intimate knowledge of events described in his chapter. Robert Berdahl and Frank Schmidtlein, who wrote the Maryland chapters, were and remain professors at the main campus affected by restructuring. I led one of the systems that would be subsumed under a new board and administration in Minnesota. As close observers and sometimes participants in the action, the authors of merger narratives in the five states had access to information denied to those at a distance. As the editor, I was happy to trade complete dispassion for the deep insights of those closer to drama. I also believe that readers will agree with me that the authors "got it right" in describing restructuring in their states. I was pleased to enlist Rich Novak from his perch at the Association of Governing Boards and Aims McGuinness of the National Center for Higher Education Management Systems to bring their broad perspectives as students of change over time and across the country.

Acknowledgments

As the lead author and editor of this book, I am indebted to the members of the Minnesota State University Board for their encouragement and insight. I greatly appreciate the valuable hours that Elizabeth Pegues, board president, devoted to our discussions of governance change. Special thanks are due to board member and former speaker of the Minnesota house of representatives Rodney Searle, my longtime friend and mentor and a remarkable observer of the political scene. I also value the insights of gifted legislators like Lyndon Carlson, Roger Moe, Peter Rodosovitch, and LeRoy Stumph, among many others; members of Minnesota's new Higher Education Board and the other higher education boards; my colleague presidents; and especially the talented staff in the chancellor's office. The word processing support from Shelly Heller was excellent. My assistant, Carol Zwinger, provided commonsense counsel throughout the process of creating this book. The contributing authors and my assistant editor, Cynthia Crist, were patient and insightful. I hope that the collective result at least equals their individual effort. My wife, Janet Warnert, took time from her busy career to cast a critical eye on much of the text. For her help and so many other gifts, I cannot think of how to thank her enough, but I know she has some ideas.

St. Paul, Minnesota   Terrence J. MacTaggart
October 1995

References

Drucker, P. "The Age of Social Transformation." *Atlantic Monthly*, May 1994, pp. 53–80.

Reich, R. *The Work of Nations: Preparing Ourselves for 21st Century Capitalism.* New York: Vintage Books, 1992.

Thurow, L. *Head to Head: The Coming Economic Battle Among Japan, Europe, and America.* New York: Warner Books, 1992.

The Authors

Terrence J. MacTaggart served from 1991 to 1995 as chancellor of the Minnesota State University system, where he is also professor of English. He received his B.A. degree (1967) in English literature from Canisius College in Buffalo, New York, an M.A. (1970) in English from Saint Louis University, an M.B.A. (1985) from Saint Cloud State University, and a Ph.D. (1976) in English from Saint Louis University. MacTaggart has served as a faculty member and administrator at Blackburn College in Carlinville, Illinois; Webster University in Saint Louis, the University of Alaska Fairbanks, and Saint Cloud State University in Minnesota. He served as vice president for academic and administrative affairs for Metropolitan State University, Saint Paul, Minnesota, from 1983 to 1986 and as interim vice chancellor for academic affairs for the Minnesota State University system from 1986 to 1987. In 1987, he was named chancellor of the University of Wisconsin—Superior, also holding an appointment as professor of English. He became chancellor of the Minnesota State Universities in 1991, serving as the chief executive officer for a system of seven regional universities in Minnesota and a two-year program in Akita, Japan. A member of Phi Beta Kappa and a Fulbright scholar, he has published and made presentations on topics including the economics of nontraditional programs, strategic planning, and relations between higher education and state government.

Robert Berdahl is professor of higher education and director of the Institute for Research in Higher and Adult Education in the Department of Education Policy, Planning and Administration, College of Education, University of Maryland, College Park. He earned his B.A. degree (1949) in political science from the University of California, Los Angeles, an M.A. (1954) from the University of California, Berkeley, an M.S.Econ. (1957) in political science from the London School of Economics and Political Science, and a Ph.D. (1958) in political science from the University of California, Berkeley. He also attended the Institute of Political Studies at the University of Paris in 1952 and 1953. Berdahl served as assistant and associate professor of political science at San Francisco State College from 1958 to 1969 and as professor of higher education at the State University of New York, Buffalo, from 1969 to 1980. He was a senior fellow with the Carnegie Council on Policy Studies in Higher Education at Berkeley between 1974 and 1976. His extensive publications in the field of higher education include *Statewide Coordination of Higher Education.*

Cynthia L. Crist is system director for educational policy research for the Minnesota State Colleges and Universities, the newly merged system described in this book. She earned a B.S. degree (1972) and an M.S. (1977) in education at Illinois State University and is a doctoral candidate in education policy and administration at the University of Minnesota. She taught elementary special education in Peoria, Illinois, and North Saint Paul–Maplewood, Minnesota, before joining the staff of Minnesota Governor Rudy Perpich in 1983. Between 1983 and 1987, she served as assistant to the director, assistant director, and acting director of the Governor's Office of Science and Technology. She became assistant to the chancellor for policy research in the Minnesota State University system in 1987 and later served as assistant vice chancellor for academic affairs (1989 to 1993) and associate vice chancellor for academic affairs (1993 to 1995).

Patricia H. Crosson is currently interim provost and vice chancellor for academic affairs at the University of Massachusetts, Amherst, where she is also professor of higher education and former chair of the Department of Educational Policy, Research and Administration in the School of Education. She earned an M.Ed. (1972) and an Ed.D. (1974) in higher education at the University of Massachusetts. She has served on the faculties of the University of Maryland, College Park; the University of Pittsburgh; and the University of Massachusetts, Amherst. She has also held a variety of administrative positions at the University of Massachusetts; the University of Maryland, College Park; and the University of Pittsburgh.

Aims C. McGuinness, Jr. is senior associate at the National Center for Higher Education Systems (NCHEMS), specializing in higher education finance, governance, and state policy issues. He holds a B.A. degree (1965) in political science from the University of Pennsylvania, an M.B.A. (1970) from the George Washington University, and a Ph.D. (1979) in social science from the Maxwell Graduate School for Citizenship and Public Affairs, Syracuse University. He served as assistant to the chancellor of the University of Maine system and became director of higher education policy at the Education Commission of the States (ECS) in 1975. During an eighteen-year tenure at ECS, he directed a national project on state policy and college learning, staffed two national task forces on higher education policy issues, and was active in initiatives on finance, governance, assessment, and K–12 and international education reform. McGuinness served as a member and later as president of the board of education of the Littleton Public Schools, Colorado. He is currently in his second four-year term, as an appointee of Governor Roy Romer, on the board of trustees of the State Colleges in Colorado.

Richard J. Novak is the director of public sector programs for the Association of Governing Boards of Universities and Colleges (AGB). He received both his B.A. degree (1973) in liberal arts and his M.A. (1975) in higher education administration/college student personnel from Michigan State University. While there, he held an administrative position in admissions and student affairs in the university's College of Human Medicine. He joined the staff at the American Association of State Colleges and Universities (AASCU) in 1979, serving for eight years as assistant director of governmental relations and for three years as director of the Center for State Higher Education Policy and Finance, where he led AASCU's efforts in state policy and governmental relations. While at AASCU, he also served as staff liaison for the association's interests in intercollegiate athletics and worked extensively in federal budget, finance, and governance issues. In his current position at the AGB, Novak monitors public sector trends in higher education and currently directs a special six-year initiative on board and presidential leadership sponsored by the AGB and funded by the W. K. Kellogg Foundation.

Patrick J. O'Rourke is chancellor emeritus of the University of Alaska Fairbanks. He served Alaska's system of higher education for over twenty-one years until his retirement. He earned his B.A.

degree (1964) in psychology and English at Saint John's University in Jamaica, New York, an M.S. (1968) in psychology at Indiana State University, and a Ph.D. (1977) in education at the University of Connecticut. O'Rourke established the University of Alaska's first rural campus in 1972, and he retains a strong interest in rural and Native American education. In recent years he has been a frequent speaker on multicultural and global issues in education, and he remains active as a consultant to a number of institutions of higher education.

Frank A. Schmidtlein is associate professor of higher education in the Department of Education Policy, Planning and Administration at the University of Maryland, College Park. He has a B.S. degree (1954) in citizenship education from Kansas State University and an M.A. (1970) in education planning and a Ph.D. (1979) in higher education, both from the University of California, Berkeley. He has served in a number of executive positions with the federal government in the Public Health Service, Office of Education, Bureau of the Budget, and National Foundation for the Arts and Humanities. He also served for four years as director of academic and financial planning for the Maryland State Board for Higher Education. At the University of Maryland, College Park, in addition to serving as assistant and then associate professor of higher education, he has held the positions of assistant to the chancellor, acting department chair, and associate director of the National Center for Postsecondary Governance and Finance, of which he was one of the founders.

Douglas M. Treadway is currently superintendent and president of Shasta Community College in Redding, California. He earned a B.A. degree (1964) in social sciences from California Western University, an M.T. (1967) in counseling from the Claremont Graduate School, and a Ph.D. (1971) in counselor education from Northwestern University. Administrative positions held include assistant dean of students at Northwestern University from 1969 to 1971; director of student development, associate dean of academic affairs, and dean of regional programs at Eastern Oregon State College between 1974 and 1985; president of Western Montana College in Dillon, Montana, from 1985 to 1987; president of Southwest State University in Marshall, Minnesota, from 1987 to 1991; and chancellor of the North Dakota University system from 1991 to 1994. He has also served on the faculty of Northwestern University, U.S. International University in Maui, Maui Community College, Eastern Oregon State College, Oregon State University, and Western Montana College. Treadway has written and spoken frequently on issues of higher education and economic development in rural America.

Restructuring Higher Education

Part One

Context for Change

Chapter One

Restructuring and the Failure of Reform

Terrence J. MacTaggart

To demonstrate the limits of power, King Canute, the eleventh-century English monarch, stood on the banks of the Thames and commanded the incoming tide to cease. He proved his point by getting wet. It remains to be seen if higher education will develop a similar sense of Realpolitik in time to address the tides of change that threaten to overwhelm it. Simply put, the challenge facing public higher education is to regain credibility by reforming itself to meet higher public expectations. A likely alternative to self-imposed improvement will be more governance change and greater regulation foisted on the enterprise by governors and state legislators.

This chapter identifies the most intensely felt external pressures on higher education today and points to new challenges that loom on the horizon. It then assesses how these forces combine, reinforce, and at times contradict one another to influence the condition and future of public higher education. It argues that the concentrated impact of these economic, social, and political forces will be to increase pressure on government, especially state government, to intrude in the affairs of the academy. A review of current attempts to improve the management, performance, and reputation of the enterprise in the minds of the public and its elected representatives suggests that these efforts at reform have not gone nearly far enough. As a result, we can expect that the pressure for greater state intrusion will result in even more widespread governance restructuring. Often the change will take an authoritarian bent as executives responsible to governors rather than lay boards of trustees become more powerful.

Pressures for Change

Clark Kerr, one of the chief architects of the higher education edifice in California and an insightful commentator on the threats to that structure, sees the future as a "time of troubles" (1994, p. 11). Facing declining public resources, more vocal claimants for those resources, and heightened expectations that higher education must contribute directly to the economy, higher education, Kerr predicts, will be the scene of "endemic internal guerrilla warfare" (p. 12) as various forces battle over the need for and direction of change in a resource-poor environment. The pressures will become more intense as the country comes to grips with its diminished role in the world economic order.

Economic Pressures

A modest upturn in many state appropriations to higher education in 1994 (Hines, 1994, p. 3) should be viewed as a temporary reprieve from the downward trend of the early nineties and the inevitability of further reductions in the future. David Breneman points to a steady decline in higher education's share of state budgets from 1968 onward as evidence of the permanency of the "new austerity" (1994, p. 6) besieging higher education. Though the recent national and international recession forced deep cuts in operating budgets and some sharp tuition hikes, the longer-term outlook has not brightened with recovery because of other claimants on the public purse. State investments in health care for the aged, education for the young, and prisons for the criminal have resulted in cuts to institutions and systems of higher learning. In spite of projected enrollment increases, no one expects state investment to rise with the tide of new students. It is likely that while students and others protest the unfairness of a deliberate "high tuition, high aid" strategy, more and more states are likely to drift in that direction, or quite possibly toward its dark twin, "high tuition, not so high aid."

What disturbs Breneman and other analysts is not only the dismal financial forecast but also the high levels of denial surrounding it. He identifies a number of possible strategies in the face of economic decline, including reducing enrollment, finding more productive delivery systems, and differentiating missions, but finds that most institutions avoid structural change (1994, p. 11). Instead, they cut discretionary-cost items, temporarily leave vacant positions unfilled, freeze salaries, defer maintenance, and otherwise hunker down.

Changing Public Attitudes

The public's more jaundiced attitude toward higher education probably stems from growing national anxiety over employment security and declining faith in many social and political institutions. Well-publicized scandals involving the use of federal overhead monies to maintain yachts, headlines citing high college loan default rates, widely read news stories about unemployed college graduates, and pungent criticism from the likes of Allan Bloom (1987) and Dinesh D'Souza (1991) have cast higher education and its leaders in a negative light. National surveys as well as those concentrating on specific states, such as the work of the California Higher Education Policy Center, confirm that many Americans believe that a college education is becoming too expensive; that mismanagement and overpaid administrators, as well as cutbacks in state support, are to blame; and that the system needs a thorough overhaul (Finney, 1994, p. 25).

The public attitude is a complex one composed partly of fear and partly of hope commingled with a good deal of distrust. Fear arises from simultaneously knowing that advanced knowledge is the gateway to a middle-class standard of living and that the toll may become more than many citizens can afford. There is hope that once endowed with a credential, graduates will indeed enjoy relative material comfort. The public's distrust in the competence and good intentions of higher education's leaders likely stems from sensationalized stories in the media and, perhaps, class conflict. Whatever the causes, this skepticism contributes to an atmosphere in which politicians, themselves under suspicion, are likely to see higher education as too important to leave to the academics.

The tight link in the public mind between education and good jobs will lead more students, and perhaps more public investment, to technical and vocational education to the detriment of the liberal arts. The emphasis on school-to-work programs in a number of states and initiatives by the U.S. Department of Labor to connect schooling and job training more closely confirm this trend. A disturbing feature of this new vocationalism, however, is that so far the economic returns to students completing two-year and shorter vocational programs lag considerably behind those of graduates with baccalaureate degrees. Students who rest their hopes too much on the currency of technical training may be disappointed, and their frustration can only contribute to further skepticism over the merits of higher education generally.

Corporate Restructuring

Pervasive examples of restructuring, reengineering, rightsizing, downsizing, and a host of other organizational changes in the corporate world also contribute to a climate in which similar massive change is expected among public enterprises. The vastly different cultures and political contexts that separate public and private enterprise are largely ignored, as is the mounting evidence that much corporate restructuring often results in lower profits and other unexpected costs (Kanter, 1989, pp. 57–60; "Trouble with Mergers," 1994, p. 13). Works by Tom Peters (1988), Michael Hammer and James Champy (1993), and Charles Handy (1994), all of which deal with structural change in the global economy and corporations, are widely read and highly influential. Scarcely a week passes without news of thousands of layoffs as a consequence of corporate restructuring. These headlines, and often hard personal experience, have inured many citizens to the prospect of similar reductions at colleges and universities. Workers in the insecure world of the modern corporation and former-managers-turned-consultants trying to make a living by their wits and energy feel little sympathy for what they regard as the extraordinary freedom and security of the academic life.

Reinventing Government

The phenomenal success of Osborne and Gaebler's *Reinventing Government* (1992), confidently subtitled *How the Entrepreneurial*

Spirit Is Transforming the Public Sector, has created a reform industry in its own right. Whereas Dan Quayle, as vice president, focused on quietly enhancing relationships with a business community frustrated by regulation, his successor, Al Gore, has been charged with nothing less than reinventing the federal bureaucracy. He and leaders across the country look to Osborne and Gaebler's bright inventory of ideas such as "funding outcomes, not inputs," "injecting competition in service delivery," and "transforming rule-driven organizations" for inspiration. The tone of much of the reinventing-government literature suggests that having conceived of the idea of shifting market-based incentives to the public government sector, the transformation itself should be easily accomplished and the benefits quickly enjoyed. Ignoring the high mortality rates among efforts to reinvent government and the difficulties of successful reengineering on the corporate side, some of the more naive proponents of reinvention assume that the inevitable next step is the successful reform of higher education. Whatever the level of sophistication of its devotees, the popularity of the reinventing movement contributes to the belief that profound change should come to higher education quickly.

Emerging Pressures

In addition to the prominent forces just noted, new social and political trends are at work to destabilize higher education. The Republican party's Contract with America, the balanced budget amendment, the Republican congressional majority's zeal for reducing government spending and services, and the Clinton administration's attempt to outmaneuver the new majority could well lead to reductions in student financial aid, an increase in the cost of student loans, and experiments with educational voucher systems. The shift of responsibility for social programs to the states will almost certainly reduce the current level of funding that supports these programs. Pressures to fund social services and health care responsibilities at the state level could well result in further reductions in public support for higher education and in tuition increases. Some states may seize this opportunity to make greater use of underenrolled private colleges, while others may cut their subsidies to private institutions in favor of state-supported schools.

The consequences of these Republican and New Democratic initiatives will be fewer public dollars for colleges, universities, and their students; greater pressure to reduce cost; and less sympathy overall for institutions and their faculties, who have traditionally been allied with the liberal Democratic tradition.

Less certain than the impact of the 1994 midterm elections, but intriguing nonetheless, is the potential growth of competition for students and support from proprietary schools and "virtual universities" that offer their wares electronically. Proprietary schools should benefit from both the increasing appetite for job-oriented education and interest in privatizing public services. Efficient, focused professional degree programs such as those offered by the Keller Graduate School of Management and the University of Phoenix could provide stiff competition to conventional institutions with their full-time, tenured faculty. The expansion of the information highway and the high level of computer literacy create a large market for entrepreneurial institutions to offer courses and degrees over the Internet and through interactive television. The ease of access to programs offered by these nimble institutions will prompt legislators and students to ask why conventional, tax-supported colleges cannot be as responsive.

A Cumulative Impact

What sense can we make of this mélange of economic trends, popular attitudes, and political movements? Part of the answer, of course, depends on the effectiveness of higher education's response to these pressures, but we will hold that issue in abeyance for the moment. This brief environmental scan leads to three conclusions: (1) there will be more, not less, state government intervention; (2) that intervention will very often take the form of governance restructuring; and (3) this restructuring will frequently take an authoritarian twist.

An axiom of social change in a democracy with a free press is that public concern, intensified by media attention, leads either to self- or government-imposed reform. Just as the work of Rachel Carson hastened tighter regulation of the chemical industry and Ralph Nader's ability to attract media attention brought about a new era of government regulation of automakers, so widely publicized critiques of higher education management have inspired state action and will continue to do so in the future. The basic lessons of the impact of public concern brought into focus by media attention is that absent self-regulation, government will intervene to correct abuse or ensure reform (Nolan, 1974).

If the fact of increasing state intervention is clear, the forms it will take in the future are more difficult to discern. The thrust of contemporary management theory and practice argues for shifting decision-making authority to the lowest practical level. However, the public's concern for access and affordability and the historical preference of legislators for control over public agencies will likely lead to more centralized control. When politicians lack money to create incentives for change in tax-supported enterprises, as they do in today's economy, they tend to fall back on regulatory control to bring it about. The widespread public anxiety over the affordability of higher education reinforces this predilection to seek greater control over the affairs of the academy. If state coffers were full and there were relatively few claimants on the public purse, tuition could be kept affordable, as in the past, by increasing the state's direct investment in institutions. But since this largesse is no longer possible, state legislators will look to other ways of constraining the cost of higher education and thus its tuition levels.

As Richard Novak points out in Chapter Two, politicos usually cannot reach directly into the operations of an institution to reduce its costs of doing business, and many are politically astute enough to avoid doing so even if they could. Instead they act in the province they do control, the governance system. And since they expect systems to deliver some specific results, such as affordable tuition and high access, as well as to meet what Aims McGuinness calls the perennial expectations of reducing program duplication and minimizing institutional competition (1994, p. 19), we can expect that many of the externally imposed governance changes will include more authoritarian elements. The instruments will often include powerful executives responsible more to the governor than to the institutions they oversee.

It should also be emphasized that there are several prominent examples of what might be called an antiauthoritarian trend in governance restructuring. Governor Christine Todd Whitman's elimination of New Jersey's Board of Higher Education in favor of a council of college presidents and Maryland's decision in 1988 to allow two public institutions, St. Mary's College and Morgan State, to remain independent of the new state governing board illustrate this trend. It remains to be seen if these and other examples of liberation management will lead to improved educational performance and thereby be revealed as a widely applicable and attractive alternative to more restrictive governance schemes. Some critics might argue that the removal of the higher education board, which insulated New Jersey's public institutions somewhat from political interference, will open the door to more direct gubernatorial and legislative intrusion.

Of course, the grim scenario of more authoritarian intrusion may be avoided, or at least ameliorated, if higher education demonstrates the capacity to reform itself.

Status of Reform

What is reform to a citizen or a legislator or an editorial writer may be anathema to a faculty member and a serious challenge to a college president. Most academics feel that whatever ails higher education could be cured with fewer administrators and a lot more money. The academy finds itself far more comfortable in the role of critic of society than it does in critical self-examination. With their decentralized forms of governance, a history of arriving at administrative as well as academic decisions through consensus, and a culture of faculty independence reinforced by the tenure system and the power of faculty unions, colleges and universities are notoriously resistant to change.

The price of that resistance may be high in the present environment. Failure to succeed at some of the reform initiatives now afoot and to communicate that success to a broad public will likely result in fewer resources overall, less opportunity for faculty development and creativity, and reduced options for self-government.

Broadly speaking, higher education's responses to its many challenges range from passive reactions in the face of budget cutbacks to more proactive efforts to reconstruct traditional ways of doing business. The passive response, much decried by David Breneman (1994) and others, has been to act as if economic hardship were a temporary condition. In the short run, this strategy of avoidance leads to across-the-board cuts, freezes in pay and discretionary expenditures, and other forms of belt tightening. As Breneman observes, this effort at denial is apt to demoralize faculty, who, believing that "the first round of cuts would be sufficient . . . may feel betrayed" (p. 11) when succeeding waves of reductions roll in. It may leave students and the general public feeling betrayed as well when tuition hikes above the inflation rate and reductions in courses and programs combine to give each new class a bit less than the one before. An aggressive and high-profile lobbying effort, which often accompanies passive internal management, may temporarily impart hope but does little to alter the underlying financial problem.

McGuinness and Ewell (1994) outline more assertive approaches to improving productivity and quality. The strategies they describe include making the current structure more efficient, as illustrated in the ideas of William Massy and Robert Zemsky. With support from the Pew Charitable Trusts (see Pew Higher Education Research Program, 1990), Massy and Zemsky call attention to the sinister features of the administrative lattice, or the growth in nonessential management positions and tasks, and the academic ratchet, the shift away from teaching to research (McGuinness and Ewell, pp. 5–6). They advocate an internal restructuring that reduces administrative costs and focuses on the role of faculty as teachers.

A second, more diffuse strategy is to apply, or attempt to apply, the lessons of the total quality movement to the academy. While academics wrinkle their noses at the thought of substituting the word *customer* for *student,* leaders in the movement plunge ahead in efforts to increase satisfaction of customer needs, engage in continuous improvement, and reexamine orthodox ways of delivering service (McGuinness and Ewell, pp. 8–9).

A third approach, which recognizes that colleges and universities are part of a much larger educational system including K–12 education on the one hand and the world of employment on the other, strives to make this interlocking network more productive as a whole. Thoughtful recommendations from Bruce Johnstone (1993) direct attention to increasing the student's intellectual growth by a variety of means rather than concentrating on the number of hours a faculty member stands in front of a class. Learning productivity, as Johnstone's strategy is dubbed, includes some time-honored ideas such as greater use of mastery learning, year-round study, and independent learning combined in a systematic effort to reduce the time to degree completion.

Virtually all contributors to the literature of reform emphasize the renewed importance of strategic planning. Robert Shirley, an experienced practitioner of the art, underscores the importance of creating a mission statement that is specific enough actually to guide decisions, targets well-defined clientele groups, and etches a comparative advantage in the marketplace (1994, pp. 5–6).

Failure of Reform

The literature of reform contains much intelligent writing, and impressive examples of constructive change can be found in various institutions and systems. Unfortunately, it is difficult to argue that the level or the visibility of these improvements adequately addresses today's intense societal and political demands. Neither a survey of the reforms that are occurring at colleges and universities across the country nor a review of either the professional literature or the mass media would lead to the conclusion that the level of response is credible.

Two examples illustrate this point. In 1993, the Wingspread Group on Higher Education set about responding to the question, What does society need from higher education? This task force, made up largely of prominent education and foundation executives, came to very somber conclusions: "A disturbing and dangerous mismatch exists between what American society needs of higher education and what it is receiving. Nowhere is the mismatch more dangerous than in the quality of undergraduate preparation provided on many campuses. The American imperative for the 21st century is that society must hold higher education to much higher expectations or risk national decline" (p. 1).

The Wingspread Group, consisting largely of insiders writing for insiders, is familiar with the usual excuses for preserving the status quo. "We understand the explanations offered when criticisms are leveled at higher education," they write. "Entrants are inadequately prepared; institutional missions vary; we are required by law to accept all high school graduates; students change their minds frequently and drop out of school; controlling costs is difficult in the labor-intensive academy; cutting-edge research consumes the time of senior faculty." Still, the group insists, "the explanations, no matter how persuasive they once were, no longer add up to a compelling whole. The simple fact is that some faculties and institutions certified for graduation too many students who cannot read and write very well, too many whose intellectual depth and breadth are unimpressive, and too many whose skills are inadequate in the face of the demands of contemporary life" (p. 1).

Without brutally honest self-appraisal and a systematic program of reform of undergraduate education, the Wingspread Group concludes, "the withdrawal of public support for higher education can only accelerate as students, parents, and taxpayers come to understand that they paid for an expensive education without receiving fair value in return" (p. 2).

The second testimony to the failure to reform comes from the Holmes Group, made up of leading teacher educators. In *Tomorrow's Schools of Education* (1995), the group criticizes the lack of progress in improving teacher education. This group advocates a five-year professional development school model as the ideal preparation for future teachers. One could argue that this model is not fully tested by empirical evaluations and that other approaches may be equally valid. But the point is that little progress has been made in what has long been a target of critics, the quality of teacher preparation.

If the public has a right to suspect the quality of undergraduate and teacher education, it also believes that higher education could make better use of its resources. Bruce Johnstone (1992) offers an all-too-apt summary of this view:

America in the early 1990s has become consumed with the specter of lost productivity and the challenge of international competitiveness. We have begun to accept the need to do business in radically different ways and to accept the loss of jobs, the wrenching changes in career paths, and the disappearance of familiar corporate names; these seem to be the prices for progress, or even for survival, in the private sector. It is in this context that higher education's continuing cost escalation and its seeming obliviousness to economic realities and to the tough decisions and real sacrifices being made elsewhere in the economy have met with such hostility in the press and among public officials [p. 22].

Later observers may decide whether public higher education in this country is simply on the wrong side of history or is itself at fault for not summoning up the ingenuity and courage to reconstruct itself. Perhaps no amount of initiative would reverse the trends. To date, at least, we have seen too little effective, recognized reform. As a result, higher education stands to become less influential in guiding its own destiny. Governance restructuring, such as described in this book, will become more and more the order of the day.

References

Bloom, A. *The Closing of the American Mind: How Higher Education Has Failed Democracy and Impoverished the Souls of Today's Students.* New York: Simon & Schuster, 1987.

Breneman, D. W. *Higher Education: On a Collision Course with New Realities.* AGB Occasional Paper No. 22. Washington, D.C.: Association of Governing Boards of Universities and Colleges, 1994.

D'Souza, D. *Illiberal Education: The Politics of Race and Sex on Campus.* New York: Free Press, 1991.

Ewell, P. T. "A Matter of Integrity, Accountability and the Future of Self-Regulation." *Change,* 1994, *26*(6), 25–29.

Finney, J. "Tough Choices for Higher Education." *Spectrum,* 1994, *67*(2), 24–30.

Hammer, M., and Champy, J. *Reengineering the Corporation: A Manifesto for Business Revolution.* New York: HarperCollins, 1993.

Handy, C. *The Age of Paradox.* Cambridge, Mass.: Harvard Business School, 1994.

Hines, E. *State Higher Education Appropriations, 1993–94.* Denver, Colo.: State Higher Education Executive Officers, 1994.

Holmes Group. *Tomorrow's Schools of Education.* East Lansing: The Holmes Group, Michigan State University, 1995.

Johnstone, D. B. "Building Rapport." In G. Budig (ed.), *A Higher Education Map for the 1990s.* New York: American Council on Education/Macmillan, 1992.

Johnstone, D. B. *Learning Productivity: A New Imperative for American Higher Education.* Studies in Public Higher Education, no. 3. Albany: State University of New York, 1993.

Kanter, R. M. *When Giants Learn to Dance: Mastering the Challenges of Strategy, Management, and Careers in the 1990s.* New York: Simon & Schuster, 1989.

Kerr, C. "American Society Turns More Assertive: A New Century Approaches for Higher Education in the United States." In P. Altbach,

R. Berdahl, and P. Gumport (eds.), *Higher Education in American Society.* (3rd ed.) Buffalo, N.Y.: Prometheus, 1994.

McGuinness, A. C., Jr. "The Changing Structure of State Higher Education Leadership." In A. C. McGuinness Jr., R. Epper, and S. Arredondo (eds.), *State Postsecondary Education Structures Handbook: State Coordinating and Governing Boards.* Denver, Colo.: Education Commission of the States, 1994.

McGuinness, A. C., Jr., and Ewell, P. T. "Improving Productivity and Quality in Higher Education." *Priorities,* Vol. 2. Washington, D.C.: Association of Governing Boards of Universities and Colleges, Fall 1994.

Nolan, J. "Protect Your Public Image with Performance." *Harvard Business Review,* Vol. 53, March 1975, pp. 135–142.

Osborne, D., and Gaebler, T. *Reinventing Government: How the Entrepreneurial Spirit Is Transforming the Public Sector.* Reading, Mass.: Addison-Wesley, 1992.

Peters, T. *Thriving on Chaos: Handbook for a Management Revolution.* New York: HarperCollins, 1988.

Pew Higher Education Research Program. "The Lattice and the Ratchet." *Policy Perspectives,* 1990, 2(4), 1–8.

Shirley, R. *Strategic Operational Reform in Public Higher Education: A Mandate for Change.* AGB Occasional Paper No. 21. Washington, D.C.: Association of Governing Boards of Universities and Colleges, 1994.

"Trouble with Mergers, The." *Economist,* Sept. 10, 1994, pp. 13–14.

Wingspread Group on Higher Education. *An American Imperative: Higher Expectations for Higher Education.* Racine, Wis.: Johnson Foundation, 1993.

Chapter Two

Methods, Objectives, and Consequences of Restructuring

Richard J. Novak

The chancellor of a large midwestern university system complained recently that his board was oblivious to the current debate over societal expectations of higher education. "They just don't see that being active in the discussions of what the public wants from us and how we can serve them better is part of governing. I'm afraid we are quickly becoming the problem when we used to be the solution." It is telling that his state is one in which the legislature has recently abolished most of its governing systems in favor of free-standing campus boards. The lesson is clear: if the public feels that higher education's governing structures and its leaders are indifferent to social needs, those structures and leaders will be traded in for other alternatives. Sadly, those alternatives may be no better than what they replaced.

Citizens have a lot at stake in the way higher education is governed. It is relatively easy to communicate the value of higher education's products, the importance of quality programs offered at a tuition rate that students can afford, and the need to provide a high level of access. In fact, the public clearly grasps these basic facts, though increasingly citizens worry that the price will rise and access will diminish. But they do not often realize that an effective governing system will help determine if those public goods are readily available. A dysfunctional or unstable system will not be able to advocate effectively for the resources necessary to maintain quality programs required by students in our knowledge-based economy. Nor will it lead, coordinate, manage, or plan the future for colleges and universities in ways that enable these institutions to serve the citizenry well in the long run. With annual expenditures close to $120 billion and more than 11.7 million students (National Center for Education Statistics, 1993), public higher education is a major enterprise. It is important that the people's representatives, if not all the people themselves, realize the linkage between stable, well-run governing structures and the ability of higher education to continue to deliver the goods. A review of recent trends in restructuring higher education will suggest that impulsive efforts to change may bring much distraction and few benefits.

This chapter begins with a review of the history of higher education governance. It discusses how structures evolved; how changes, especially centralization of forms and functions, were meant to improve governance; and the consequences of those changes. The chapter then explores the current ambiguity in the relationship between state government and higher education, especially the conflict over whether to centralize or decentralize decision-making authority. The chapter concludes with a discussion of options for governance restructuring, including strategies for improved performance of governing and coordinating boards.

First, some definitions are in order. State higher education governance structures are the formal, established mechanisms by which all public colleges and universities are overseen. Each consists of lay boards supported by large or small administrations headed by presidents, chancellors, commissioners, or executive directors. Authority has been granted by state constitutions or statutes for these boards to govern, coordinate, or regulate public colleges and universities and sometimes, albeit in limited ways, private and proprietary institutions as well.

There are essentially two types of state higher education governance structures: "governing" and "coordinating." Governing boards have legal management and control responsibilities for a single institution or for a cluster of institutions called a multicampus or university system. In a given state, there may be one or more governing boards. Coordinating boards, of which there is never more than one per state, were established in large part after World

War II and have been charged with ensuring orderly growth in higher education, free of political or parochial interests (Callan, 1991). Coordinating boards shape public debates on higher education and exercise limited, though sometimes significant, authority over colleges and universities by issuing regulations and rendering decisions that have a wide-ranging impact on institutional or system governance. The lines of authority between the two types of structures are often murky.

The citizen members and paid executives of these boards and organizations seek to balance the needs of society, expressed through government, with those of educational institutions. They have the final word in many decisions affecting colleges and universities, yet their authority sometimes faces practical limitations as it intersects with the desires of major external stakeholders, such as elected officials, or internal stakeholders, such as faculty.

Higher education governance structures have evolved differently in the states, but they are more similar than they are different, due in part to the ways in which educators and policy makers have observed and borrowed ideas from each other. Every year, a half dozen or more states undergo rigorous debates on the adequacy of their structure. Such debates center around the effectiveness of governing and coordinating structures in sustaining or enhancing the state's overall postsecondary delivery system. The student of higher education policy development will be struck by the complexities that emerge within a given state when such a debate occurs. The political alliances and maneuvering of institutions and university systems can be fascinating. The influence of personalities and the strength of political champions for change or the status quo can never be underestimated. In some cases, intense debates mask deeper, legitimate concerns of public policy makers about the education of their citizenry; in others, political motives overshadow policy goals and educational philosophy.

Governance restructuring (a term used interchangeably here with governance reorganization) is an organizational change in the formal mechanism affecting either an institutional or system governing board and its senior administration or the state-level coordinating board and its staff. Structural changes, which must be authorized in state law or, in some cases, university system policy, can vary considerably in scope and complexity. Some are seemingly modest, increasing the size of a governing board, for example, by adding faculty, student, or other representatives. Others can result in one institution's being subsumed by a larger multicampus or university system board or, in a major reorganization, creating a new public university system with authority over previously independent institutions whose single governing boards are dissolved. Still other changes can call for a state coordinating agency to assume authority for all new college and university academic programs and budget requests.

In all of these examples, decision-making authority has shifted within the state governance structure between boards or within boards and consequently in the relationship of the governance structure to the state. A brief history of such changes over the past several decades will present a clearer picture of recent trends in governance restructuring.

The Movement Toward Consolidation and Centralization

The bulk of governance restructuring that occurred from the 1950s through the early 1970s moved toward a consolidation of authority into the hands of fewer boards and higher-level administrators. The exceptions were few. By 1972, as McGuinness (1994) notes, "forty-seven states had established either consolidated governing boards responsible for all senior institutions (and in some cases community colleges also) or coordinating boards responsible for statewide planning and coordination of two or more governing boards" (p. 19).

Although the move by states to centralize decision-making authority by consolidating boards and institutions became widespread in the 1960s and 1970s and even continued into the early 1980s, actions by some states and national policy discussions came much earlier. By 1931, thirteen states had single governing boards, most in states west of the Mississippi River. As the nation entered the Great Depression and resources became severely strained, government and education leaders recognized a need for greater unified control. "To build a State-centered program of higher education to replace the uncoordinated development of the separate institutions has become the determined effort of leaders in

State after State," reported The Carnegie Foundation (Kelly and McNeeley, 1933, p. 179). The American Council on Education complained of the costs of "regionalism" within states and advocated greater cooperation and coordination (Klein, 1938). But only a handful of states made changes in the 1930s and 1940s. In 1947, President Truman's Commission on Higher Education issued its landmark report and wrote, "During the past 35 years States have become increasingly aware of the excessive cost, in both money and public favor, of the incoordination represented by many of the present arrangements. Accordingly, a score or more of States have changed the machinery for the control of their public colleges and universities" (President's Commission on Higher Education, 1947, p. 28). After issuance of the report—but not necessarily as a result of it—the move to centralize planning and decision making accelerated. By 1959, a third of the states had coordinating agencies. According to Glenny (1959), the ease with which the coordinating agency could be established by statute without changes in the state constitution or existing higher education laws made them a popular means of restructuring.

By the 1960s, the reasons for consolidation were fairly consistent across states. They included the need to coordinate enrollment growth among institutions, to minimize institutional competition and conflict over resources and academic programs, to control a proliferation of graduate and professional programs, to improve overall coordination and cooperation among institutions, and to ensure adequate oversight of new and emerging institutions (McGuinness, 1991, pp. 8–9; 1994, pp. 19–21). In many states undergoing consolidation, state lawmakers also wanted to put some political distance between themselves and higher education. Many clearly felt the need for objective, professional advice to help them make decisions or to free them from having to make politically difficult choices. Advice was also needed to help part-time legislators with small staffs find their way through a maze of issues on their way to enacting effective policies.

Almost all of these centralizing efforts—the creation of statewide coordinating boards and consolidations to create larger university systems—were initiated by state legislatures or governors who watched and learned from each other's actions. They, or their predecessors, had written the laws that created the original governance and management structures of state colleges and universities, and they had the power to change them, often over educators' objections. This reality was best exemplified in a report by the Education Commission of the States in the early 1970s. Addressing the need for increased statewide coordination, the report says, "Institutions have not always recognized that their own long-range interests lie in complementation, development of role and scope, and cooperation to meet public postsecondary educational needs. . . . The impetus for coordination to date has come primarily from the political world" (Task Force on Coordination, 1973, p. 6).

If one were to visualize a "governance continuum" (a term coined by my colleague Edgar Schick, although I have altered his usage to fit my own needs) with consolidation and centralization at one extreme and institutional independence and autonomy at the other, one would see the majority of states clustered somewhere close to the consolidation or centralization end of the continuum. Specifically, twenty-three states have coordinating boards with significant powers. Among the many reasons for creating coordinating boards, six were most common: to address overall challenges before higher education in the state, to represent the broad public interest in higher education, to serve as a special staff to state government on higher education matters, to act as advocates for higher education, to mediate differences between institutions or types of institutions, and to conduct multiyear strategic planning. "Statewide" university system structures governing all public senior institutions (and in some cases all two-year institutions as well) exist in twenty states, half created prior to 1968 and the other half between 1968 and 1981. And when one counts the full array of multicampus, statewide, and university system structures, overseeing from two to sixty-four institutions, the number of system states rises to forty-one. These systems assumed authority over colleges and universities that had been established earlier with their own independent governing boards, had been part of smaller university systems, had answered to state departments of education, or had evolved from parent campuses. In many states, multicampus and university systems coexist with other systems, with institutions still retaining independent governing boards, with private institutions, or with state coordinating boards (McGuinness, 1994, pp. 9–18). They were created for many of the same reasons as coordinating boards, as well as to increase student access and allow (or, in some cases, force) institutions to lower costs and benefit from the visibility, status, and shared resources derived from acting as a collective entity. Examples of the benefits of collective action are pooled assets for capital financing, shared faculty, loaned resources among institutions, central leadership and collective decision making, and joint advocacy (Schick, Novak, Norton, and Elam, 1992). As the next section makes clear, consolidation has not always resulted in unalloyed benefits.

Some Major Consequences of Consolidation

The consequences of governance consolidation are far-reaching, affecting the many participants in higher education in a variety of ways. Among the many positive results have been the realization of the goals mentioned earlier as well as increased student access, fairer resource allocation, and better planning. The downside includes a diminution of presidential authority, an overextended span of control, a decline of "federated" systems, and a lack of clarity of lines of authority. Let us examine each more closely.

Lessening of presidential authority. The period of major restructuring and consolidation that began in the 1950s and continued through the 1960s, 1970s, and early 1980s saw many university systems create "system administrators" and "central offices" with new administrative positions called "system heads" bearing such official titles as chancellor, commissioner, or president of the system. These individuals were vested with considerable administrative authority over campus presidents as they built large central staffs to set overall educational and fiscal policy. With the creation of university systems, many campus presidents found themselves reporting to a system board through a system head and sometimes to a coordinating board executive as well. Consolidation thus lessened the authority of college presidents and created more boards and individuals to whom they were accountable.

Expanded governing board responsibilities. With the creation of large, sometimes statewide, university systems, governing boards became responsible for many institutions and students. The Board of Trustees for the State University of New York, for example, oversees the nation's largest system with thirty-four senior institutions and thirty community colleges. As noted by Kerr and Gade (1989), in the 120 public systems in the nation that govern two- and four-year colleges and universities, the ratio of students per board member is 4,333 to 1. Such ratios "affect the quality of trustees' decisions, which are based less often on practical direct contact than on political or economic considerations, ideologies, statistical data, or what they are told secondhand by administrators" (p. 120). System boards thus often make important policy decisions at a considerable distance from students and institutions.

Decline of "federated" systems. Consolidation precipitated the gradual decline of the "federated" university system, in which multiple institutions fall under one system governing board with college presidents reporting directly to that board. The boards in these systems were served by a small staff, usually headed by an executive secretary or a director. Despite the weaknesses deriving from diffuse authority, federated systems nevertheless worked well for institutions of similar mission and history. State teachers colleges, all similar in scope and mission, that were removed from state departments of education and not given independent governing boards comprised many of these federated systems. Only a handful of federated systems remain.

Unclear lines of authority. Consolidation also created unclear lines of authority in many states between the powers that govern and those that coordinate. In many instances, coordinating decisions have overlapped governance decisions or vice versa, creating situations that are confusing at best and rife with potential conflict at worst (Schick, Novak, Norton, and Elam, 1992).

As mentioned, many statewide coordinating and advisory boards were created or had their powers enhanced between the 1950s and the mid 1980s. Strong coordinating boards have authority in a number of areas, including the review of existing academic programs, approval of new degree requests, and setting of tuition rates, although exercising such authority can be tricky or politically risky. Widespread consolidation has also left a majority of senior institutions in only twelve states with an independent governing board despite the fact that, to many observers, this remains the ideal model for all college and university governance, maximizing autonomy and local decision making. Yet as a consequence of the creation of coordinating boards, even the vast majority of the institutions in these twelve states function within a context that places limits on their discretion and authority. The overlapping authority between coordinating bodies and university or multicampus system structures has led to resentment over who makes final decisions on academic and fiscal matters.

Restructuring: Improvement, Dysfunction, and Instability

Some observers claim there is little evidence to prove that changing the governance structure makes any difference on such bottom-line issues as quality of teaching, learning, public service, and research, let alone issues such as institutional conflict, growth, and resource allocation. In fact, it seems clear that despite the benefits brought about by consolidation in some states, the "blessings" overall are mixed at best. Perhaps the most important factor is leadership at the board and top administrative levels. "While a poorly conceived structure may hamper effective leaders, the best of structures will not suffice if they lack quality lay and paid leaders of integrity, vision, and competence" (Schick, Novak, Norton, and Elam, 1992, p. 13).

To have any chance for lasting success, structural change requires effective leaders who must work in concert with and have the support of state policy makers to exert leverage on the governance structure for sustained improvement of higher education. Broadly speaking, restructuring may be said to result in one of three conditions: improvement, dysfunction, or instability.

Improvement

Spokespersons for many institutions that have been part of consolidations will say that centralization has had a detrimental effect by diminishing institutional independence and identity, reducing flexibility to respond quickly to state or market needs, and limiting the discretion of senior administrators. But if one observes higher education in Pennsylvania, one comes away assured that the State System of Higher Education, a fourteen-campus system of similar colleges and universities overseen by a strong chancellor and a strong board of governors, has improved the quality of its member institutions, enhanced local control and institutional autonomy by preserving campus governing boards with prescribed but meaningful campus-level authority, and freed the hands of senior campus administrators from unnecessary state controls. Supporters in Wisconsin and North Carolina would argue that despite the size of their systems, early problems in transition, and the occasional complaint from the flagship campuses, the leaders of their consolidated systems have been able to foster a diverse set of quality institutions with expanded access for state citizens. And in Kentucky, where independent governing boards coexist with a strong coordinating board, nearly everyone, including institutional presidents, would agree that with the right personalities in place, state coordination has been effective and institutional governance has improved. In these four states, detractors may point out that some institutions have benefited more than others or that state government has benefited the most. However, it appears that consolidation has indeed improved higher education for the students and the taxpayers while enhancing institutional autonomy.

Dysfunction

It has become clear that in some states, consolidation has created dysfunctional university systems and coordinating agencies characterized by institutions that resist any sense of common purposes and by boards that argue publicly, intrude improperly into campus management, and fail both to represent institutional and system interests and to understand the needs of the state. Persons in a dysfunctional structure will spend time refighting lost battles over power and authority or arguing over regional differences and political turf and be distracted from providing leadership to the educational programs of their institutions. Furthermore, they will not have the unity or the time to tackle salient policy issues such as quality, access, affordability, and budget shortfalls. By deferring action on such issues, boards and administrations will see higher levels of government erode their policy-making authority and see campus needs diminished as a state priority in relation to other public services. Dysfunctional structures also make it difficult to attract or retain good individuals for system, coordinating agency, or campus administrative positions.

An interim chancellor at one dysfunctional system described a situation filled with bitterness and distrust. Tensions were particularly high among the regents over the dismissal of one of the system presidents and the granting of tenure at one of the system campuses to the previous chancellor. In the local newspaper, students complained of archaic computer labs, inadequate library hours and resources, parking fees, and potholes in commuter lots. Faculty complained to reporters that "the chancellor and regents offered little reason for faculty to believe they would change their mode of operation" (Solochek, 1992, p. 1A).

Instability

In some states, the debate over higher education restructuring seems endless. Their educators and policy makers fail to come to grips with the broad underlying causes of institutional and legislative discontent. These ongoing debates are inevitably tied to competition for scarce state resources, often among too many institutions vying for too few students, or to bitter institutional fights over new programs. They may also be tied to perceived shortcomings of key education leaders and to a perceived weakness in the state coordinating agency's power and influence. Dissatisfaction of faculty leaders over their institution's share of the pie can spill over into the legislature. As a result, cooperation among institutional or system leaders to negotiate agreements over budgets, institutional missions, and new programs may be difficult to achieve. The political influence of these same leaders is often enough to defeat proposals for major structural reorganization.

Broadening the jurisdiction of a coordinating board is sometimes selected as a strategy because it is seen as a means to resolve institutional conflicts while heading off legislative impulses for more radical action, such as the creation of a single, consolidated university system. A middle-range reorganization of this kind results in further centralization, addresses legislative concerns, and quells complaints about higher education but generally serves only to defer action on the underlying causes of problems. Thus the situation remains unsettled and the structure impermanent. Conflicts between boards and institutions in Colorado leading to increased powers for the Colorado Commission on Higher Education is a good example. At the same time, the broadened jurisdiction of the coordinating board can be undercut or eroded by the political influence of institutional leaders. If institutional advocates and policy makers allow debates to drag on from one legislative session to another, the lack of action can seriously undermine higher education, lower the confidence of supporters, frighten away current and new leaders among both governing boards and administrators, and place the state on the path to dysfunction.

Most of the states in this situation have a "mixed" structure consisting of one or more systems coexisting with one another or with independent campuses and overseen by a coordinating agency. It is ironic that enhancement of the coordinating agency's authority may further increase overlapping responsibilities with governing boards and possibly foster further conflict. Among the states that seem to be perpetually debating change are Colorado and Washington; Nebraska, Illinois, Connecticut, and South Carolina are on the verge of such deliberations. Texas, after years of debate, may have finally come to resolution.

New Developments and Realities Affecting State Governance

As we move into the latter half of the 1990s and prepare for the twenty-first century, the relationship of public higher education to state government appears to be more uncertain and in greater flux than ever before. In state after state, new realities and developments are pulling higher education in opposite directions along the governance continuum. In many states, this will affect not only the process of governance but also the governance structures themselves. As uncertain relationships continue to evolve, the outcomes will be unpredictable and uneven.

The uncertain relationship between higher education and state government is the result of a number of factors, among which four related and sometimes overlapping developments or realities are most prominent. The first is an *erosion of public confidence in higher education*. A number of events have shaken the faith in postsecondary education among the public and among lawmakers, including highly publicized scandals in athletics, improper reimbursements of federal research costs, and alleged price fixing of tuition and student aid. Although some of these events occurred at private institutions, they have affected all of higher education as witnessed by calls for greater scrutiny by a public that appears to make little distinction between public and private. In addition, various groups have raised a plethora of concerns: about the depth of commitment of college leaders to the education of minority populations, about college quality, about the lack of emphasis on undergraduate education, about the increase in college costs and its effect on access, about disengagement on the part of colleges and universities from efforts to solve social and economic problems, and about higher education's reluctance to address issues of institutional productivity and efficiency. For a growing number of citizens and critics, higher education is no longer seen as a national resource above reproach or as a guarantor of the "good life."

The erosion of confidence may not have reached all quarters, but it affects the opinions and actions of legislators and governors who themselves have few qualms about criticizing their own state institutions on myriad issues. Ultimately, questions are raised in the minds of lawmakers and the public at large about the ability of current governance structures to "fix" the problems at hand.

A *changed fiscal environment* contributes to greater uncertainty in the higher education–government relationship. The National Conference of State Legislatures and the National Governors' Association have documented threats to state revenues due to changes in the American economy, the population, and federal fiscal policy that have undermined tax bases and made state taxes less responsive to economic growth (Snell, 1993). In addition, it seems a certainty that political and citizen pressures to reduce state and local taxes will not subside. This pressure has already led to the enactment of a number of revenue limitations. On the expenditure side, states will be forced to spend large amounts on infrastructure; health, welfare, and related federal mandates; corrections and law enforcement; and imbalances in local funding for elementary and secondary schools. A number of states have also enacted constitutional spending limits.

Johnstone (1993) and Gold (1989), among others, have predicted that funding for higher education will never again reach the levels formerly attained, percentagewise or in terms of priority in overall budgets. Even if the fiscal situation for higher education stabilizes on a national level, the funding patterns for institutions in individual states and regions will likely be downward.

Increases in tuition and fees have in part made up for the appropriations shortfall, but students, parents, and many legislators have let institutions know that there are limits to the increases they will tolerate. In most states, short-term cost cutting, tuition increases, and limits on student enrollment can enable an institution to survive financially from one fiscal year or biennium to the next. However, such measures are not sufficient to sustain a viable system of higher education over the long term.

The concepts of *reinventing government* and *less government* are the third influential development. The notion of reinventing government, in particular, views competition, rewards, financial incentives, and contracting out to the private sector as desirable and feasible for government agencies. It is essentially a restructuring of government agencies, applicable in sum or in part to all operations, and has proved to be extremely popular with governors and legislators attempting to reduce the size and cost of state government.

There are implications for higher education in the reinventing-government philosophy. It may be that declining state resources and the need for efficiency and productivity will lead to efforts to decentralize either the operations of existing coordinating and governing structures or the structures themselves. The concept of less government may lead to these same changes as well as less overall funding for higher education. Recent and proposed changes in governance structures incorporate elements of both concepts.

Finally, *institutional restructuring* is redefining the state–higher education relationship. Articulated best by the groundbreaking scholarship of William Massy and Robert Zemsky conducted for the Pew Higher Education Roundtable (1990), institutional restructuring provides a framework for recasting colleges and universities to take on current and projected fiscal realities. This approach is characterized by a new vocabulary that includes such expressions as "growth by substitution," "administrative entrepreneurship," "cost-plus pricing," the "administrative lattice," and the "academic ratchet."

Institutional restructuring is a campus-based self-examination requiring no changes in state governance laws. It is essentially the internal reordering of both administrative and academic priorities by reexamining the incentives for growth and cost escalation. It goes beyond cost cutting or retrenchment to change internal administrative and academic work processes through resource reallocation and applications of new educational technologies designed to increase efficiency, productivity, and consumer orientation. Its proponents favor campus-level flexibility and entrepreneurship but also centralized decision making by key campus leaders when and where necessary (Pew Higher Education Research Program, 1992).

It is important to understand that institutional restructuring and state governance restructuring are related but distinct endeavors and that one can be initiated independent of the other. Because both have many of the same goals, including greater productivity and efficiency, they may tend to be thought of as the same by the public, state policy makers, and the press. As individual institutions struggle with their own campus-level restructuring and as restructuring becomes better understood when its success stories are disseminated to people outside higher education, pressures and expectations may build on state governing structures to reorganize to achieve similar results.

The Uncertain and Evolving Relationship

The relationship between higher education and state government will continue to evolve in uncertain and unpredictable ways. The immediate future seems to offer opposite and contradictory trends, including movement toward decentralizing established governance structures and movement toward centralization. Overlaying both of these trends will be confusing messages on the relationship of governance to accountability.

Decentralization

The decentralizing trend clearly manifests itself in proposals to disaggregate university systems or diffuse their central authority. Of the sixteen proposed or enacted governance changes affecting four-year colleges and universities in the late 1980s and early 1990s, nine involved significant decentralization. Four of these changes deserve brief descriptions:

- West Virginia abolished its statewide board of regents and put in its place two new boards, one for a state college system and the other for a state university system.
- Massachusetts reconstituted its statewide board of regents into a hybrid coordinating council–governing board with continued governing authority over the state and community colleges. It then removed the University of Massachusetts system from the governing authority of the council while retaining the council's authority to coordinate the system in certain specific areas.
- Illinois abolished two university systems that had been in existence since the mid 1960s and created seven new independent campus governing boards. A concomitant proposal to strengthen the authority of the state coordinating board failed.
- Puerto Rico diminished the powers of the Council on Higher Education, a commonwealth-wide board that served both as a governing board for the University of Puerto Rico system and as a commonwealth coordinating board for all public and private institutions. An entirely new and separate governing board for the system was created while the coordinating authority of the council was retained.

In addition to these governance changes, there is also a move afoot to decentralize some aspects of state government relations within consolidated university systems. This is occurring because some educators fear that unified system approaches to state governmental relations have overly concentrated advocacy efforts at the state capitol and weakened political linkages between local legislators and institutions. This, they feel, diminishes the ability of the whole system to leverage adequate state support. While some fear that a decentralized approach to state relations will result in institutions' developing political connections and alliances to the detriment of other institutions and system unity, it seems clear that a better balance between system office and campus-based advocacy will occur as educators seek new strategies for adequate funding.

Decentralizing authority in multicampus and university systems has also manifested itself in the increasing number and authority of local governing and advisory boards within existing university systems. Currently, local advisory and governing boards exist in twenty-seven states that have multicampus systems or institutions with branch campuses, and their numbers are increasing (Schick, 1994). The creation of such boards allows a degree of local control and decision making within a larger overall structure, most often as a complement to the university system or parent campus. Local boards can, however, become an impetus for changing the system when allowed to become strong and independent of the system board and administration. For example, they can call for their own freestanding institution, as happened recently when Coastal Carolina University separated itself from the University of South Carolina system.

An increase in the number and authority of local boards demonstrates the value placed by lawmakers in many states on campus autonomy, decentralized management, and local power bases. "Campus-based boards can give more intense consideration than system boards to buildings and grounds issues; to relations with faculty, students, alumni, and local communities; to fund raising; to the performance of the campus head; and to the appointment of officers below the CEO level" (Kerr and Gade, 1989, p. 123). Look for even larger roles for these boards in the future.

A second form of decentralization is set forth in proposals to alter state coordinating functions. New Jersey Governor Christine Whitman proposed and signed legislation in 1994 eliminating the New Jersey Board of Higher Education and the Department of Higher Education. The board and the department, both created in 1966, had considerable power over public institutions, all of which also have their own independent governing boards. Under the New Jersey plan, some coordinating functions have been assumed under cabinet-level agencies, but most higher education decisions will be made by two new entities: a president's council for voluntary coordination between all public and private institutions and a new commission on higher education for long-range planning, budget recommendations, and mission establishment. New Jersey's plan may be the single most dramatic effort to deregulate colleges and universities in any state since the movement toward consolidation began. Although maintaining a role for state coordination through the new commission on higher education, the plan delegates to institutional governing boards and college presidents many responsibilities previously within the purview of the board and the department.

A related proposal, discussed in South Carolina, would eliminate the Commission on Higher Education and replace it with a new coordinating body consisting of members appointed by the institutional and system governing boards, with the governor appointing additional members and the staff director. Although it failed to pass in the 1994 legislative session, it will be pressed by institutional and legislative interests in future sessions.

In general, state higher education coordinating agencies have been most effective when they serve as arbitrators between the interests of large, competing state universities and, to a lesser extent, between higher education sectors or regional interests in the state. Empowered by legislatures to arbitrate these differences and to develop an overall plan for higher education, some agencies feel new pressures to demonstrate their value in the face of declining budgets and dwindling reliance on government. The roles of state coordinating agencies may well be dramatically defined for the first time since their inception.

State-assisted institutions, public corporations, and charter schools are three interrelated concepts being considered or developed that embody the third major guise of decentralized governance, particularly since the late 1980s as appropriations for postsecondary education have declined rapidly in many states.

The term *state-assisted* implies that the institution is exempt from certain state controls. Constitutionally established universities, with some variations among states, have almost always operated as a fourth branch of government, dependent on state monies but free from controls of other state agencies (Glenny and Dalglish, 1973). They receive significant private and federal financial support and generate substantial revenues of their own, and many have chosen to be defined as state-assisted. Institutions established by statute rather than by constitution are beginning to use the term as well, implying a level of independence from the state that has been attained by virtue of the continued decline in state support.

A growing number of university systems that are not constitutionally based are also showing interest in the idea of becoming "public corporations." Some desire to re-create their systems as

501(c)(3) public corporations of the state, a status held by the University of Maine and the University of New Hampshire. Public corporation status as a 501(c)(3) has freed these systems and their institutions from a number of state bureaucratic controls over business operations. For example, with this status, the system can establish its own payroll, procurement, and accounting procedures and retirement plans. Other efforts to create public corporations will be attempts to widen the existing corporate status of the governing board (as granted in founding statutes or as interpreted by the courts) for purposes of legally distancing the university system from many forms of state oversight. The board of regents of the Oregon State System of Higher Education has asked its legislature for this broader definition. Other systems are watching closely and may attempt to follow suit.

A related development is the concept of charter schools. The term, applied primarily to elementary and secondary schools, implies even greater freedom than *state-assisted*. Charter schools can be of any size, but the concept conjures up images of small, public liberal arts institutions operating with financial and academic freedoms approaching those of private colleges. It also brings to mind institutions given a green light to reinvent themselves. The result may be to pilot unique approaches to teaching and learning, to the tenure system, and to other conventional practices. State and higher education leaders in Virginia, Wisconsin, and California have seriously explored the idea of charter schools in higher education, in Virginia as independent institutions and in California and Wisconsin as part of university systems. None have gone so far as Maryland, where Saint Mary's College, a fifteen-hundred-student public liberal arts institution, enjoys a large measure of freedom from state control. Maryland Secretary of Higher Education Shaila Aery stated, "The St. Mary's model allows the college to plan on predictable [state support] and to have greater control of its own destiny. The college is still able to fulfill its mission and pursue its goals for national prominence" (Lewis, Muller, and Aery, 1994, p. 25). All of these developments are being watched closely in other states, particularly those continuing to experience declines in state support. If successful, charter schools could represent a wave of the future without regard to levels of state support.

Although fiscal flexibility and management autonomy are conditions desired by colleges and universities regardless of state governance structure or fiscal circumstance, the interest in state-assisted institutions, public corporations, and charter schools is fostered by the state disinvestment in colleges and universities. It has both positive and negative implications. On the one hand, these approaches offer the promise of autonomy, flexibility, and freedom for both business operations and academic affairs. Proponents of the three concepts have borrowed from the "new accountability" idea developed in the relatively good fiscal years of the 1980s. The new accountability focuses on demonstrable student and institutional outcomes to distinguish it from the "old accountability" and its reliance on measurable inputs, such as the size of the library or the number of faculty members with doctorates.

On the other hand, many people in state government and higher education are uncomfortable with these concepts, feeling that any leverage that could be exercised over public colleges and universities to meet future state needs, especially educational or economic goals, might be lost forever. Clearly, many are seeking an appropriate balance between institutional independence and the public agenda.

How extensive is the trend to decentralize? Are we approaching a time when new developments and realities, in combination with the restlessness or displeasure of state policy makers over their higher education governance structures, will inevitably lead to changes that tend to move states away from the consolidation or centralization end of the governance continuum? Based on the recent actions of the states noted here, one could answer with a guarded yes. After years of centralization in government and higher education, the pendulum is beginning to swing the other way. But to answer too quickly in the affirmative may oversimplify the public policy debate and the political dynamics in states across the country and thus mask contradictory views held by state policy makers about higher education and its relationship to state government.

Centralization

The impetus toward centralization of state governance structures continues. It is based on the belief that efficiency and productivity are best achieved through centralized operations and decision making or that more, rather than less, scrutiny is called for during times of declining resources.

The impulse to centralize has played out in one familiar form and in a few new ones: consolidated or strengthened systems and coordinating boards, institutional mergers within existing statewide systems, and realignments in response to desegregation orders.

Of the sixteen proposed or enacted state governance changes affecting four-year colleges and universities in the late 1980s and early 1990s, six moved in the direction of strengthened systems and coordinating boards. Four states offer the most notable examples:

- Maryland created the eleven-campus University of Maryland system through consolidation of the University of Maryland system with the State Universities and Colleges of Maryland and set up a higher education commission with new and enhanced powers.
- Minnesota consolidated three separate systems (the Minnesota State Universities, the Minnesota Community College system, and the Minnesota Technical College system) under the new Minnesota Higher Education Board.
- Texas subsumed the University System of South Texas into the Texas A&M system, and Pan American University became part of the University of Texas system.
- Nebraska created a new and significantly stronger coordinating board, the Coordinating Commission for Postsecondary Education.

In some statewide university systems with one board governing all institutions, budget cuts have dictated further centralization of administrative decision making through institutional mergers designed to improve efficiency and productivity.

There are two kinds of institutional mergers. In an *administrative merger*, the offices of the president and other senior administrators of two or more institutions are combined, resulting in a reduction of administrative cost, even though the merged campuses may be many miles apart. The smaller of the merged institutions essentially becomes a satellite campus of a larger institution, yet retains a large degree of institutional identity. Alaska, experiencing a severe fiscal crisis caused by a drop in world oil prices, was one of the first states to implement administrative mergers during the late 1980s. More recent administrative realignments have been implemented in North Dakota, Montana, and Massachusetts, with serious discussions also taking place in Oregon. States under desegregation orders have also completed or contemplated institutional mergers.

The second kind of institutional merger, sometimes referred to as a *pure merger,* is one in which two or more of the merged institutions lose their separate institutional identities (Martin and Samels, 1994). These are more common in the private sector but have occurred and are still possible for public institutions. Examples include the merger of Gorham State College into the University of Maine, Portland, in the early 1970s, later to be renamed the University of Southern Maine, and a merger of Federal City Teacher's College and Washington Technical Institute to create a new university in the nation's capital, the University of the District of Columbia.

Downsizing through mergers may or may not have major disruptive effects on the institutions involved. In some states mergers appear to work, while in others the mere mention of them is tantamount to invoking outright closure of a campus, sparking a political firestorm. They almost inevitably have significant human costs as duplicative staff and faculty positions are eliminated.

The 1992 Supreme Court ruling in the case of *Ayers* v. *Fordice* continues the legal battles over desegregation of higher education and has drawn attention to governance reconfiguration as a means to respond to desegregation orders. In *Ayers* v. *Fordice,* the Court said that Mississippi has to do more than just end discrimination by race in admissions; it must examine the total system and "educationally justify or eliminate" all traces of its dual higher education system (Smothers, 1994). Although the decision directly affects only Mississippi public colleges and universities, it has implications for an additional eighteen states that are in various stages of implementing court decisions or plans approved by the U.S. Office of Civil Rights (Jaschik, 1994). In February 1994, the Office of Civil Rights notified these states that the review of their progress on desegregation would be held to the same standards as Mississippi, one result of which could be the reopening of their cases.

Governance reorganizations have often been part of desegregation plans, sometimes driven by state fiscal realities in addition to efforts to cnd a dual higher education system. For example, one of Louisiana's attempted desegregation plans (later rejected) included a proposal for a single statewide board. An institutional merger was part of Tennessee's desegregation plan, and proposals for institutional mergers are being forwarded in Mississippi and Alabama. The merger of historically black institutions with white institutions or, as had been proposed but later rejected in Louisiana, the merger of the nation's only university system of historically black colleges into a single statewide system is particularly controversial. Black leaders have made clear their intentions to fight to keep black colleges independent, arguing for facilities and program enhancements as a way to attract white students while maintaining their historical identity and current governance arrangements. But it appears increasingly likely that mergers, institutional cooperative arrangements, and other governance consolidations will eventually occur.

Future Governance Trends

Where are we headed on the governance continuum? It appears that states will continue to struggle with consolidation or centralization and decentralization issues when considering the restructuring of state higher education governance. For example, as declining state revenues may lead one legislature to seek scale economies through consolidation, another holds that institutions will be more cost-effective if freed from some central controls.

Governance changes have also become increasingly sophisticated and more complex. Decentralized approaches can contain elements that limit the degree of institutional freedoms. Illinois offers an example with its proposal to eliminate university systems and create independent boards while at the same time significantly enhancing the authority of the state coordinating board, although, as noted, the latter was not passed into law. Even within a plan for centralization, strategies can emerge to protect institutional autonomy, local decision making, and campus presidential leadership and increase the political standing of institutions, as in the case of the Pennsylvania State System of Higher Education.

And although actions in New Jersey significantly diminished the authority of its state coordinating agency and swiftly caught the attention of many education and political leaders, other states may seek more subtle changes to relax regulations or controls on institutions. What was written in the first known national study on state coordination still rings largely true: "It is important that the place which each institution is to occupy and the policy which it is to pursue be determined in the light of the whole state problem of higher education . . . in order to advance the cause of higher education and the public good" (Leonard, 1923, p. 3). The vast majority of states will continue to rely on various forms of central authority.

Confusing Messages on Governance and Accountability

Governors and legislatures can sometimes hold ambivalent, even contradictory, views on higher education's need for autonomy and independent governance and their own needs for control and oversight of fiscal and, increasingly, academic matters. Lawmakers, for instance, may express support for autonomy and academic freedom, honoring the authority of institutions to set course and degree requirements, yet demand that senior universities develop full articulation and transfer agreements with two-year colleges. They may encourage universities to raise funds from private sources, yet demand open access to all university foundation reports and records. Others may regret the degree of budget authority granted previously to coordinating and statewide governing boards in states with consolidated budget requests or lump-sum budgeting and seek fiscal accountability directly from institutions, thus bypassing the state boards. These contradictory views stem from legislative frustration over institutional accountability to the state, responsiveness to public or political demands, or a perceived disregard for the satisfaction of student "customers." Sometimes confusing messages emanate from different branches or agencies of government, and colleges and universities find themselves caught in the middle.

The demands of accountability put explicit or implicit pressure on the state governance structure to work with legislators to sort through the contradictions, to buffer institutions from unnecessary intrusion, to see that questions of accountability are resolved, and to ensure institutional flexibility in meeting state accountability standards. Legislatures may, if issues are not resolved to their satisfaction, place mandates on boards and commissions, make laws around them (thereby weakening their authority), or pass laws to eliminate them.

Reorganizing college and university boards is sometimes seen as a means by which lawmakers can improve accountability. Because elected officials cannot directly control a campus or university system as they can most cabinet-level agencies, they instead change those factors over which they can exert control—the laws that determine how boards are constituted or that define the extent of their authority. Lawmakers may see centralization of governance not only as a way to merge boards and administrations but also as a way to centralize institutional academic practices, which they increasingly perceive as being characterized by "unaccountable" academic departments and faculty who operate with great independence and with little interest in the overall needs of the institution, let alone the needs of the state. Unfortunately, too often these strategies (as well as the tendency to legislate around boards by passing legislation on academic policy) are more drastic measures than necessary to achieve desired outcomes, especially when it may be more effective to foster positive change by encouraging campus-initiated institutional restructuring or state-level incentive funding programs as suggested by Ewell (1985), Folger (1984), and others.

Creating Successful Alternatives to Major Governance Restructuring

In a number of states, including some in which one or more rounds of governance reorganization have taken place or where rigorous debates have occurred over serious educational and resource problems, consensus is emerging that current structures offer the best mechanisms to address fiscal and other challenges. To reach consensus in support of current governance, both educational and governmental leaders must be able to agree on reforms only where truly needed and develop viable alternatives that do not require governance changes. States that can achieve such a consensus can avoid bitter, divisive battles and the distractions that accompany major organizational change.

If state officials wish to sustain existing governance structures, they must respect and support the integrity of such structures. They must understand that boards, commissions, and their administrations are the legally created link among higher education, the state, and the public. Likewise, legislatures must discourage geopolitical differences from spilling over into higher education.

Schick, Novak, Norton, and Elam (1992) suggest that even before considering changing state governance structures, state officials need to realize six key realities:

1. No single structure or organization is best for every state. Changes can be counterproductive and disruptive, distracting key parties from the main purposes of higher education.
2. Demonstrable improvements after reorganization may be hard to recognize and may be delayed or barely tangible.
3. A structure must be created that transcends the talents of particular leaders.
4. The number and types of institutions within a university system structure may have a major impact on how the system functions. For example, large systems may find it difficult to attend to local needs, and systems made up of institutions with divergent missions may need policies that support institutional differentiation.
5. Similarly, in the state structure, policy makers must consider the overall balance of institutions and boards, perhaps placing some institutions within a system and allowing others to remain independent.
6. States must create structures that grant as much autonomy and fiscal flexibility as possible, conferring sufficient authority on leaders while clearly expecting accountability.

McGuinness (1994) has also made six cogent suggestions to states considering reorganization:

1. Before reorganizing, clarify the state vision, goals, and objectives for higher education. Recognize reorganization as a means to an end rather than an end in itself.
2. Be explicit about the specific problems that were the catalyst for the reorganization proposals.
3. Ask if reorganization is the only means or the most effective

means for addressing the problems that have been identified. Have the costs of reorganization been weighed against the short- and long-term benefits?

4. Recognize that a good system takes the needs of state, society, and colleges and universities into consideration but recognize also that state interests are not necessarily the same as the sum of institutional interests.

5. Distinguish between state coordination and institutional governance.

6. Examine the total policy structure and process, including the roles of the governor and agencies of the executive branch and the legislature, rather than focusing exclusively on the formal education structure.

State leaders may come to realize that it will be internal institutional restructuring (something they can foster, encourage, and support) that makes a difference in institutional performance, resulting in higher quality, greater productivity, and improved accountability; that institutional restructuring can occur without major changes in state governance; and that it can in fact best be accomplished with stable boards and administrations. Undoubtedly, state government structures are influencing institutional restructuring by fostering, encouraging, and supporting campus-based change.

Some Suggested Improvements for Boards of Current Structures

The uncertain relationship between higher education and state governments requires stable, cohesive governing boards capable of thinking and acting strategically and serving as vital links between society and institutions. Recognizing the financial and human costs associated with state governance restructuring and realizing that there is little evidence that reorganization makes a difference in the performance of institutions, state and education leaders may need jointly to develop a reform agenda to improve governing and coordinating board performance and, in some cases, chief executive performance as well. Improving board performance will not prevent all efforts to reorganize governance structures—many reorganizations have occurred for many reasons other than ineffective boards, as mentioned earlier.

Nevertheless, improved boards capable of inspiring confidence on the part of state officials and the public they represent are a critical first step for board and institutional stability, growth, change, and future success. What might the reform agenda include? The following suggestions have been culled from state, institutional, and board practices in a small but growing number of places, as well as from scholarship on effective governance and board behavior.

First, states must improve the process for selecting citizens to serve on governing and coordinating boards and commissions. These selections are of enormous importance to higher education but too often fall low on the priority lists of the governors and legislatures who make them. In many states, competent individuals are overlooked or never considered, and too often, selections are made to repay political favors.

Ideally, each state's governor and legislature should appoint a ten- to twelve-member standing committee or citizens' nonpartisan screening committee whose job it is to solicit nominations and review candidates for vacancies on all public higher education boards. The committee would not make or confirm final selections but rather would provide two or three names for each seat to the appointing authority—the governor in the vast majority of states. The appointing authority would then choose one name to place in nomination for each seat. Thirty-four states use an analogous process to make district and appeals court nominations. A committee of this kind would largely depoliticize the selection process and ensure that persons chosen for such critical positions can balance a state stewardship role with understanding and caring for higher education. New Mexico, Minnesota, Kentucky, Massachusetts, North Dakota, and the District of Columbia have created such bodies.

Although not a substitute for a third-party screening committee, legislatures themselves can improve the selection process by developing fair, rigorous, publicly stated criteria for use in the confirmation process. The governor, the public, and all nominees would then get the appropriate message that seats on public higher education boards were viewed as prized appointments (Callan and Honetschlager, 1992).

Second, there should be a yearly orientation program for all board members, both new and experienced, that is separate from the orientation to the institution or the university system. Eleven states have such orientation programs, of which five are required by statute, one is required by executive order, one was initiated by the governing board itself, and the others were begun by the state coordinating board. This type of orientation is especially useful in states with multiple boards whose members rarely, if ever, have an opportunity to discuss the role and responsibilities of boards, issues occurring at other institutions, or matters of statewide significance. In the annual governor's conference on trusteeship, Kentucky trustees have an opportunity to discuss not only board "process issues" but also issues before the governor and legislature and those facing private and community colleges. In that sense, the orientation helps trustees develop nonparochial perspectives that are in the best long-term interests of their institutions. Developing nonparochial perspectives is particularly important in states like Kentucky where independent governing boards predominate. In these uncertain times, independent boards must be effective if they are to be justified as viable alternatives to system governance and representative of how institutions can best be governed. These governing boards must think and act strategically and be willing to achieve a balance in their roles as both institutional advocate and state overseer. A statewide orientation program would help in accomplishing this.

States with statewide multicampus governing boards can also hold orientations focused on issues outside the immediate experiences of those within their own system. The Wisconsin Board of Regents has developed a strong program centered around such issues as relationships with internal and external constituents and the appropriate balance between the roles of resource manager and system advocate.

Third, boards should undergo an annual internal self-assessment and a periodic external assessment of performance, with the results used in future strategic planning. Although self-assessment can be incorporated into regular board meetings (Chait, Holland, and Taylor, 1993), an annual one-day retreat, facilitated by a neutral third party, can not only build board cohesion but also clarify the role of the board and its relationship to and expectations of the chief executive (and vice versa). An internal self-assessment will allow the board, president, or system administration to review its past year's performance in order first to determine what it has done well, what it has done not so well, and what it may want to do differently and then to help set goals for the upcoming year.

In addition to the internal self-assessment, an external assessment of the board should be done every few years. External constituents hold many opinions about institutions and systems and their boards, and in that sense informal assessments occur constantly. Listening to and discussing these opinions systematically (no matter how contradictory they may be) could prove extremely useful. Included should be the opinions of elected officials, elementary and secondary educators, local community leaders, employers, the media, and, most important of all, the general public. External assessment may be viewed as a high-risk endeavor, but if the assessment instrument is realistically and thoughtfully designed, it will open up communication among the board, the administration, and major external constituencies.

As term limits, retirements, and elections contribute to an increasingly high rate of turnover among legislators and governors, it is imperative that higher education maintain regular communication with lawmakers. Hence as either part of or follow-up to external assessment, board and executive leaders might consider a meeting with the legislative leadership and the governor's office to discuss the results. Carried too far, however, an external assessment could undermine board authority and independence or give the impression that the board is a deputy legislature or governor's agent. If discussions focus on disagreements over the results of assessments, the board and chief executive can help determine which areas require institutional or system remedy, state remedy, or both.

Long-term external assessments might explore a number of critical issues, including the degree to which the board balances institutional advocacy with state oversight; its success as a vehicle for communication with its many constituents; its ability to manage human and physical assets, handle fiscal autonomy and responsibility, and stay focused on policy and not institutional micromanagement; its effectiveness in setting institutional missions and keeping the institution focused on state educational and economic priorities; and if a system board, its ability to allocate resources fairly to its member campuses.

Fourth, states should revise open-meeting laws (sunshine laws), as far too many do not allow public boards to make important decisions in private. All fifty states have open-meeting laws, varying in degrees of required openness (Cleveland, 1985). Open-meeting laws that are too extensive inhibit cohesion among board members, encourage boardroom behavior that plays to the media or special constituents, and discourage citizens from serving on boards. The inability to discuss legal, real estate, financial, personnel, or labor relations issues in private or executive sessions limits board effectiveness and hinders the decision-making process. Most unfortunately, by being forced to conduct chief executive searches in public or release names of candidates, sunshine laws discourage many qualified individuals from seeking positions. At many institutions, the privacy of presidential searches has been challenged by the popular media, necessitating the intervention of the courts, which have tended to rule in favor of the press (Davis, 1994).

As politically difficult as it is to change sunshine laws, states must seek to balance the "public's right to know" with the need for collective "privacy" within the board. We should not expect public boards to make all decisions behind closed doors, but neither can we expect them to function at the highest levels of effectiveness under the laws that are now on the books.

Fifth, limitations on the service of board members and especially the length of term for board chairs should be reexamined. On too many university, system, and state coordinating boards, chairs serve for one year and then are either rotated out of the chairmanship or face reelection. To understand their roles fully, all board members must serve terms of adequate length. Laws or policies that force board members to vacate the chair after just one year do not allow boards and the institutions they govern or coordinate to benefit sufficiently from the leadership and experience they have attained. In addition, important time and effort are wasted on internal board politicking.

State and institutional leaders may wish to develop additional ideas to improve current performance, based on the literature on presidential leadership and board effectiveness. The scholarship on board effectiveness, sporadic throughout the 1960s and 1970s, has mushroomed recently through works sponsored by the Association of Governing Boards of Universities and Colleges and the National Center for Nonprofit Boards and is beginning to rival the literature on presidential leadership.

Conclusion

We are in a period of major change in higher education. Downward pressure on state spending due to lowered taxes or a sustained national recession may lead to radical changes for the financing, governance, and coordination of nearly all public colleges and universities. And developments in technology will have unknown effects on how institutions are governed or coordinated.

Although we appear to be moving toward governance structures consisting of more decentralized university systems and institutions, we are also moving toward one in which students and parents, due to declining state and federal aid, will be paying a larger portion of educational costs than any other source. The questions raised by such arrangements for the financing, accountability, and governance of institutions are many and as yet unanswerable. What demands on governance, for example, are students entitled to make if they pay for a greater share of their education than the state? What sustained and consistently applied measures can demonstrate institutional accountability and satisfy state policy makers?

Given the uncertain relationship between higher education and state government, states must build and support higher education governance structures that are stable yet adaptable, and higher education's leaders must constantly be alert to broad change and be the first to recognize when the roles and responsibilities of their organizations have become static. State leaders must not be too quick to embrace governance restructuring as the vehicle for change in the behavior or performance of institutions. Again, disruptions may distract from higher education's main purposes for long periods of time.

No matter how they are constituted, governance structures that encourage good communication with the state and the public, foster institutional cooperation and the resolution of conflict without external intervention, assure institutional involvement in pressing public policy issues like school reform and minority access, and ensure quality and accountability are necessary now and will be in the future. A weak governance structure creates myriad problems that can undermine leadership, academic freedom, and institutional quality. A sound structure does make a difference in the bottom-line issues that really matter: the quality of teaching, learning, public service, and research.

References

Callan, P. M. *Perspectives on the Current Status of and Emerging Policy Issues for State Coordinating Boards.* AGB Occasional Paper No. 2. Washington, D.C.: Association of Governing Boards of Universities and Colleges, 1991.

Callan, P. M., and Honetschlager, D. A. *Policies for Improving Trustee Selection in the Public Sector.* AGB Occasional Paper No. 13. Washington, D.C.: Association of Governing Boards of Universities and Colleges, 1992.

Chait, R. P., Holland, T. P., and Taylor, B. E. *The Effective Board of Trustees.* Phoenix, Ariz.: Oryx Press, 1993.

Cleveland, H. *The Costs and Benefits of Openness: Sunshine Laws and Higher Education.* AGB Special Report. Washington, D.C.: Association of Governing Boards of Universities and Colleges, 1985.

Davis, C. H. "Scaling the Ivory Tower: State Public Records Laws and University Presidential Searches." *Journal of College and University Law,* 1994, *21*(2), 353–368.

Ewell, P. T. *Levers for Change: The Role of State Government in Improving the Quality of Postsecondary Education.* Denver, Colo.: Education Commission of the States, 1985.

Folger, J. (ed.). *Financial Incentives for Academic Quality.* New Directions for Higher Education, Vol. XII, no. 48. San Francisco: Jossey-Bass, 1984.

Glenny, L. A. *Autonomy of Public Colleges: The Challenge of Coordination.* New York: McGraw-Hill, 1959.

Glenny, L. A., and Dalglish, T. K. "Higher Education and the Law." In J. A. Perkins (ed.), *The University as an Organization.* New York: McGraw-Hill, 1973.

Gold, S. D. *The Outlook for State Support of Higher Education.* Denver, Colo.: National Conference of State Legislatures, 1989.

Jaschik, S. "Whither Desegregation?" *Chronicle of Higher Education,* Jan. 26, 1994, p. 33.

Johnstone, D. B. *Learning Productivity: A New Imperative for American Higher Education*. Studies in Public Higher Education, no. 3. Albany: State University of New York, 1993.

Kelly, F. J., and McNeeley, J. H. *The State and Higher Education: Phases of Their Relationship*. New York: The Carnegie Foundation for the Advancement of Teaching, 1933.

Kerr, C., and Gade, M. L. *The Guardians: Boards of Trustees of American Colleges and Universities*. Washington, D.C.: Association of Governing Boards of Universities and Colleges, 1989.

Klein, A. J. *Cooperation and Coordination in Higher Education*. Washington, D.C.: American Council on Education, 1938.

Leonard, R. J. *The Coordination of State Institutions for Higher Education Through Supplementary Curricular Boards*. Berkeley: University of California Department of Education, 1923.

Lewis, E. T., Muller, S., and Aery, S. R. "Metamorphosis of a Public College." *Trusteeship*, 1994, *2*(5), 20–25.

McGuinness, A. C., Jr. *Perspectives on the Current Status of and Emerging Policy Issues for Public Multicampus Higher Education Systems*. AGB Occasional Paper No. 3. Washington, D.C.: Association of Governing Boards of Universities and Colleges, 1991.

McGuinness, A. C., Jr. "The Changing Structure of State Higher Education Leadership." In A. C. McGuinness Jr., R. Epper, and S. Arredondo (eds.), *State Postsecondary Education Structures Handbook: State Coordinating and Governing Boards*. Denver, Colo.: Education Commission of the States, 1994.

Martin, J., and Samels, J. E. "A Closer Look at Mergers." *Trusteeship*, 1994, *2*(2), 15–18.

National Center for Education Statistics. *Digest of Education Statistics*. Washington D.C.: U.S. Department of Education, 1993.

Pew Higher Education Research Program. "The Lattice and the Ratchet." *Policy Perspectives*, 1990, *2*(4), 1–8.

Pew Higher Education Research Program. "Testimony from the Belly of the Whale." *Policy Perspectives*, 1992, *4*(3), 1–8.

President's Commission on Higher Education. *Higher Education for American Democracy*, Vol 1. Washington, D.C.: U.S. Government Printing Office, 1947.

Schick, E. B. *The Local Board in Public Systems and Multicampus Universities*. Washington, D.C.: Association of Governing Boards of Universities and Colleges, 1994.

Schick, E. B., Novak, R. J., Norton, J. A., and Elam, H. G. *Shared Visions of Public Higher Education Governance: Structures and Leadership Styles That*

Work. Washington, D.C.: American Association of State Colleges and Universities, 1992.

Smothers, R. "Mississippi's University System Going on Trial." *New York Times,* May 9, 1994, p. A10.

Snell, R. (ed.). *Financing State Government in the 1990s.* Denver, Colo.: National Conference of State Legislatures/Washington, D.C.: National Governors' Association, 1993.

Solochek, Jeffrey S. "L. V. Consultant Visits Students, Faculty, Deans." *Beaumont Enterprise,* Oct. 23, 1992, p. 1A.

Task Force on Coordination, Governance and Structure of Postsecondary Education. *Coordination or Chaos?* Denver, Colo.: Education Commission of the States, 1973.

Part Two

Five Case Studies

Chapter Three

Restructuring That Works: North Dakota

Douglas M. Treadway

North Dakotans, a small and declining population of about six hundred thousand, are deployed across a vast prairie that could swallow the New England states with room to spare. North Dakota offers a stage where a handful or two of able leaders can truly make a difference in the course of events. This is a good thing, because the taxpayers of the state are reluctant to provide money when they believe perpetual effort will do.

The attempt at restructuring higher education in North Dakota is remarkable because it has been largely successful. And it succeeded because it was characterized by the homespun virtues of common sense, responsibility, and courage in its leaders and participants. It offers a host of applicable lessons for practitioners and policy makers in larger and more complex states that have to date failed to get this reorganization business right. North Dakota's transition in the 1980s and early 1990s from a loosely federated collection of colleges and universities to an integrated system of higher education was powerfully influenced by ideas of the national academic reform agenda, declining state resources for higher education, and innovations associated with the total quality movement.

Responding to unmistakable signs of long-term economic decline punctuated by voters' refusals to raise taxes, the Board of Higher Education accepted its responsibility to restructure and reform. Experienced academic leaders developed a blueprint for change that drew inspiration from various national agendas and the unique challenges of this sparsely populated agricultural state. As the new chancellor, I inherited solid board support, a coherent and visionary agenda, and an experienced staff who had personally invested in the change. What I did not inherit was broad-based public or legislative confidence in the new system, a condition that continues to hamper the new way of doing things. This chapter presents the contemporary history of restructuring in North Dakota, then offers a summary of the lessons provided in this northern laboratory for change.

A Constitutionally Mandated System

The modern history of higher education in North Dakota is one of consistent strengthening of the authority of the board. The North Dakota Board of Higher Education, established by the state's constitution, oversees eleven campuses, each with a specific mission. The constitution provides the board with broad powers and specifies that the board retains any powers it does not specifically delegate to the chancellor and the presidents.

In 1985, the board acquired authority beyond the eight colleges and universities to include the state's three community colleges as well. The funding base of these institutions migrated from local funds to state appropriations. Soon after the addition of the community colleges, the four-year institutions were given university status. One two-year institution at Devils Lake was designated as a branch campus of the University of North Dakota, as had been done to Williston some years earlier. Bottineau, another two-year college, had become a branch of North Dakota State University years before. The community college at Bismarck was renamed Bismarck State College.

Under its board-dominated hierarchy, each of the university presidents reported not to its executive but to the board itself. Throughout the 1980s, the board developed policies that would turn a collection of institutions into a system. The journey toward consolidation accelerated at the end of the decade when a fiscal crisis prompted the board to reorganize its governing and management pattern.

As prices fell in on the agriculture and energy markets and federal mandates shifted more costs for health care and other human services onto the states, state support for higher education dwindled. North Dakota's long-term population decline meant that fewer residents shouldered the tax burden. In December 1989, a voter-initiated referendum killed a tax increase passed by the legislature and precipitated a financial crisis for the colleges and universities.

Board Action

The tax vote forced the state board to act with resolve, which it did by establishing the North Dakota University System, headed by a chancellor. The board; the commissioner, John Richardson; and institutional leaders recognized, albeit with some reluctance, that continuing to compete for fewer state dollars would erode the quality of the entire system. In February 1990, the board adopted the "one-university system" concept and formally established a statewide, cohesive system of public higher education. The presidents would report to the board's executive, now called a chancellor, rather than to the board itself. Public policy issues affecting higher education were to be dealt with at the system level, while the presidents of the institutions retained authority for campus management.

Three features distinguish restructuring in North Dakota from that in other states. The move to what North Dakotans called the one-university concept grew organically out of a history characterized by gradual consolidation of authority. It was not a radical departure from the familiar. Once the voters spoke by turning down the tax measure, the board acted responsibly and with dispatch. Unlike peers in other states, its members did not wait for the governor or legislature to intervene. Finally, the board insisted from the start that while this restructuring would enjoy strong executive leadership, it would unfold in a carefully planned way with substantial involvement from the presidents of the colleges and universities. This communal approach would serve the system well in the difficult times ahead.

Of immense help in the re-creation of the system was a statute enacted in 1989 that mandated a strategic planning process for higher education. Known as the Seven Year Plan, this process required that the board meet every other year with the governor and legislative leadership to discuss issues and opportunities for higher education. Following consultation, the board was required then to submit to the legislature (in its biennial sessions) their short- and long-range strategic plan as an accompaniment to the biennial budget request. The first of these plans became the blueprint for the new system.

This first Seven Year Plan, written in 1990, was a comprehensive and visionary document that acknowledged not only the harsh realities of North Dakota's economy but also the lofty aspirations of the national reform movement in higher education. The plan reflected the key elements of the reform literature of the 1980s as well as the emerging national interest in total quality improvement (TQI).

For the first time, the state had placed before it a specific higher education agenda emphasizing undergraduate teaching, investments in faculty development, diversity in admissions, hiring and curriculum in international opportunities, linkages with K–12 education on the one hand and employers on the other, and technology as a means of expanding access in a large, sparsely populated state. The board looked after its own development. It retained professor Lawrence Sherr of the University of Kansas to coach members and staff on the principles of total quality. The board came to believe that a total quality effort would be instrumental in addressing the need to achieve greater unity of purpose and hoped it would also lead to measurable enhancements in efficiency, programs, and services. The Seven Year Plan, driven by a total quality philosophy, became the cornerstone for the leadership priorities of the first full-time chancellor for the North Dakota University System.

Leadership Transition

The chief architects of the one-university system were John Richardson and key members of his staff. Dr. Richardson held the position of commissioner of higher education and felt strongly that when the move from a commissioner to a chancellor role took place, a new leader would be better positioned actually to implement the change he championed. He therefore declined to seek the permanent leadership role, and Dr. Thomas Clifford, president of the University of North Dakota, was appointed by the board to serve as interim chancellor while a national search was conducted. Working closely with both Richardson and Clifford were Ellen Earle Chaffee and Larry Isaak. Chaffee, who had been chief academic officer in the earlier regime and who wrote the new system's educational reform agenda, stayed on and became the system's first vice chancellor for academic affairs. Isaak, formerly the chief administrative officer, became vice chancellor for administrative and student affairs. His prior experience in the state budget office, his credibility with state legislators, and his leadership in establishing statewide administrative systems in higher education throughout the 1980s would prove vital to the next stage of restructuring. Thus the new chancellor would enter the state with a plan to pursue and an experienced and respected staff to help carry it out.

On July 1, 1991, I assumed responsibility as chancellor of the restructured system of higher education in North Dakota. I came to North Dakota from the neighboring state of Minnesota, where I had served for four years as president of one of its rural universities. I brought experience with reform initiatives undertaken by the Minnesota State University System and by the Minnesota Council on Quality, a statewide industry-education partnership, as well as experience in national rural educational leadership.

During my first week in office, I met for two days with the board and campus presidents in a planning retreat. I subsequently gathered more than one hundred campus leaders for a similar planning retreat and with them developed a vision for implementing the state's one-university system concept. I set forth seven principles that would guide the one-university system in its development (Treadway, 1991):

1. There would be a shared vision of the future firmly grounded in the national reform agenda and realistically cast within the fiscal constraints of North Dakota.
2. The institutions would create, in partnership with the public schools, a "seamless educational delivery system."
3. The system approach would empower people to responsibility and action at their own level in the organization and would reward creativity and risk taking by all concerned.

4. The system would support development of higher education as one of the primary growth industries of North Dakota.
5. Administration and delivery systems would be organized around the changing needs of the state and would be decentralized as member institutions would assume shared leadership in creating the system. The central office would not grow in personnel.
6. A balance between campus autonomy and systemwide unity would flow from a consensus decision-making process in the chancellor's cabinet (presidents, chancellor, and vice chancellors) and the state board.
7. Allocation of a restricted base of resources would be addressed through focusing campus missions, reducing duplication, administratively downsizing and streamlining, and developing partnerships with other entities in pursuit of resource sharing and other mutual benefits.

Rather than taking the one-university system creation as a mandate for centralization of authority through restructuring, I pursued a communal agenda. As much as possible, decisions would be reached by consensus and plans implemented in a decentralized fashion. The first real test of this communal style came as legislators and editorial writers pressured me to address the economic crisis triggered by the 1989 tax referral vote by closing a campus.

Campus Closing Issue

The idea of closing one of the smaller campuses has been a recurring theme in discussions of alternatives for higher education in the upper Midwest. Wisconsin converted one of its two-year campuses to a prison in the early 1980s, as did South Dakota. The University of Minnesota announced in 1991 that it would shut down a rural campus with an agricultural curriculum. Pressure mounted on me and the board to show similar resolve.

In 1987, the board supported a measure to revise the North Dakota constitution by eliminating the specific naming of the campuses and their missions. As long as each campus had a constitutional designation, the board did not have authority on its own to enact a campus closure. This constitutional revision move was soundly turned back in the halls of the legislature and never made it to the electorate for a vote. Rural legislators from towns hosting small campuses were angered at the board over their actions.

Knowing this, the board urged me not to come into this line of fire early in my tenure of office. Leaders within the system insisted that any campus closure would seriously damage a region of the state. They made a convincing case for the more complex alternative of simultaneously reducing costs and improving service in the system as a whole. Eventually, this argument won the day. By the close of 1993, the governor, legislative leaders, and most (but not all) newspaper editorial boards had taken a position of supporting the plan to refocus and make better use of the small campuses and thus to support their otherwise economically fragile rural communities.

One of the reasons there was a hiatus of pressure for closure of one or more campuses was the recognition that other alternatives for addressing costs and duplication were being actively pursued by the chancellor and the board. Having rejected a no-win strategy of proposing closure, the strategy of mergers and consolidations, which were to a greater extent matters of board authority, were openly discussed.

A successful and intriguing structural change occurred within the consolidation of the administration of two small universities under a single president. The administrative alliance of Mayville State and Valley City State universities has not only saved dollars but signaled to some at least that there were going to be new ways of doing business in higher education. The arrangement, perhaps unique in American higher education, keeps the two universities separate for budgets (constitutional provision) but joins the staff and faculty in a cooperative-type organization (a rural model for mutual endeavor strongly rooted in the Midwest farming culture). Under the cooperative structure, the two campuses became experimental colleges for the demonstration of new college teaching strategies and advanced learning technologies. Ellen Chaffee moved from her position as vice chancellor for academic affairs to the combined presidency, which gave further credibility to the new cooperative, along with some specially designated state appropriations for the experimental college mission.

Concurrent with the alignment of Mayville and Valley City

universities, the board and I attempted to align or merge North Dakota State College of Science with North Dakota State University. This attempt at consolidation met fierce opposition from constituents of the State College of Science and created controversy that flowed into the legislative session in a mode not unlike the previous board attempt to revise the constitution. Informal discussions to form mergers or alliances among four colleges in the western half of the state never became public proposals; they were sidelined, under intense legislative pressures, along with the College of Science merger.

Despite the fact that only one consolidation had been accomplished, it nevertheless showed resolve of the system to strengthen its members rather than eliminate weaker members. This near-term victory for the collectivist approach carried a downside as well. Having forgone the bold stroke of proposing closing an institution and having fallen short of accomplishing mergers and consolidations on a broad scale, the new system found it difficult to make a convincing case to the public generally that important reforms were nevertheless being accomplished.

A Collaborative Model That Works

Four years after the State Board of Higher Education established the university system, concerns remain over loss of autonomy among the institutions. Griping is still common, particularly at the state's largest universities, over the loss of local autonomy. Some legislators complain that they can no longer campaign for their hometown college exclusively but must instead support the system as a whole. However, it is also widely recognized that the chancellorship and the one-university system makes sense. As one external reviewer said, "Together they are seen as the only way to reduce duplication, promote cooperation, and improve quality without spending any more money" (Oster, 1993, p. 9).

Though the chief organizational change under the new system is simple (namely, that campus presidents now report to a chancellor instead of directly to the board), the cultural change within the system is dramatic and continuous. Its chief feature, as outlined in Table 3.1, is a shift from competition among institutions to collaboration.

Table 3.1. Changes Under the New System.

Old Commissioner System	New Chancellor System
Competition for programs	Collaboration and sharing; mission differentiation
Proprietary lobbying of legislature	Coordinated legislative plan
Eleven campus administrations	Ten administrations; accelerated system streamlining
Central office separation	Chancellor's cabinet and systemwide councils
Little systemwide delivery	Systemwide delivery methods added or enhanced for statewide interactive video, on-line library services, economic development, human resource expertise, motor pool administration, customized training, and other services
Classified staff under state personnel program	System's own human resource program
Minimum long-range planning	Seven-year strategic plan
Competition with K–12	"Seamless" partnership with K–12

There are numerous internal groups working together for the first time in their history, with significant results. The Council of College Faculties, for example, a statewide organization with representation from all eleven campuses, has a designated position on the Board of Higher Education. Although this remains a nonvoting membership, still the council has become more proactive under the system structure than it had been previously. In the early 1980s, the statewide student association gained a nonvoting position on the board. Creation of the university system brought this organization more actively into the governance process as well, to the point that the 1993 legislature passed a bill to give the student representative full status as a voting member of the board.

To keep the structure as streamlined as possible, the chancellor's cabinet serves as the clearinghouse for all policy development and coordination systemwide. Ad hoc groups, usually representing all campuses, are established to assist in major policy making and problem solving, but no standing committees exist at either board or cabinet level.

Lead Campus Model

An important example of collaboration is in the development of a focused academic mission for each institution and the award of "lead responsibilities" to different campuses for the various academic and service programs offered by the system. Previously, each campus had prepared plans for new programs in secrecy and from a highly competitive vantage point in an effort to build student enrollments. Under the focused-mission scenario, the campus with lead responsibility has "first call" for a new program in its area of the curriculum. If it will not be offering the program, it is nevertheless expected to provide leadership to site the program appropriately and articulate it with existing programs in the same field of study.

As Table 3.2 shows, responsibility to serve as a lead campus is spread across the system to large and small institutions.

Changing the Academic Structure

Within two years, the new system accomplished a number of changes in the academic array, changes that would have been all but impossible to implement in the era when each campus could act independently. The board approved new and more focused missions for each campus. About a dozen degree programs were eliminated, institutional agreements were finalized to ensure the transferability of courses between campuses, and all quarter-calendar institutions converted to the semester system. The system created and enforced a common admissions standard based on a core high school curriculum for enrollment to the universities in the system. The system also created a planning and coordinating mechanism for secondary and two-year college vocational-technical programs in collaboration with the Department of Vocational Education and the North Dakota Job Service. Finally, a new mission was established for Valley City State University as the systemwide

Table 3.2. Assignments of Lead Responsibility.

Center for Innovation in Instruction	Valley City State University
Quentin Burdick Center for Cooperatives	North Dakota State University
Center for Social Policy and Research	University of North Dakota
Center for International Development and Exchange	Dickinson State University
Center for Rural Health	University of North Dakota
Institute for Cultural Diversity	North Dakota State University
Institute for Writing and Critical Thinking	Minot State University
North Dakota Center for Disabilities	Minot State University
State Forester	North Dakota State University, Bottineau
State Demographer	North Dakota State University
Center for Aerospace Studies	University of North Dakota
Customized Training Center	North Dakota State College of Science
Vocational-Technical Curriculum Services	Bismarck State College
State Adult Education Resource Center	Bismarck State College
North Dakota Tech Prep	Bismarck State College
College Technical Education	System/Vocation Education

laboratory for innovation in teaching and learning at the college level, with support received from the North Dakota legislature as a line item in the Valley City State University budget and through grants from the U.S. Office of Education and other state and private organizations.

Some people at the campuses were and continue to be unhappy with these changes, especially the program discontinuances and restrictions on faculty hiring. Had this discipline not been exercised by the system office, the legislature would surely have intervened with more draconian measures.

Reinventing Administrative Services

The system had pioneered in the use of statewide computing as early as the 1970s, with the Higher Education Computing Network offering a central student records function based at the University of North Dakota and a central financial function based at North Dakota State University. Through a number of projects that capitalized on the network as a shared set of programs and databases, it became the foundation for an array of reports and services done simultaneously for all eleven campuses, rather than being done eleven times over. These systems are currently being rewritten to take advantage of new technology.

A common admissions form has been developed, and touchtone telephone registration is in place on about half the campuses. Teams of staff, faculty, and administrators continue to work on system streamlining and resource sharing projects under broad authority of the chancellor to institute changes as brought forward from the campuses.

Downsizing the Administration

In response to harsh economic realities, the administration has been significantly downsized. A 10 percent systemwide reduction in administrative budgets was achieved, along with a reduction in the chancellor's office staff, including elimination of one vice chancellor position. A portion of the system operating budget was dedicated to support professional development for faculty, staff, and administrators, and each campus budgeted a prescribed minimum percentage of its payroll for training for all personnel.

A university system human resources program was established, enabling the system to separate from the state central personnel system. The system embarked on a systemwide facilities management and development program. Finally, new computerized financial systems were designed and a planning process was developed to support further streamlining of administrative services across all campuses. The new system received national recognition for implementing total quality improvement methods within the chancellor governance model.

Using Technology to Expand Service

Among the dozens of multicampus cooperative activities that have taken place, none is more visible than the statewide network for distance learning. The North Dakota University System has moved aggressively to provide courses to site-bound learners through an interactive television network and related computer interactive systems support. All eleven campuses, the state capitol, and the state hospital are on-line with this interactive system. Soon to be connected is Standing Rock Tribal Community College, and the four other tribal colleges (Fort Berthold Community College, Turtle Mountain Community College, Little Hoop Community College, and United Tribes Technical College) plan connection in the near future. The system has hired a full-time coordinator who is housed at the University of North Dakota, and each campus is represented on a planning council for the network that develops policies and procedures for the network as well as protocols for determining delivery system priorities.

The distance learning technology network serves multiple purposes. A range of full degree programs is offered over the interactive video network, including an associate degree in mental health; two bachelor's degrees in nursing; master's degrees in counselor education, business administration, public administration, and rural health nursing; and specialist degrees in educational administration and early childhood education. Between two or more campuses, courses in foreign languages, teacher education, the sciences, and the humanities are shared using one common instructor.

Valley City State University has been designated as the lead institution for the training of teachers in using the new distance learning technologies. Another shared activity over the network is a common electronic library catalogue and retrieval system known as ODIN (On-line Dakota Information Network), established in the 1980s but reaching full implementation in the 1990s. Every public and school library has access to ODIN, with its network of university system library resources as well as external databases. Significant progress has been achieved in plans for further integration of technology-based systems, including interactive television, library services, academic computer services, and student and administrative services.

More Effective Service to the State

Much of the reform in North Dakota higher education has been introspective, focusing on streamlining the academic program and reducing administrative costs. Indeed, the bulk of the national reform movement calls for internal change, and this has been a priority for North Dakota as well. Still, restructuring has enabled higher education to respond to pressing state needs, notably economic development, job creation, and the needs of the state's significant Native American population.

To apply its shoulder to the economic development wheel, the system developed a statewide, integrated network through which the campuses assist business and industry. Known as the University Business Assistance Network, UBAN has brought together the teaching, research, and extension expertise of all eleven campuses and related entities into a coordinated outreach program. The system entered into agreements with the Department of Economic Development and Finance to colocate regional coordinators on campuses of the university system and extended the colocation model to include other local, state, and federal agencies to evolve "one-stop shops" at the regional colleges. In addition, a plan was developed to track all North Dakota citizens engaged in education and job training through employment placement; a comprehensive delivery system for customized training was developed, with North Dakota State College of Science serving as coordinating institution; and a system-level economic development advisory committee of leaders from agriculture and industry was set up.

Thanks to restructuring, the system could act in a more comprehensive way to stimulate job creation. A complete statewide program of cooperative education, including the tribal colleges, was developed, and the U.S. Department of Labor funded it as a national demonstration model of statewide cooperative education coordination. The system established a center for training public school teachers in the uses of interactive TV and other technologies and expanded the distance learning network to include public school sites. In addition, the system entered into agreements with the Board of Public Schools and the Board of Vocational Education for collaborative efforts in education at all levels in the state, including teacher training, teacher in-service, workforce training, library services, administrator competence-based credentialing, and cultural diversity program sharing.

Collaboration also extended to diverse populations. The system developed articulation agreements with the five tribal colleges in North Dakota and enhanced coordination with the tribes for economic development and outreach. Four campuses developed cultural diversity programs as part of the Western Interstate Commission on Higher Education diversity program. Dickinson State University agreed to serve as the system center for exchanges with China.

Lessons Learned and a Few Surprises

The drama of change unfolds in unique ways in each state. What works with one political, economic, and cultural context will not apply entirely in another. Yet six lessons from the North Dakota experience should help guide others.

1. *Crisis creates the opportunity for leadership.* Although the movement toward a unified system had been under way for some years, a major financial crisis accelerated structural change. The North Dakota Board of Higher Education recognized the looming crisis as an opportunity to unite the campuses further in a communal response. Most observers contend that if the board had not taken action, the state legislature would have enacted sweeping changes by statute. Almost certainly, these would have been less congenial than the changes wrought from within.

2. *The process for change must reflect the values of its participants.* Resistance to centralizing power or control in any group or person is a strong social force in North Dakota, thanks to its populist traditions. In this climate, the strategy of shaping the new system by consensus and by decentralizing service responsibilities to member campuses yielded positive results. Aims McGuinness points out that the higher education systems of the future must achieve "two

seemingly contradictory changes": they must redefine "centralized functions related to policy leadership, while at the same time transforming leadership and management to achieve far more differentiated, decentralized, adaptive and innovative units" (1991, p. 18). North Dakota is well on the way to balancing these twin imperatives.

Within the first three years of the Seven Year Plan, forty-four of fifty-two goals had been accomplished or were well under development in the university system. The pace of change and the magnitude of system-driven activity surprised even the most optimistic leaders in education.

3.   *Rapid, major change extracts a toll on the participants that calls for a less intense, more focused second phase.* The pace of change in the first cycle of the new structure could not be effectively maintained in the next cycle. The remaining twelve goals of the Seven Year Plan will be systematically addressed and two or three new ones added. There will not be another list of forty or fifty items in future plans. In retrospect, the reform agenda placed in the charge of the new chancellor was too ambitious and multidimensional for the initial phase of creating a unified system. The new system was overlooked for what its small staff would carry at several critical points in the first three-year period of major change. Other systems would be well advised to develop a more manageable agenda.

In the private sector, where total quality improvement is practiced, businesses estimate that it takes three to five years to begin seeing significant changes and ten or more years to turn an organizational culture completely around. Though it is widely agreed that the unified system is now a reality, it is also agreed that the change agenda in the next few years must be much more focused. A few high-priority targets of opportunity must be selected with an eye to the likelihood of success in accomplishing identified goals. The changes that have already been initiated need further cultivation and reinforcement in order to remain firmly rooted in the organizational culture.

4.   *Structure makes a difference in pursuing a unified agenda.* An important factor in North Dakota's success has been the single governing board that oversees all of public higher education. Although the presence of a single authority does not guarantee that the coordinated pursuit of common goals will occur, it creates

that potential, which does not exist where sector boards divide authority. The tangible threat posed by the voter referendum on taxes, a history of good intrasystem communication, and able system leadership were also necessary ingredients in this successful restructuring effort.

The effectiveness of restructuring in North Dakota owes much to its linkage to worthwhile educational reform. The purpose of organizational change was not merely to reduce costs or tighten accountability but also to enable a diverse set of institutions to deliver better educational services. The national educational reform agenda in higher education has enjoyed strong support and acceptance in North Dakota. There has been significant movement toward placing undergraduate education at the top of the agenda and experimenting with new ways to enhance learning. There are many initiatives to internationalize the campuses and to reach out to surrounding communities to form economic development partnerships. K–12 public school systems are working in tandem with higher education at both the state planning level and across districts. Cultural diversity, with an emphasis on providing higher education opportunities for members of the Native American tribes in North Dakota, is strongly supported on all campuses and by the chancellor and the board. Site-bound learners of all ages are served through a major technology-supported learning network, which continues to expand. These initiatives would not have been conducted as systematically as they were without restructuring. At the same time, they become an important part of the raison d'être for the reorganized system.

5. *Strenuous public communication efforts must accompany internal reform.* Throughout the first three years of my tenure in the new system, I traveled extensively throughout the state, engaging campus and community leaders in dialogue and meeting with representatives of the media. Appearances on radio talk shows, television news interviews, newspaper stories, and editorials told the public of a new era seeking to find its foothold in North Dakota higher education. I was criticized in some quarters for this extensive outreach to the public. However, the lesson learned is that an extensive public communication effort is indispensable to undergird confidence in leadership for change.

A state agenda dominated by resource issues and political tensions between rural and urban locales and between small and large campuses has held center stage in the public view of higher education in North Dakota. Despite the importance of educational reform to the campuses and their constituents, political leaders have not come forth with endorsements, nor are they convinced that these are the salient issues to be addressed by the board and the chancellor. Without the firm backing of executive and legislative leaders who promote the educational agenda, the North Dakota system, like its counterparts in every other state, is severely handicapped in its ability to tell its story and garner widespread support.

Perhaps the truth is that if you want strong public support, you must give people what they think they want, not just what educators feel has value. The system must do a better job of telling its story, if for no other reason than to bolster the morale of its own members. The system is also coming to grips with the stark reality that it has not yet gone far enough in creating what in the public's mind is an affordable and "right-size" system for the present-day realities.

6. *Board leadership and self-development are essential.* During any major change in a system, no single element is more crucial to success than the leadership provided by the board of trustees. In North Dakota, board members are appointed by the governor to seven-year terms. It was the board that set into motion the restructured one-university system and hired a chancellor to manage the reform agenda. The board brought in consultants from the Maine university system, the Western Interstate Commission on Higher Education, and the New Hampshire system. It took time to undergo training in total quality improvement. It brought in consultants, once the chancellor had been hired, to help rethink the appropriate roles and responsibilities of the board, the chancellor, and campus leaders. Through a series of planning retreats, the board came to understand decentralization and its consequences, set priorities within the constraints of limited resources, and developed policies to support enhanced institutional effectiveness in meeting the state's changing needs. The board has

made it clear that it intends to make its program of self-education a continuous one.

In 1993, the Association of Governing Boards of Universities and Colleges (AGB) published a special report on policies and practices in multicampus systems. Of the sixteen recommended ideas the AGB put forth for consideration, fourteen are in practice to some degree in the restructured North Dakota University System. The two not involved are graduate program duplication and the development of campus-level physical plans. In the comprehensive system in place in North Dakota, undergraduate instruction is necessarily a focus of coordination in program planning. And under the requirements of the legislature and the fiscal realities in the state, involvement in campus facilities planning is necessary at the board and system levels. Otherwise, the principles of practice for a multicampus system that the AGB set forth appear to be demonstrated in North Dakota.

Serious Challenges Ahead

The unified system in North Dakota faces a number of serious challenges. The state's economy and the public's ability and willingness to support higher education will remain precarious. Perhaps the most fundamental challenge is to support and otherwise sustain leadership to pursue the reform vision in the face of scarce resources and public preoccupation with issues of size and affordability rather than quality and relevance.

Stronger ties with peer systems in neighboring states and Canadian provinces will be in order and may help assure citizens in the near term that affordable educational delivery systems will be available. Joint ventures in telecommunications are being pursued as well as shared research, faculty and student exchanges, and regional curricula differentiation. The North American Free Trade Association and other North-South alignments in both the public and private sectors will reinforce the need for the states of Minnesota, North Dakota, South Dakota, Nebraska, Montana, and Wyoming and the Canadian provinces of Saskatchewan, Alberta, and Manitoba to work more closely together.

These states and provinces will face continuing difficulties in serving the needs of their rural populations undergoing major social, economic, and demographic changes. Within North Dakota, continuing population losses from the small and isolated counties will make it difficult for the campuses in those areas to maintain their enrollments. Historian Earl Robinson (1966) dubbed North Dakota the "Too Much State": it has too much education, health care, local government, and other services for its small population and rural-based economy to sustain.

There is once again talk in political circles of the need to close one of the smaller campuses. If the state experiences continued rural population decline in the 1990s of the magnitude of the 1980s, and even if the urban areas offset this decline to some degree, unparalleled pressure may build for reduction in the number of campuses overall and a review of the appropriateness of supporting two comprehensive research universities.

Without the talent and courage of a handful of leaders among the board and its staff and at the universities and colleges, the positive changes described in this chapter would not have occurred. I left the state in the summer of 1994, after three years of service as chancellor. My replacement accepted the position only to withdraw abruptly shortly thereafter. This leadership gap prompted critics to propose a return to the federated system of colleges and universities. Wishing to avoid a second long and costly national search and to short-circuit a public debate over the structure of the system, the board named Larry Isaak, the system's vice chancellor for administrative and student affairs, to a two-year term as chancellor. Isaak brings several key assets to the position that history may well prove are essential at this point in the evolution of the system. He is a well-respected North Dakota native who understands its culture and has established personal credibility with executive and legislative leaders. It was he who raised again, in 1990, the old but previously unfeasible idea of unifying the campuses into a system instead of a federation. Not only is he committed to the concept, but he recognizes when and how important ideas can come forth. Isaak has the background and the experience to guide the system in the difficult balancing of its commitments to educational reform and innovation with the economic and political realities of his home state. As North Dakotans know perhaps better than anyone in American higher education, necessity is indeed the mother of continuous invention!

References

McGuinness, A. C., Jr. *Perspectives on the Current Status of and Emerging Policy Issues for Public Multicampus Higher Education Systems.* AGB Occasional Paper No. 3. Washington, D.C.: Association of Governing Boards of Universities and Colleges, 1991.

Oster, A. *Prospectus for Presidential Search Process.* Consultant's Report to the Office of the Chancellor. Bismarck: North Dakota Board of Higher Education, 1993.

Robinson, E. *A History of North Dakota.* Lincoln: University of Nebraska Press, 1966.

Treadway, D. M. *Vision Statement for the North Dakota University System.* Bismarck: North Dakota Board of Higher Education, 1991.

Chapter Four

Where All Politics Is Local: Massachusetts

Patricia H. Crosson

The story of restructuring in Massachusetts is instructive and important for several reasons. Within a ten-year period, the commonwealth of Massachusetts has overhauled the way it governs and organizes higher education not once but twice. Though neither of these bold attempts at reform achieved its goals, they do offer rich lessons for others across the country who seek to reinvent the way higher education is managed.

The underwhelming record in Massachusetts owes much to the tumultuous political life of a state where a favorite son coined the phrase "all politics is local," to the savage economic decline of the early 1990s, to the chronic inability of the state's higher education interests to find common ground, and sadly, to a consistent failure of leadership from the statehouse to old main.

Politicians, some with presidential ambitions, and local operators were all too willing to ignore a looming fiscal crisis and to meddle in higher education. System and institutional leaders resigned rather than remain to take on tough battles on behalf of higher education.

The creation of a "superboard" in 1980, the first reorganization analyzed in this chapter, represents what had been for some time conventional wisdom that increased authority under one board would result in better planning, coordination, and use of scarce resources. It illustrates a classic response of the time to the pressures of growth. Adequate enough when there were resources sufficient to feed higher education's appetite for development, this system gradually devolved into a regulatory agency with the power to constrain but not to lead.

Governor William Weld's reinvention of higher education governance some ten years later, the second restructuring of this chapter, resembles attempts in other states to redesign their public systems. Strongly influenced by the work of Osborne and Gaebler (1992), the governor wished to downsize public higher education and to make it more accountable to the executive branch. These and other examples of reinventing state government are hot topics in policy debates but have proven very difficult to implement.

This chapter tells the tale of these two major restructurings, with an emphasis on trying to make sense of what happened in each case and on finding lessons for ourselves in Massachusetts and our colleagues in other states.

Stories usually reflect personal experiences and points of view, and this one is written by an academic who has observed the play of events in Massachusetts for nearly a decade as a faculty member on one of the public campuses. It is also based on three years of interviews and conversations with board and staff members, legislators, and college and university officials and on a review of formal documents, reports, and newspaper articles.

The Context of Massachusetts Education

Massachusetts likes to consider itself a national leader in the higher education business, in part because of its early history of college founding and support for the school movement, in part because of the abundance of institutions (more than ninety private colleges and universities and twenty-nine public ones), and in part because of a long tradition of pro-education legislators, congressional representatives, and business leaders.

The public system of higher education, however, is smaller, of later origin, and, with some exceptions, of much lesser renown than the public systems in many other states. Relying on its independent institutions, the commonwealth took nearly a century to develop a full-fledged public university from the small agricultural college founded in Amherst in 1863 and was quite slow to build both university and community college systems. It was more than a decade behind other populous states in recognizing the need for a state system for higher education.

The current public higher education system is comprised of the five-campus University of Massachusetts system, nine state colleges, and fifteen community colleges. Total enrollment in the public system in 1994 was over 120,000 full-time-equivalent (FTE) students, and the state appropriation exceeds seven hundred million dollars. In 1993, the average state appropriation per student was $3,817. In 1994, more than 56 percent of all students enrolled in higher education in Massachusetts were enrolled in independent institutions.

There is a strong sense among the public institutions in Massachusetts that they have never received the recognition or funding they deserved. This feeling of deficiency has fostered a sometimes bitter rivalry between the state's public and private institutions and between the University of Massachusetts and the less well funded state colleges. This discontent has typically prevented public higher education leaders from establishing a united front, just as it has fueled interest in restructuring as a way of securing advantage.

Massachusetts is rightfully proud of its traditionally high participation rates in higher education. Until recently, low tuition and fees in the public sector, together with generous financial aid and scholarship programs, have given Massachusetts residents access to higher education and the freedom to choose between public or private attendance. These characteristics have largely been lost, however, as the fiscal crisis led to dramatic tuition increases in the public sector and deep cuts in scholarship programs. From approximately the midpoint among the states in tuition and fee levels in the late 1980s, by 1992 Massachusetts had become among the most expensive for students in the public sector. Under the current governor, William Weld, the state has moved to a policy of high tuition and limited financial aid.

Massachusetts was among the first states to experience the recession of the late 1980s. As tax revenues plummeted, the state made cuts in all areas of spending. The largest item in the discretionary budget, higher education, was hit particularly hard. Deep cuts were made in appropriation levels, and large expenses for fringe benefits and other items were shifted onto the higher education accounts. Between fiscal 1988 and fiscal 1992, state appropriations for higher education dropped by a third while tuition and fees rose 112 percent. Institutions still had to reduce costs by cutting programs, services, and quality (Breneman, 1994).

Politically, Massachusetts is a liberal state. There are usually large Democratic majorities in both the house of representatives and the senate. The governor is usually a Democrat as well. Profound differences in political philosophy between Republican Governor Weld and the majority of state legislators have led to an unusually high level of political turmoil in a state already well known for political infighting. Massachusetts is considered an "executive state" in the sense that the governor initiates appropriations bills and other legislative packages. The legislature is active and often even intrusive in university affairs, and many fundamental policies are made through amendments to budget bills.

Public Higher Education on the Eve of the First Restructuring

In 1980, the commonwealth of Massachusetts supported three public higher education systems—the three-campus University of Massachusetts, a community college system with fifteen campuses, a state college system with ten campuses—and two freestanding universities. Each system was governed by a board of trustees whose policies were carried out by a separate central office in Boston. The two universities that were not part of a system had separate boards of trustees.

The levels of centralization and decentralization for policy and management decisions varied among the systems and institutions. For example, the state colleges and community colleges were more centralized and more closely regulated by state civil service and fiscal controls. The University of Massachusetts had achieved a significant level of autonomy from state bureaucracies in the legislation creating the multicampus system in 1970. As a system, the University of Massachusetts was made up of quite diverse institutions. There was a research, land grant, and "flagship" campus in Amherst with twenty-five thousand students; an urban, primarily undergraduate campus in Boston with eighty-five hundred students; and a medical school in Worcester with fewer than one hundred students.

A Gentleman's Agreement

The Board of Higher Education, established in 1965, provided a coordinating mechanism for both public and private institutions. Headed by a chancellor, the board held regular meetings of college presidents and sought consensus on educational policy issues but rarely engaged in self-regulation or control. The presidents honored a tacit gentleman's agreement not to disagree in public, but rarely did the higher education community speak in a single voice on any subject. The board had approval power over new academic programs in both public and private universities but rarely turned down a proposal, except an occasional program in the public sector that a private college found duplicative.

The weaknesses of this arrangement from a state policy perspective were not terribly obvious in the 1960s and early 1970s, while attention was focused on institution building, but they began to emerge by the mid 1970s as each institution clamored for more resources and more programs. There was increasing competition in the Boston area between the University of Massachusetts, Boston, and Boston State College. The gentleman's agreement was broken by an open battle between Robert Wood, a strong incoming University of Massachusetts president advocating growth for the Boston campus, and John Silber, the equally strong and assertive president of Boston University, who argued that increased state support for private institutions would better serve the higher education needs of state residents. A variety of state commissions had examined issues of statewide structure and governance without much progress until Laura Claussen (now Laura Coelen), education adviser to the governor in the new Executive Office of Educational Affairs, worked with a small group of key legislators and higher education officials to craft a bold plan for reorganization. The legislation, which passed in a late-night amendment to the budget bill, took the higher education community by surprise.

The Board of Regents

Massachusetts had created a single system for public higher education and one of the most powerful superboards in the country, the Board of Regents of Higher Education (BOR). Newspaper accounts at the time noted that the governor and the legislature (in

Massachusetts known as the Great and General Court) had grown weary of the constant barrage of institutional pleading and wanted a buffer between the state and its institutions. They also wanted an entity with enough power to control increasing costs in the public sector, as well as increasing competition and program duplication between systems and between public and private institutions.

Officially, the purpose of the BOR was "to develop, foster, and advocate a comprehensive system of public higher education of high quality, flexibility, responsiveness, and accountability" and to provide access and choice for the citizens of the commonwealth. The BOR was awarded all the powers previously vested in the Board of Higher Education, the Executive Office of Educational Affairs, and the boards of trustees of all public institutions. Trustee boards were transformed from lay governing to lay advisory boards, although they retained some governance powers.

The legislature gave the BOR an impressive list of powers, ranging from policy setting and planning to day-to-day management oversight. Suddenly, the regents had authority over decisions that had long been jealously guarded by separate institutional trustee boards. The board of regents' failure to exercise this authority at the policy level was one factor that led to its demise.

When the BOR was created, the community college and state college systems' trustee boards were abolished, but the system board for the three-campus University of Massachusetts was retained. Boards for the University of Lowell and Southeastern Massachusetts University were continued, while new lay boards were appointed by the governor for each community and state college—twenty-nine different boards in all.

The ramifications of the power and authority delineations between the BOR and trustee boards were many, varied, and important to the play of restructuring events. The university trustee boards, because they had been continued but with considerable loss of power and authority, were often inclined to challenge the BOR and its actions as contrary to the best interests of "their" institutions and of higher education in general. The state and community college boards, as new boards, were less inclined to resent the BOR, but they often displayed little concern for the "public interest" or a statewide perspective on higher education, and, even worse, little awareness of their responsibilities for management and oversight.

Duff: A "President's Chancellor"

The initial period under the BOR was relatively undramatic. Democratic Governor Edward King appointed many strong and well-respected individuals to the board, and except for consternation over the appointments from private colleges, the board was well received. The governor appointed James R. Martin, an insurance executive from Springfield, as the first chair of the BOR, and the BOR chose first Paul Guzzi, secretary of state, as acting chancellor and then John Duff, president of the University of Lowell, as the first permanent chancellor.

Although the chancellor selection process angered many in the higher education community because there had been little consultation with college and university leaders, Duff turned out to be a "president's chancellor" in that his perspective on higher education was influenced by his years at the University of Lowell. He emphasized the advocacy role of the regents on behalf of specific colleges and universities as well as for the new system of public higher education.

The BOR quickly delegated extensive powers to the trustee boards so that institutions could continue to operate while the regents system was put in place. Duff concentrated on developing the capacity to govern by building processes for planning, budget development and analysis, fiscal oversight, and data gathering and analysis. Gradually, colleges and universities came to learn the language of system and state policy, although it was invoked rhetorically more often than it was reflected in practice.

In an early action, the BOR forced a merger between Boston State College and the University of Massachusetts, Boston. The merger was decreed in 1981 and fully accomplished by 1984, despite intense efforts to block it on the part of the Boston State unionized faculty, its alumni, parents, and some legislators. This consolidation produced some savings in staff and facilities costs, although some costs were simply shifted to the University of Massachusetts, Boston.

The president of the University of Massachusetts followed a policy of cooperation with the regents during this period. Quiet and accommodating, David Knapp had succeeded the more assertive Robert Wood. Knapp believed that the new statewide system had the potential to increase public and political support for higher education and for the University of Massachusetts. Ironically, years later, a Knapp initiative would contribute to the regents' downfall, but during the early years, despite considerable trustee dissatisfaction, there were no major confrontations between the university and the BOR.

It has become clear that the regents' unwillingness to assert strong leadership over the development of higher education paved the way for greater political intrusion. Although staff size continued to grow and the groundwork for statewide policy was being laid, no embracing new master plan or important initiatives were announced. The competition over resources and programs continued, and the BOR seemed unable to control its institutions or buffer them from legislators.

Scandals and Politics

The laissez-faire stance of the regents and the Duff administration hardened up somewhat in the face of a series of well-publicized scandals. One instance involved a male college president and a $10,000 payment to a male student he was accused of seducing. In another, a president was caught falsifying entertainment expense reports. These scandals undermined public confidence and forced the regents to exercise more intrusive oversight than they would have liked. At the close of 1985, Chancellor Duff himself resigned amid charges of "improper political fundraising" (Hogarty, 1988, p. 16).

As the BOR members who had been appointed to staggered terms by Governor King were replaced by appointees of Democratic Governor Michael Dukakis, who had been reelected in 1982, political infighting became more intense in the board's deliberations. Open confrontation erupted during the search for Duff's replacement as chancellor in 1986. The search committee, composed of board members, made a recommendation that was rejected by the full board during a regularly scheduled meeting. In the same meeting, the full board, contrary to the wishes of its appointed search committee, selected James Collins, an incumbent Democratic state representative, for the post. Governor Dukakis promptly condemned the appointment and, at the urging of members of the

BOR search committee, intervened in the only way he could. He ousted the board chair and appointed a new one, Edward Lashman, who would later become secretary of administration and finance. Lashman promptly forced a resignation from the new chancellor and reopened the search. It was clearly a confrontation between governor and legislature. Collins had been the choice of the legislative leaders and their friends on the BOR, and he had the active support of key labor unions. All three groups were infuriated at Dukakis's interference.

Political intrusion had serious consequences. According to a student of this battle, "The relationship of the Board of Regents to the other institutions within the system was damaged; and its struggle for autonomy was lost. The agency's credibility was not only weakened, but the legitimacy of its governance was undermined. . . . The viability of the Board of Regents itself was called into question" (Hogarty, 1988, p. 35).

The Jenifer Era: Oversight and Conflict

Franklyn Jenifer was selected to replace Collins in 1986. He brought from his experience as senior academic officer for the Board of Higher Education in New Jersey a strong sense of the responsibilities and prerogatives of statewide boards. He inaugurated a much more activist and intrusive era on the board of regents.

In his first months, on affirmative action grounds, Chancellor Jenifer successfully persuaded the regents to "decline to approve" several local board recommendations for college presidencies. Gradually, more women and people of color were selected as college presidents, but the willingness of the regents to overrule trustees increased tensions.

Jenifer also increased the size of the BOR staff by hiring experienced academic, fiscal, labor relations, and legislative liaison personnel, often from out of state. Over time, staff size increased severalfold to nearly a hundred employees. As the staff grew, activity levels increased. Institutions were asked to prepare planning documents, budget requests and justifications, and reports on such matters as academic programs and activities, affirmative action, student services, and undergraduate education and to supply increasing amounts of data to the regents' staff. From the regents' perspective, all of this activity was consistent with their mandated duties and responsibilities and essential to the creation of a strong system of higher education. From a college or university perspective, however, the regents' activities were experienced as a vastly increased workload that often competed with ongoing responsibilities for institutional management. Many colleges and universities claimed that they added several staff members to handle the flow of paper between campus and the BOR.

In 1988, Paul Tsongas was asked to replace Lashman as chair of the BOR. Tsongas had been a well-liked local politician and United States senator whose popularity increased during his successful battle with cancer. Tsongas promised to devote his time and energy to public higher education. Most legislators and college and university leaders were pleased with the appointment, believing that it augured well for increased state support. This optimism proved unfounded. Although the fiscal crisis was not of Tsongas's making, it dominated his tenure as chair of the BOR.

Meanwhile, legislative dissatisfaction with the BOR began to increase. Although some legislators worked well with Jenifer, many legislators continued to be angry about the Collins ouster and to blame Chancellor Jenifer for it. Others felt that the regents had been slow to provide adequate educational opportunities for the growing population centers in the eastern part of the state and had failed to produce needed reforms in a number of small state and community colleges in western Massachusetts. Others did not like the regents' consolidated single-line-item budget process because it limited their opportunities to champion and intervene on behalf of specific campuses in their legislative districts. In short, the regents interfered with "politics as usual" for Massachusetts.

Unhappiness at the University of Massachusetts

Over time, the regents system came to be perceived as having a negative effect on the University of Massachusetts system. As the laissez-faire stance of Duff gave way to the authoritarianism of Jenifer, the president and trustees of the University of Massachusetts witnessed an erosion in the university's autonomy, so hard won when the system had been established in 1970. The university itself became fragmented. The chancellors on the three campuses began routinely to bypass the president's office and work directly with the chancellor and staff of the BOR. Each campus, for example, took its budget request directly to the regents and separately sought to influence the regents on its own behalf.

In 1988, President Knapp and the university trustees asked David Saxon, former chancellor of the University of California, Berkeley, and then head of the MIT Corporation, to chair a study commission on the future of the University of Massachusetts. The Saxon commission reported that the growth and development of the University of Massachusetts system was being impeded by inclusion within the regents' public higher education system. The Saxon commission recommended that University of Massachusetts form a separate system, autonomous from the BOR and the state, and further that the University of Lowell and Southeastern Massachusetts University be merged into the University of Massachusetts system. This proposal launched an extensive governance debate that contributed to the second restructuring in higher education and will be taken up later in this story. First, however, it is important to describe the fiscal situation and the end of the Jenifer era.

The Looming Fiscal Crisis

Although politics and growing resentments toward the BOR from public colleges and universities created an unstable governance system, it was the fiscal crisis that was to highlight the most serious weaknesses in the BOR. Oddly, the situation began on a positive note, as during the early and mid 1980s, the commonwealth enjoyed remarkable fiscal health. Tax revenues increased each year thanks to prosperous high-technology industries, a booming real estate market, big defense contracts, and high employment rates. Governor Dukakis's presidential aspirations grew as the rest of the country yearned to emulate the "Massachusetts miracle." The largely Democratic legislature fully endorsed Dukakis's White House ambitions.

The bright economic picture faded rapidly during late 1987 and 1988 as state revenues began to fall far short of projections. Expensive entitlement programs in health and welfare consumed unusually large proportions of state revenues, but the governor and the legislature were reluctant to alter them because they had been showcased nationally to promote Dukakis's candidacy. The state began to borrow to balance the budget. Bond ratings fell. It was no longer possible to hide the real fiscal mess in the commonwealth. His presidential hopes dashed by a fading economic miracle and a lackluster campaign, Dukakis finally made deep cuts in state appropriations in 1989.

Although all parts of the state budget were affected by the fiscal crisis, higher education was among the hardest hit. Moreover, no cost-of-living increases or merit raises were granted to faculty and staff members in public colleges and universities—a situation that was to obtain from 1988 to 1993. State support for higher education declined steadily through 1992. The actual experience for colleges and universities was especially wrenching because annual cuts were usually followed by additional midyear budget recessions.

Disillusionment with the Regents

The board of regents had no choice but to try to manage the process of cutting higher education budgets, which further compromised its standing with the colleges and universities. The BOR spread out a $35 million recision in the fall of 1989 by imposing a 5 percent reduction on each college and university. Because nearly all faculty members and most staff in the state's public institutions belong to unions, the BOR declared a financial exigency, setting the stage for institutional boards to do likewise so that layoffs and terminations could be pursued. The board approved a very large tuition increase for the 1990–91 academic year, and individual institutions approved even larger increases in mandatory fees.

Colleges and universities scrambled to find the required savings without cutting programs or firing faculty and staff. Some layoffs were imposed, but most economies were achieved through a combination of unfilled vacancies, creative bookkeeping, deferred maintenance, deep cuts in support accounts, and passing costs on to students in the form of increased fees. Campus staffers looked to the BOR to advocate the interests of higher education and protect them against the budget cuts, and when that did not succeed, to make allocation decisions that would spare their particular institution or program. Disillusionment with the regents accelerated. Most institutions began end runs to the legislature around the regents in efforts to protect their budget base.

Many people in the legislative and executive branches were

equally unimpressed with the performance of the regents, but for different reasons. They looked to the BOR to use its ample power during the crisis to create a leaner and more focused system of higher education. They were disappointed when the board distributed cuts equally across the system and made no proposals for the closure or merger of campuses or programs.

Although much negative feeling was directed toward the BOR during these early years of the fiscal crisis, many observers felt that the regents were managing as best they could in a situation that did not allow for orderly responses and effective planning. The BOR did try to serve as the advocate for public higher education. The chair, BOR members, and the chancellor, individually and collectively, made repeated public statements arguing that higher education could not absorb such deep cuts without harm to the educational enterprise. Perhaps they staved off even deeper cuts; perhaps they did not. Public higher education was cut more deeply than other state agencies, but it was one of the largest discretionary items in the state budget, and it was well known that costs could be passed on to students through tuition and fee increases.

Changes in Leadership

Leadership changes came at a crucial moment in the fiscal drama as Franklyn Jenifer resigned to assume the presidency of Howard University. Over the next months, an additional half dozen senior administrators on the BOR staff also announced their resignations. A committee was established to search for both an interim and a permanent replacement for Jenifer.

Randolph Bromery, former chancellor of the University of Massachusetts, Amherst, and former president of Westfield State College, became interim chancellor of the BOR in April 1990. Several other important changes occurred during this period as well. Paul Tsongas declared an interest in the governor's race, which had been abandoned by Dukakis months earlier but was now beginning to attract interesting candidates, including John Silber, president of Boston University and an outspoken advocate for private higher education. David Knapp retired as University of Massachusetts president after eleven years of service. Given the fiscal situation, the University of Massachusetts trustees asked Joseph Duffey, chancellor of the Amherst campus, to serve concurrently as chancellor and president and to reduce the size of the University of Massachusetts president's office. Widely respected in Massachusetts higher education circles, Duffey was hailed as a good choice.

A frequently told story from this period illustrates the worsening relations between the university and the regents. After a public announcement had been made about Duffey's appointment as president of the University of Massachusetts, the trustees and Duffey belatedly remembered the regents' power to approve trustee presidential selections. Duffey attempted to make amends by attending the next BOR meeting (Bromery was not yet serving as chancellor), but the regents offended both Duffey and the trustees by subjecting him to a long wait in an anteroom and a long interview to determine his "fitness" for the position. This episode accelerated a growing University of Massachusetts resolve to free itself of the regents by any means possible.

At his first meeting as chancellor, Bromery made an impressive speech about the fiscal crisis, noting that excellent faculty members would leave Massachusetts if the situation did not improve. Over the next several months, he supported tuition increases and advocated a policy, first introduced by Jenifer in 1988, to allow colleges and universities to keep the tuition revenues, or at least the increases in tuition revenue, that normally reverted to the state. He was successful in that colleges and universities were allowed to keep the tuition increase revenue during fiscal 1991 and for several years thereafter. Although the BOR worried about the increased burdens for students and their parents, it was difficult for them to withstand the pressure for increases from college and university leaders who argued that there was no other way for them to adjust to the state cuts without harm to curricula and programs.

Bromery was also required to manage the deep cuts in the fiscal 1991 budget and two budget recessions, in September and October 1990. Two of the cuts were apportioned equally across all colleges and universities, but Bromery distributed one disproportionately, with the universities taking the deepest cuts because they had the greatest flexibility to buffer their losses with other sources of revenue. This action was not well received by university leaders, who firmly believed that academic quality should have been the major criterion used for deciding about budget cuts. Fiscal exigency and hiring freezes were again imposed, and the vacancy counts continued to rise. Paul Tsongas, now no longer a candidate for governor, also made repeated statements about the devastation in higher education.

Not long after Republican Governor Weld's election, Randolph Bromery announced his resignation as chancellor, citing philosophical differences over education policy with the governor. The resignation was clearly a protest over the governor's proposals to downsize public higher education. It was widely rumored at the time that BOR chair Tsongas had hoped that the entire board would resign in protest, but this did not happen because several regents believed that a mass resignation would leave no one to fight on behalf of higher education in the state.

Paul Marks, a regent of long standing and a former University of Massachusetts trustee, was named interim chancellor after Bromery's resignation. Two fiscal decisions, made by Governor Weld but implicating the BOR, occurred during the spring of 1991 and further angered the higher education community. First, Weld rejected a collective bargaining agreement that had been negotiated over many months and would have provided long-delayed raises for the faculty. Weld also initiated an emergency cost reduction plan to furlough state employees. Faculty were all declared "essential personnel" in the furlough scheme so that they would have to complete the academic year and take pay cuts. Eventually, the furlough monies were returned to faculty, but throughout the spring, faculty members were angry not only with Weld but also with the BOR, which had been put in the unfortunate position of having to work out the details of the furlough program.

Paul Tsongas, the courageous but beleaguered champion of higher education, resigned as chair of the regents in June 1991 to seek the presidency of the United States. This provided the opportunity for Governor Weld to put his own man at the helm, Richard A. Wiley. The change in leadership at this crucial time paved the way for the dramatic reorganization of higher education as a whole.

Proposals for Restructuring

The growing dissatisfaction with the regents, along with the state's deepening fiscal crisis, heightened interest in several quite different proposals for restructuring higher education governance.

The 1989 Saxon commission's recommendations for including

the University of Lowell and Southeastern Massachusetts University in the university system and making the system autonomous from the regents gained considerable support from the trustees and from campus leaders during 1990. Trustees and the presidents of the University of Massachusetts, the University of Lowell, and Southeastern Massachusetts University now believed that a larger, more geographically dispersed university system would have greater political support and would fare better in the heavily politicized fiscal battles. The situation of the University of Lowell was somewhat more complicated, with all parties—the president, the trustees, and Paul Tsongas, chair of the BOR but a longtime supporter and former trustee of the University of Lowell—taking different positions on the issue. In fact, Tsongas's divided loyalties and political ambitions had become a serious problem for the BOR by the early 1990s. In July 1991, just before he left to assume the presidency of American University in Washington, D.C., Duffey was authorized by the University of Massachusetts trustees to file legislation to effect the structural and governance changes recommended by the Saxon committee.

When the Saxon committee's report had been released in late February 1989, it had been opposed by the BOR. At that time, BOR Chancellor Jenifer hastily unveiled an alternative proposal that would break up the University of Massachusetts system by eliminating the office of the president and system trustees, create separate universities at Amherst and Boston, merge the Worcester Health Center into the University of Massachusetts, Amherst, and change the names of the University of Lowell and Southeastern Massachusetts University to the University of Massachusetts, Lowell, and the University of Massachusetts, Dartmouth, respectively. The proposal would not have altered the BOR's powers or structure. There was very little support for the Jenifer proposal when it was announced and even less after his departure.

In May 1990, the house of representatives amended a budget bill to call for the abolition of the BOR. Representative Ellen Rourke (D, Lowell) sponsored the amendment, arguing that it would save $3 million and eliminate a layer of bureaucracy. Paul Tsongas, chair of the BOR and also from Lowell, charged that Rourke's motivation was political and aimed personally at him. Although the amendment was defeated, no alternative proposals came forward. During fall 1990, all energy was taken up with the election season, and by the following spring, under the new Republican administration, the action had shifted to the Joint Committee on Education, Arts and Humanities, commonly called the Joint Committee on Education.

During his brief tenure as chancellor of the board of regents during the summer and fall of 1990, Bromery had developed a proposal that was much less ambitious and far reaching than the Jenifer plan. Bromery's Regionalization Plan called for grouping all public institutions in each of three geographical regions into coalition entities that would collaborate much more closely on programs and services and achieve administrative savings. The regionalization proposal did not receive a great deal of support from campuses or legislators or even from individual members of the board of regents, although the governor appeared to like it and it was endorsed in concept by the board. The existence of the proposal, however unsatisfactory, made it awkward for the regents to develop an alternative governance proposal during a crucial period of debate and political jockeying.

In late fall 1990, after his election as governor but before the inauguration, William Weld hired a law professor from a private university to advise him on education matters. The professor's report was confidential but widely reported and discussed. It called for the closing of four or five public colleges, combining the five university-level campuses under a single board of trustees, and deep cuts in scholarship and other programs. Many of these proposals reappeared in Weld's January budget message calling for a 17.5 percent cut in the higher education appropriation.

Early in the spring of 1991, Weld produced legislative proposals calling for the elimination of the board of regents and the board of education (the lay board responsible for K–12 education) and their replacement by a cabinet-level secretary of education; he also sought to set up a commission to study the merger or closing of three to five public colleges. The proposals were taken up by the Joint Committee on Education, co-chaired by Democrats from both the house of representatives and the senate. In open hearings in March and April 1991, considerable opposition was expressed to all aspects of Weld's proposals, especially the elimination of lay boards. It is telling that in all this debate, not a single voice defended the board of regents or the superboard system of governance.

Weld campaigned on promises of "reinventing government" and gave much public play to the book of the same name. The state and community college presidents understood this slogan to mean that he was committed to pushing management responsibility and authority to operating levels and to strengthening accountability, including quantitative performance measures. As it turned out, there was no additional delegation of operating authority to the campuses of the state and community colleges. This was a major disappointment to their advocates.

After lengthy open hearings and considerable debate, the Joint Committee on Education, Arts and Humanities crafted a bill that gave Governor Weld much of what he wanted, especially the secretary of education. The committee also responded, however, to the wishes of legislators and campus leaders by creating a lay board and by mandating a series of studies desired by the legislature. As the bill was debated on the house and senate floors, a variety of attempts were made to amend it, including an effort to transform one of the state colleges into a university institution and one to include strong alumni membership on the University of Massachusetts board of trustees. Amendments implementing major substantive changes were rejected by both houses of the legislature. Chapter 142, "An Act Relative to Public Education in Massachusetts," was passed with large majorities in both house and senate in late June and early July 1991, respectively, and promptly signed by Governor Weld. The new structure was scheduled to take effect on September 1, 1991.

A Reinvented System of Higher Education

The new Massachusetts organizational scheme responded to political pressures, especially the desire of advocates of the University of Massachusetts for more autonomy, but it also illustrates some of the attempts at structural reform advocated as part of the larger reinventing-government movement. Its ingredients include a strong executive in the person of Piedad Robertson, the cabinet-level secretary of education. At the same time, it decentralized authority for one of the systems by granting the University of Massachusetts the substantial independence it desired. It also merged the five universities under the control of the University of Massachusetts executive.

The state colleges, despite legislative initiatives sponsored by state college presidents, remained under the thumb of the Higher Education Coordinating Council (HECC), which acts as their governing board while it serves as a coordinating board for the University of Massachusetts. These changes are outlined in Figure 4.1. Finally, it dramatically downsized the central office management staff. In theory, these shifts were supposed to lead to a series of benefits, from lower-cost administration to greater responsiveness to the needs of the state and greater accountability to their public masters.

A Strong Executive

Perhaps the most profound change was the creation of the cabinet-level position of secretary of education. Piedad Robertson, former president of Bunker Hill Community College, was named to the new post on September 1, 1991. The secretary of education has responsibilities for elementary, secondary, and postsecondary education and is the chief adviser to the governor on all education matters. The secretary makes recommendations to the governor on funding for education and assists the governor in the preparation of appropriation legislation. The secretary is the chief spokesperson for education in the state and chairs the Committee on Educational Policy, which brings together representatives from K–12 as well as higher education. On matters of K–12 education, the secretary works with a board of education and, on matters of higher education, with the HECC.

A Coordinating Board with Reduced Staff

The HECC is an entirely different structure from the board of regents, but it has many of the same powers and duties. Although it is called a coordinating board and is mandated to coordinate the activities of the system, it has many powers traditionally accorded governance boards. The relationship of the HECC with the community and state colleges can best be described as a governance relationship, while the relationship with the University of Massachusetts is a coordinating one.

The law stipulates that there is to be an office of the chancellor with a staff to carry out the work of the HECC. From the beginning,

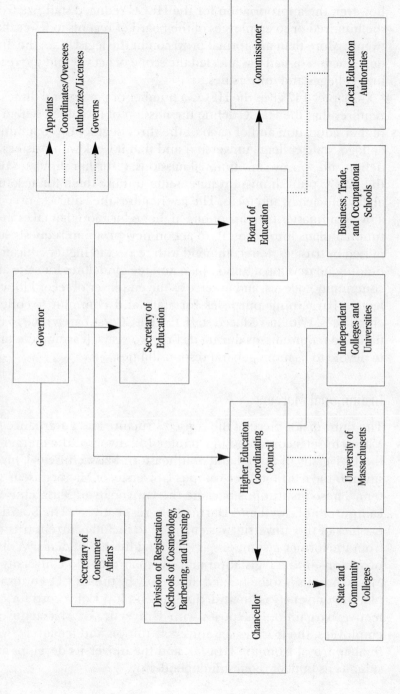

Figure 4.1. Massachusetts Educational Governance Structure.

however, the appropriation for the HECC reduced staff size from the hundred or so employees of the board of regents to fewer than twenty. More than any formal provision in the legislation, the drastic reduction of staff has affected the scope of activity and the reach into colleges and universities.

Chapter 142 gives the HECC a number of powers and duties. It requires that the HECC define the mission of the state's system of higher education and of each of the three segments (community college, state college, university) and that it work with trustees to define and approve institutional missions. It further stipulates that the HECC publish mission statements and use them for accountability, efficiency, and focus. The law requires the HECC to prepare a five-year master plan for public higher education that takes institutional plans into account, to act on new program requests submitted by trustees, to recommend with respect to higher education funding, to develop a tuition plan and fee guidelines for state and community colleges, and to serve as the employer of record for collective bargaining purposes for state and community college employees. With its reduced staff, the HECC was barely able to fulfill these requirements during its first two years, leaving little time to devote to its more general responsibilities.

Institutional Mergers

The third major piece of the revised structure and governance for Massachusetts contained in Chapter 142 involved the merger of the University of Lowell and Southeastern Massachusetts University into the existing three-campus University of Massachusetts system. These institutions became the University of Massachusetts campuses at Lowell and Dartmouth, respectively. The board of trustees of the university was enlarged to include current trustees from the former institutions as well as additional students. Various provisions in the legislation make it clear that the University of Massachusetts is to be treated differently by the HECC. For example, the university is identified as the employer of record for collective bargaining purposes with University of Massachusetts employees, the trustees set university tuition and fee levels (with final approval from the HECC), and the university develops and submits its budget request independently.

The HECC in Action, 1991–1994

The HECC has not emerged as a major player on the higher education stage. Paul Marks, who had served as the final chancellor of the BOR after Bromery's resignation, became the first chancellor of the HECC. He assisted the transition from the regents to the HECC and the integration of the new secretary. Mild-mannered and accommodating, Marks supported Secretary Robertson's efforts to become the visible chief spokesperson and policy maker for education, including higher education.

During the first year of the HECC, there were repeated complaints about the fact that it was chaired by the secretary of education. Many people believed that it had turned into a rubber-stamp board. Others were concerned about the conflict that resulted when the council did not support the governor's budget proposals but its chair, the secretary of education, was obliged to do so. After a year, the legislation was changed so that the chair of the HECC would be chosen by the members of the council, who would also have the ability to choose the chancellor.

Marks resigned from the post of chancellor after the transition year, and Peter Mitchell, who had been a vice chancellor of the BOR and then on the HECC under Paul Marks, was named interim chancellor while the HECC board continued its national search for a permanent chancellor. In September 1993, Stanley Koplik, a man with system experience in Kansas and Missouri, was hired as chancellor. Koplik seems to possess a clear sense of the strengths and limitations of coordinating boards, but his lack of grounding in Massachusetts politics has raised fears that it will be difficult for him to be effective.

The HECC has developed a mission statement for the system and for each sector of higher education and has worked to ensure that each institution has a mission statement that is consistent with these. It has approved the mission statements for every institution and published a large book containing all mission statements. Many authorities believe that the new mission statements are overly broad and fail to address program duplication in the state.

The long-standing debate over duplication versus regional service has yet to be resolved. With the exception of the state's maritime academy and its art college, the state colleges assert their role as comprehensives that should offer a broad array of programs. Proponents of the Amherst campus highlight its flagship status and its comprehensive array of undergraduate, master's, and doctoral programs, many of which the other university campuses seek to duplicate to secure their status as university campuses. The HECC has failed to mediate the conflict between state colleges and the university and among university campuses.

At the time the HECC was established, some observers thought that the appropriate structure for Massachusetts was a coordinating board structure and that the complex coordinating and governing provisions of Chapter 142 were intended only as temporary provisions. One of the tasks mandated by the legislation was the creation of the Commission on the Future of the State College and Community College Systems. Presidents of the colleges argued strenuously for segmental governing boards and autonomy from the HECC similar to that enjoyed by the University of Massachusetts. Others wanted mergers or consolidations of institutions. Both groups were disappointed. Closely guided by the secretary of education and staffed by the HECC, the commission recommended clearer differentiation of mission but no governance change and no mergers or closures. The HECC formally received the report but did not act on it in any official manner.

The HECC has approved only a very small number of new degree programs. Many new programs have been stalled for several years because the HECC considered all University of Massachusetts proposals "deactivated" until acted on by the new University of Massachusetts board. In the areas of planning and the review of existing programs, the HECC has been somewhat active with state and community colleges, but it has left these matters to the trustees of the University of Massachusetts for the five university campuses. Even for state and community colleges, however, there is little evidence that planning and program review are receiving systematic attention or are related in any way to resource allocation processes.

Elusive Budget Reform

The HECC's attempts to introduce a new formula-based budget process illustrates the difficulty of implementing structural change. The new budget process was designed to use objective measures such as analysis of historical enrollment data by level and discipline and the size and nature of physical plant to determine the appropriate level of funding for the present mix of programs and enrollment at each state and community college.

For fiscal 1994 and again for fiscal 1995, the HECC presented the higher education budget request to the governor and the legislature in formula terms and provided a full description of its methods. Whereas the senate, for the most part, accepted and used the formula, the house of representatives did not. For 1994, the conference committee worked out complicated arrangements, but for 1995, it sided with the house, meaning that all funding was given directly to colleges on the basis of an across-the-board spreading of resources. As a budget official noted off the record, "The supreme irony of the budget formula is that just as we finally have an objective method of determining allocations that is supported by the college presidents, the house takes away the HECC's authority to make allocations." Clearly, the house leadership is unwilling to give up the political clout that goes along with making allocation decisions.

The HECC is struggling mightily to have a voice in higher education and to fulfill its mandated responsibilities. Though on paper the HECC retains an enormous amount of power over the community and state colleges, in practice it is often disregarded or circumvented. The state and community colleges continue to view the HECC as a critic and a potential adversary. They routinely turn to their legislative friends for help. The university, in an extraordinarily activist phase under a new president, pays very little attention to the HECC. The HECC continues to operate with an very small staff, and Massachusetts continues to be a highly politicized environment in which it is difficult for the HECC to fulfill its mandate and coordinate the statewide system of public higher education.

Themes and Lessons

The first restructuring in Massachusetts higher education created a powerful central board in order to develop a single statewide system of higher education and formulate coherent higher education policy. The second restructuring dismantled this system and put in its place a stronger executive presence, a board with both governing and coordinating responsibilities, and a larger and more autonomous University of Massachusetts.

The board of regents structure did not work well. It was considered intrusive by colleges and universities and ineffective by state legislators and the executive branch. When the budget crisis hit, colleges and universities felt unprotected and unsupported by the regents, while both executive and legislative branches were frustrated by the regents' seeming inability to manage the crisis and make the right, albeit difficult, choices. The structure itself became a target.

The second restructuring created a confusing arrangement that also has not worked. The Higher Education Coordinating Council does not have the power, the staff, or the credibility to have much impact. The secretary of education does have the power and the position, but the demands of oversight of all levels of education and the close alignment with the executive branch make it difficult to forge the necessary alliances with the legislature and with colleges and universities. The University of Massachusetts has become a more visible and more powerful entity but still represents five quite different campuses being forced to work together by a large president's office. State and community colleges seek greater independence for themselves. In truth, there is no coordinated system of public higher education in Massachusetts and little coherent state policy.

Though each restructuring in Massachusetts had its own context, actors, play of events, and hence its own story, certain themes run through both changes.

1.   *Chronic conflict between the state-level higher education board and the state legislature results in instability.* Massachusetts has failed to manage the conflict between the state legislature and whatever structure is in place at the state level for higher education management. The Great and General Court has never set or supported clear goals for higher education. With the board of regents, the legislature created one of the strongest governing boards in the country, but then legislators often criticized the board for actions that were clearly within its mandate. They also criticized the regents for not accomplishing a reform agenda in higher education. The current structure locates authority for higher education centrally in the executive branch of government. Not surprisingly,

this has elicited considerable legislative opposition. The HECC is often blamed by the legislature for not having as much influence as the old board of regents, even though its influence has been deliberately constrained by a too small staff and insufficient resources. Although the legislature has been supportive of colleges and universities and their budget needs, it has not supported the HECC or the secretary of education. The need for reform is often mentioned in connection with higher education, but there is no explicit reform agenda, and no end in sight to the conflict.

2.   *Public stewardship takes second place to political ambition.* Over and over again, political ambition rather than public stewardship has dominated decisions on the structure of higher education. Political ambition is seen at the individual level in the actions of governors, legislators, board chairs, chancellors, and college presidents and at the collective level as higher education policy matters get caught up in the ongoing struggle between executive and legislative branches of government. The best of public stewardship was needed during this difficult period for higher education in Massachusetts, but, sadly, it was in short supply. Although many individuals and groups—legislators, board members and staff, college leaders—worked to do what was best even if they often disagreed on specific policies and courses of action, this work was all too often undermined by political agendas that did not serve higher education well.

3.   *Fiscal crisis undermines rational planning and policy development.* The board of regents had clear mandates for planning, program review, and program approval. The HECC has these same mandates, as well as the responsibility to ensure that each institution and each sector has a clear and distinct mission and that mission statements guide planning and resource allocation. The fiscal crisis, however, undermined rational planning and policy development under the BOR and continues to do so under the HECC, as well as in the colleges and universities. It was impossible for colleges and universities to plan in any coherent fashion with annual budget cuts and several midyear budget recisions. Over several years, cuts were managed by taking resources from wherever they were available, which meant an unplanned readjustment of priorities. As most institutions scrambled to avoid chaos, others struggled to avoid

closure or merger. Tuition "policy" debates were less about policy and more about shifting costs onto students to protect the operations of colleges and universities. A policy of privatization was not formulated or debated but emerged over time.

Just as there are some common themes to this story of restructurings, there are also some lessons that can be drawn from the Massachusetts example.

1. *Distinguishing between statewide policy formation for higher education and micromanagement is a difficult but essential task for statewide boards.* The board of regents was expected to create a statewide system and to formulate coherent policy for that system. Slowly, it made progress on this agenda, but it also began to get deeply involved in management and operational issues. The move toward micromanagement was fostered by legislative demands and a series of scandals involving several college and university leaders, but all institutions were affected. By the late 1980s, the management tasks had begun to drive out the larger policy agenda. There were directives, regulations, and required reports on a wide variety of subjects but not much policy concerning higher education priorities, mission, or program development and not much genuine educational reform. The current structure, with its mix of governance and coordination, has not improved the situation. The HECC continues to get deeply into management with state and community colleges. Efforts at statewide policy formation involving these sectors and the University of Massachusetts often get bogged down because of the university's continual need to reassert its autonomy. The result is lack of progress in the formulation of statewide policy, continuing lack of direction for the system as a whole, and the ineffective use of scarce state resources.

2. *A superboard is not necessarily the best structure in a fiscal crisis.* A state board with extensive legislated powers and a large staff had been in place for seven years when the fiscal crisis in Massachusetts began to have an impact on higher education in the late 1980s. The BOR was unable to provide the leadership that was needed, however, in part because it did not have the support of the colleges and universities, the legislature, or the governor and in part be-

cause, despite years and years of planning, it did not have a coherent picture of the priorities and essential strengths of the system. The board itself quickly came under attack, and eliminating the BOR came to be seen as a partial solution to the fiscal problems. Because of the gradual lessening of the fiscal crisis, there is no way to tell from Massachusetts events whether a coordinating board structure or a cabinet-level executive would have been better or worse than the regents, but it is clear that strong power at the center is not always the answer.

3.   *The restructuring process itself saps energy and resources and diverts attention from fundamental questions and issues.* It was unfortunate for Massachusetts that the restructuring process began two years into the fiscal crisis. The board of regents and its staff spent increasing amounts of time and attention on organizational survival when the system should have been concentrating on access and quality, on setting priorities, and on helping colleges and universities manage in difficult circumstances. The University of Massachusetts has been negatively affected by restructuring. An extraordinary amount of attention has been diverted into questions of campus versus system authority, and extensive resources have been diverted into the central systems office. Benefits may ultimately emerge for the University of Massachusetts, but at the moment that prospect is far from clear.

4.   *Leadership—and the consistency of that leadership—matters.* For a variety of reasons, Massachusetts experienced an extraordinary amount of leadership change from 1988 to 1993. There were multiple chancellors, first of the regents then of the HECC; changes in the leadership of the governing and coordinating boards; large numbers of new board members; a new secretary of education; new presidents for the University of Massachusetts and several other colleges and universities; and changes in other senior staff. Some of these changes meant a real loss of leadership and others were welcomed, but they all had a negative effect on stability in policy and practice. Throughout these years, there was no strong, respected advocate for public higher education in Massachusetts who stayed in a leadership position long enough to make a real difference either in the level of state support and recognition or in the amount of institutional change.

It is tempting to look back over the recent past and ask how the condition of higher education might have been improved had leaders been more responsible. Had Dukakis acknowledged the early-warning signs of the fiscal crisis, would the inevitable reductions have been less harmful to students and focused more on, say, unnecessarily redundant programs? Had the board of regents focused more on leadership at the policy and master-planning level, would higher education have enjoyed stronger public support and been able to manage the economic decline more gracefully? Had college and university leaders been able to find common ground, would not the entire enterprise have fared better in the legislature? This is not the place to assign blame, nor has this author the wisdom to do so; but it is difficult to imagine that a bit more statesmanship would not have produced better results during the crisis.

It was clear in 1980 and it remains clear today that Massachusetts needs an effective structure for governance and policy formation for higher education at the state level. It needs a well-planned system of public higher education and constructive working relationships between public and private institutions. It needs effective planning and coordination if the state's resources are to be well used to provide access to a quality education. The tale of two restructuring efforts suggest that we still have not got it right. But we need to keep trying; otherwise Massachusetts risks losing its long-held and historically deserved reputation for commitment and dedication to public education.

References

Breneman, D. W. *Stabilizing the Commonwealth's Investment: Toward a Five-Year Financing Plan for Higher Education.* Cambridge, Mass.: Massachusetts Task Force on Fair Share Funding for Higher Education, 1994.

Hogarty, R. "The Search for a Massachusetts Chancellor: Autonomy and Politics in Higher Education." *New England Journal of Public Policy,* 1988, *4*(2), 7–38.

Osborne, D., and Gaebler, T. *Reinventing Government: How the Entrepreneurial Spirit Is Transforming the Public Sector.* Reading, Mass.: Addison-Wesley, 1992.

Chapter Five

Restructuring As a Way of Life: Alaska

Patrick J. O'Rourke

With a landmass fully one-third the size of the "lower forty-eight" yet populated by less than a million inhabitants, Alaska can rightly claim to be unique among states. From the days of the gold rush to the development of the Prudhoe Bay oil reserves, the history of the last frontier is one of economic booms followed by busts. This rugged state has attracted a population that prides itself on its fierce independence, citizen activism, and a readiness to shape and reshape its institutions, including colleges and universities, in response to the demands of the moment. This impetuousness with respect to organizational change lies at the heart of the political character of the state and cannot be underestimated.

Alaska's institutions of higher education fall into familiar categories: a land-grant research university with doctoral programs in Fairbanks; a regional university located in the capital, Juneau; a large urban university in Anchorage, the state's largest city; and an array of two-year institutions distributed across the state. It shares with other states a history of competition among institutions, difficulties in establishing a stable sense of distinct missions for each, a mix of both unionized and nonunion faculty, and most important for this book, a recent experience with reorganized higher education in response to a precipitous drop in state income.

The story of restructuring on the last frontier offers a number of important lessons for policy makers and educators in other states. As we shall see, reorganization in Alaska has yet to successfully accommodate the culture of the community college and that of the research university within one system. The reinvented system remains hobbled by a failure during the planning phase of the restructuring to recognize the political clout and legal rights of the community college union. Despite some benefits to traditional baccalaureate-level students and some genuine dollar savings, restructuring in Alaska remains plagued by old conflicts that threaten its stability.

The Scene

The crowd gathered early on October 31, 1986, to hear the president of the University of Alaska system address the statewide assembly of faculty and staff. The gathering was larger than usual and included representatives of the board of regents, administrators from many campuses, and students, faculty, and staff who were not members of the assembly. Although atypical, the crowd was not unexpected, for the financial plight of the state of Alaska had been regularly making headlines, and everyone knew that it was impacting higher education. Rumors had been afoot for weeks that the president and key staffers had been meeting regularly to devise major changes in the structure of the system and that these were going to be unveiled in his address this Halloween afternoon. They were not to be disappointed.

In the next forty-five minutes, the assemblage heard a dramatic proposal to modify the system into "a new university, one which is smaller, one with a restricted mission," offering "high quality" but "built on sound educational premises rather than political considerations," (O'Dowd, 1987, p. 1) which had characterized such decisions in the past. This hope would prove elusive, for Alaska is a state that is fiercely divided geographically and economically; but the president's words did express the goals of the latest restructuring effort of the University of Alaska system. Once again, experienced administrators and staff members prepared to modify the directions in which they were heading and braced themselves for the tumultuous period that was sure to follow.

A History of Conflict

To understand the 1987 restructuring, it must be viewed in the context of Alaska's higher education history, a history begun in

1922 in the interior city of Fairbanks when the territorial legislature opened the Alaska Agricultural College and School of Mines, which became the University of Alaska (Cashen, 1972, pp. 129–152). The advent of World War II and its related military buildup of Alaska brought a significant shift in development, and the city of Anchorage, four hundred miles south of Fairbanks, rapidly emerged as Alaska's major population center. It became the first site for higher education expansion with the establishment of a community college there in 1954.

In 1962, the state legislature passed the Community College Act, which sought to build partnerships between the university and local political subdivisions (usually school districts or municipalities) to establish and finance two-year colleges. While primary control remained with the board of regents, the act intended that academic instruction be funded by the university while noncredit, vocational-technical education was to be funded by the local entity. In actuality, most local funds came from state grants for postsecondary vocational education, which in subsequent years were directly appropriated to the university. From the start, there was strong central control and almost 100 percent state funding of these "community colleges." Because all significant governance was vested in the university's board of regents, local communities took little ownership and provided little financial support, factors whose significance became apparent with later restructuring.

By the late 1960s, Anchorage had grown to a city of more than one hundred thousand people and was no longer satisfied with just two-year postsecondary education opportunities (Naske and Rowinski, 1981, p. 158). In response to citizen and student pressure, Anchorage Senior College was established in a two-plus-two arrangement similar to those being instituted in Texas and Florida. By 1970, the University of Alaska had evolved into the state's single public higher education system, consisting of a main campus in Fairbanks, a senior college and a community college sharing a single campus in Anchorage, and six other community colleges that had been established by either the board or the legislature in smaller population centers. With the establishment of a senior college in Anchorage came similar requests from Juneau in the southeast, and in short order, four-year programs were extended there as well. Rural Alaska, in the meantime, had begun to emerge as a broker of political power, and in 1972, the legislature appropriated funds to establish the first rural community college campus in Bethel, a city of about three thousand people in western Alaska.

Despite its evolution, the system still operated much like a single campus and failed to distinguish real differences in need and type of education at various sites. The constitutionally established board of regents governed the university, and its president had direct responsibility for the main campus and for the branches as well. Policies established in Fairbanks were extended to other campuses with little input from them. The knowledge that all real power and control vested in the older, more established main campus caused the resentment of other institutions to build. Many complained that it took too long to establish new courses and programs because they "had to be approved in Fairbanks." Despite local needs, new program requests were often denied as duplicative of Fairbanks offerings. In the tenure and promotion processes, community college faculty, many of whom did not have terminal degrees, were held to standards of teaching and research more appropriate to the research mission of the university in Fairbanks. Neither the board, its administration, nor the faculty in Fairbanks really understood the differences between a community college and a research university, for they had known only the latter. In their minds, the community colleges were small universities and should be treated as such. Consequently, these newer campuses, tired of being branches and feeling like second-class entities, sought greater autonomy over their own affairs. Tension and discord continued to build.

Alaska is an enormous land whose map, if overlaid on an outline of the forty-eight contiguous states, would stretch from Chicago to Seattle and from the Canadian border to the Gulf of Mexico. Yet in 1992 the total population was a mere 585,000, over half of it in the greater Anchorage area. The state suffers geographical isolation not only from the rest of the United States but also within its own borders, for the only way to cover most of its vast distances is by air. Mountain ranges divide the state, and only a small portion of it is connected by road. Its economy, built largely on boom-or-bust cycles, has always been extremely fragile and highly regional. This geographical isolation and economic regionalism have bred intense rivalries and jealousies over the years. Juneau, in southeastern Alaska, saw its economy revolve around the Capitol; Anchorage, in south central Alaska, was the business and transportation hub; and Fairbanks, in the northern interior, had the university. As long as this economic balance remained, people could accept the variability of services, but once it was broken, every section wanted what the other had, and most often for the economic activity generated rather than for the intrinsic value of or need for the service itself.

Beginning in 1970, however, the board of regents began to acknowledge the need for a more decentralized system of management that would allow more responsiveness to local needs. The university was divided into three regions, each headed by a provost. Limited responsibility for the affairs of the regions was extended to each, but important decisions were still made centrally, preventing campuses from responding to identified needs and concerns as quickly and completely as many people would have liked. Then, in 1975, the board acknowledged the need for greater autonomy by creating the University of Alaska Statewide System of Higher Education. It separated the system administration from the university in Fairbanks, established three universities and a division of rural education affairs, and made each responsible for its own administrative functions. Each of the universities had one or more community colleges as part of its structure (O'Rourke, 1987a).

In an effort to speed the establishment of the two newer universities in Anchorage and Juneau, the board and the president conducted what amounted to a raid on the Fairbanks institution by offering many of its faculty transfer opportunities to these newer institutions. With each transfer went the actual position line, resulting in faculty losses in Fairbanks. Even though quite a few transfers were made, both Anchorage and Juneau felt shortchanged in the total number of new faculty their campuses received, and Fairbanks felt its destiny and strength diluted by the loss of so many positions. It was still expected to operate the same programs, but with a substantial staffing reduction, while the transferred faculty frequently formed the basis for establishing competing programs at their new universities. None of the institutions felt fairly treated, and all shared much antipathy toward the central administration and the board.

Mismanagement and Missed Opportunity

Overall, the 1970s were a very difficult time. During this period, the financial accounting systems collapsed and the system experienced its first strike, underwent three reorganizations, and had five system presidents in six years. Marred by serious rifts within its membership, the board neglected serious planning on how to serve the population then exploding throughout the state. Instead, it responded to the loudest and strongest pressures brought to the fore. Its actions, though alleviating immediate tensions, did little to lay the groundwork for a strong, stable university system. In fact, some actions, like the shift of faculty from Fairbanks to Anchorage and Juneau, weakened it for a period of time. The system seemed unable to deal with growing geographical divisions or the distinctions between the community colleges and the universities, factors that resulted in the onset of collective bargaining among community college faculty. During this period, the system expanded by five community colleges and one university center, all in response to citizen demand rather than clear evidence of need or carefully constructed plans for the delivery of services throughout the state. Some community colleges harbored desires to become four-year institutions regardless of population base or expense, and the newer universities wished to become doctorate-granting institutions. The board did little to dispel such wishful thinking, and at times its public commentary actually seemed to encourage these unrealistic ambitions.

The university's troubles were regularly chronicled in the newspapers. As public and legislative confidence in the system's ability to handle its affairs eroded, legislation was enacted to reduce its autonomy in fiscal matters. This could not have happened at a worse time. In 1975, Alaska's major north coast oil discovery became a reality with the completion of the Trans-Alaska Pipeline, and the flow of oil resulted in a government spending spree the likes of which few states have ever experienced. Unfortunately, the university had no effective plan to take advantage of this largesse, and in the general absence of public confidence in the system, financial support came piecemeal from powerful legislators responding to entrepreneurial local administrators rather than proceeding in accordance with board plans and priorities. As a result, the opportunity to invest in its newer campuses and refurbish its older ones passed it by.

The system organization created in 1975 lasted only one year. In 1976, it was modified to create a new component: the division of Community Colleges, Rural Education and Extension, made up of all community colleges and extended campus programs, leaving three single-campus universities in Anchorage, Fairbanks, and Juneau (O'Rourke, 1987a). Although this organization reflected the commonality of interest among community colleges, it also added a fourth chancellor-level administration and created a system within a system, thereby adding to cost and bureaucracy. This approach did, however, reduce strife between community colleges and universities as the two-year institutions felt for the first time that their interests were represented in systemwide policy considerations.

Despite its drawbacks, this 1976 reorganization ushered in a period of calm that helped restore public credibility in the system and lasted until 1982, when Anchorage Community College, then serving nineteen thousand students, persuaded the board to separate it from the other community colleges and create a fifth chancellor-level administration. Again, the board reached its decision with little apparent consideration of the consequences of its actions, including how costs would be met with the inevitable depletion of oil reserves and its consequent loss of revenue.

This period of unbridled and uncharted state growth was reflected in its higher education system, and the University of Alaska emerged from the seventies with three universities, eleven community colleges, and a number of extension centers. By 1985, the system's state appropriation had grown to approximately $170 million, more than double its 1979 level. However, much of this growth was the result of regional politics and legislative "add-on" funding for projects and programs the board had not requested. Systemwide administration had grown as well. The reluctance of the board and the administration to establish a system of indirect rather than direct controls resulted in a central administration that, compared to other states, seemed inordinately large and expensive for the number of campuses it served.

The Oil Crisis and Its Aftermath

Reality dawned, however, with the unanticipated world oil glut of 1985. While the rest of the country cheered declining oil prices, the oil-producing states began to shudder. Alaska faced particularly

intense financial problems since more than 90 percent of its revenues were derived from oil. As prices plunged from more than
$30 per barrel in 1985 to approximately $10 per barrel a mere
eighteen months later, Alaska lost two-thirds of its annual revenue,
and the governor and the legislature began a continuing process
of budget cutting. Unfortunately, their approach showed little commitment to basic state-supported services, and across-the-board
reductions became the most politically palatable approach to managing state revenues. Although a few policy makers were willing to
take up the hard issues of defining what the state was constitutionally responsible for funding, most lacked the courage to chart
such a course. Electoral politics does little to encourage solutions
that look beyond the next election, and consequently, legislators
tend to see budgets in two-year cycles, paying little attention to historical trends.

With fiscal 1986, the legislature required the system to absorb
its first reduction in more than a decade, an effective 4 percent loss,
and belt tightening ensued. By March 1986, oil revenue projections
had slipped again, leading the governor to declare a freeze on state
hiring and impose further limitations on spending in that fiscal
year. That spring, the board of regents directed the president "to
begin a process of examining every aspect of the University system
and to make recommendations to the Board for changes that would
be appropriate in these extraordinary circumstances" (O'Dowd,
1987, p. 2). Specifically, it sought to simplify the administrative structure in recognition that the system would be "smaller, serve fewer
people and provide a narrower array of programs" (p. 2).

The governor and the legislature, continuing their across-the-
board reductions, reduced the system's appropriation for fiscal
1987 by another 9 percent. The university scrambled to produce a
spending plan that would match its reduced revenues, which now
totaled 13 percent over twelve months' time. The budget adopted
by the board in the summer of 1986 contained severe spending
limitations and significant reductions in administrative and academic support personnel.

The ink on this plan was barely dry when the governor, by executive action, announced an additional 15 percent reduction. The
crisis was now full blown, and in August, the president presented
to the board a series of recommendations that included reductions

to teaching, research, and service programs; increases in fees; and a declaration of financial exigency that would allow the system to reduce both the compensation of employees and the length of their teaching contracts.

The regents, in what some analysts felt was one of their finest moments, refused to adopt the recommendations and requested an emergency meeting with the governor to explain the permanent harm such reductions would wreak on the colleges and universities, as well as the system's national credibility. A compromise was reached in which the operating budget recision for the current fiscal year was reduced in exchange for the lapsing of certain previously appropriated capital funds and an understanding that the balance of the operating budget recisions would be accomplished during the following fiscal year. Although the most serious consequence of the crisis, the declaration of financial exigency, had been avoided, the need to curtail expenditures even further persisted. The system had been given a little more time, and as it turned out, with a new governor, a slight rise in oil prices, and a more sympathetic legislature in office the following year, not all of these deferred reductions became reality. In eighteen months, though, the system had suffered an effective 25 percent budget decrease.

Restructuring in a Crisis

The crisis brought on by the governor's executive actions in the summer of 1986 and exacerbated by his order that the university prepare a 1988 budget request that pared costs by an additional 15 percent caused the organizational review of the system to be accelerated. This review became a response to a crisis rather than a planned process of conserving future resources. A broad program review was undertaken at each of the universities by the president and key members of the central staff during the late summer and early fall of 1986. They examined costs, the hows and whys of services, and the organizational structures used to deliver those services. Unfortunately, the budget reduction process was now in crisis mode, and each review lasted only a day and a half. Upon completion of their task, the reviewers concluded that the range of services had to be narrowed but continued to all existing constituencies and locations.

The president and his staff became the restructuring team and, following their campus reviews, went into an intense series of meetings exploring various organizational structures to reduce administrative costs while preserving the system's ability to deliver services at numerous sites. Because the president doubted, perhaps justifiably, that individuals from the system's colleges and universities could be objective in reviewing options, their input was not solicited at this point. The restructuring team soon narrowed its focus to three main options for merging the fourteen separately accredited institutions within the system: reinstituting a single multicampus university administered centrally; forming three universities and a single statewide community college; or forming three multicampus universities with both traditional university and community college missions embedded in each.

In a few weeks, a proposal emerged endorsing a three-university model, and it was shared with the chancellors of the universities and community college divisions. Despite much discussion and debate, serious reservations were expressed by only one person, and the president, sensing fairly wide support, proceeded with this model with only a few minor changes (O'Rourke, 1987b). The main objections expressed at the time concerned mixing what appeared to be two rather distinct cultures: the community college—with its concentration on rapid response, part-time students, and local community service—and the university's more traditional values. Could a stretch from vocational certificates to Ph.D.'s receive equal attention and support? Could the open admissions of the community colleges be accommodated without the universities' losing their attractiveness to more traditional students? How could a collectively bargained faculty be meshed with a nonrepresented faculty? It was the continued deferral of this last issue and its inadequate consideration that ultimately undermined much of the restructuring process and subsequently proved to be the major drawback to the objectives sought.

Under the proposal unveiled on October 31, 1986, the two community colleges in the southeastern part of the state would merge with the University of Alaska Juneau, which would become a size-limited undergraduate institution without graduate or vocational programs. The few graduate programs currently in existence would be delivered by the other two universities, and vocational programs would be offered by a statewide vocational-technical unit reporting to the University of Alaska, Anchorage. In the northern and interior part of the state, a number of rural extension centers, three rural community colleges accessible only by plane, and the local community college in Fairbanks would be merged with the doctoral-granting institution in that city. Because of the strength of its marine sciences institute, it would also assume responsibility for the fisheries program in Juneau.

In Anchorage, the community college (twenty thousand students) would be merged with the university (roughly thirty-six hundred students), as would the four regional community colleges in south central Alaska. Because of its strong vocational-technical programs, it would have a statewide role in the delivery of these to other areas of the state. With the merger of the colleges and universities, the two chancellor-level community college administrations could be eliminated.

Fourteen separately accredited institutions would become three, and it was projected that there would be a savings of approximately $6 to $7 million, mostly from reduced administrative overhead but some of it from the narrowing of mission and the limiting of services like vocational education outside of the major population centers. Because most of the restructuring savings would occur in south central Alaska, an additional $4 million was reduced from the University of Alaska Fairbanks, to achieve some political balance. Finally, it was also announced that the statewide administration in the next few years would be streamlined and narrowed to assume a more policy-oriented role in the overall system, a project that was never completed.

Hostility Toward Restructuring

Interpreting the general lack of expressed opposition as approval, the president proceeded with this model with only minor modifications. Public hearings were scheduled in various cities, and the stage was set for a major confrontation between community college interests and university concerns and among regional rivals. As Brian Rogers and Tom Gaylord, two system administrators, were to describe it later: "The public response was immediate and intense. Community college councils, the unionized community

college faculty, and concerned citizens attacked the President and
his plan. At public hearings throughout the state, hundreds of people criticized portions or all of the plan. A coalition of opponents,
the Community College Coalition of Alaska, was formed. Opponents saw the plan as denying the mission of community colleges,
changing the nature of the college commitment to students,
removing the community service role . . . , abridging local control
and autonomy, and possibly breaking the community college teachers' union" (1988, p. 7).

Although commentary on the proposal was solicited from
within the university community, it had little effect on the plan's
direction in the long run. The public hearing process produced a
few minor changes, but in the main, the proposal remained intact.

It seemed that the fiercer the criticism, the more the administration dug in behind its proposal. There was sufficient testimony
both in support and in opposition that the president concluded
he should proceed. One significant change did occur during the
public process, though, that modified an underlying tenet of the
savings plan. As public criticism of the narrowing of services
increased, attempts were made to assuage the critics by assuring
them that no staff or faculty would be moved and that each community would retain the same level of services. Having made such
assurances publicly, it became impossible for the system to carry
out the desired narrowing of missions and services.

In December, the regents considered the restructuring plan.
Having attended some of the public hearings, they were aware of
the hostile public mood, and had there not been a financial crisis,
they might well have abandoned the effort, but savings had to be
found. They also suspected that the public would be no more satisfied with alternative financial reduction proposals, and they
remained committed to preserving, to the extent possible, the system's direct instructional services within the scope of a narrower
mission. Where the board may have faltered was in not adequately
considering alternative restructuring approaches or carefully
weighing those prior to the hearing process. Some people within
the university sincerely believed that these particular mergers were
not in the long-term best interests of the system and its students
but felt that substantial administrative savings could be achieved
along with the continuation of a community college identity.

Although these alternatives were provided to the president, they were neither shared with the board nor discussed internally within the broader administration. Despite the importance of the issue, the board never considered other approaches and began to view all who did not support this particular direction as enemies and saboteurs of the effort. Thus different internal views were effectively silenced rather than explored for their merit, and the board adopted the broad outline of the proposal, albeit with a few political changes of its own, reflecting particular regional interests.

Politics

Internal politics further hampered the restructuring process. For example, consulting groups made up of representatives of the units being merged were established to formulate recommendations. They were to advise on administrative arrangements, advisory organizations, and key elements to be included in the revised missions to be drafted over the next year. For parity reasons, representation from the units being merged into the "new" universities was equal to the representation from the "old" universities regardless of differences in size and complexity. This may have conveyed a sense of participation and equity in the new organization, but the political agendas of some members complicated the effort, and what might have been a relatively easy task became more complex as political jockeying occurred for placement within the new institutions.

Due to the collective bargaining issue, the universities were directed to integrate the faculties fully into the various departments and disciplines so that there would be no distinction between community college and university faculty. In this way, it was presumed that the collective bargaining unit could be eliminated because there was no longer an identifiable "community of interest," that is, a community college faculty. This directive skewed some natural organizations. For instance, at the University of Alaska, Fairbanks, bringing in the local community college, which had virtually no academic transfer component, as a college of the university dedicated to serving local training needs was not acceptable because it would suggest a separate "community of interest" among the community college faculty. This, in turn, might negatively affect the ability to merge the large academic transfer component of the community college in Anchorage with the academic departments of the university there. Thus, the existence of a collective bargaining unit and questions about what to do about it in the restructured university system began to drive some of the decisions, although total resolution of the issue continued to be deferred.

Concerns of community college activists, meanwhile, fueled political action. In January, the house of representatives introduced a resolution requesting that the board of regents reconsider the restructuring plan and examine alternatives that "would preserve the unique goals and functions of the Community College System" (Meyers, 1988, p. 19). The senate took stronger action, reintroducing a bill that had circulated periodically over the years to separate the community colleges from the University of Alaska system. A school district with which the university had an agreement under the Community College Act filed suit, alleging an abridgment of its 1977 agreement with the university. In March, the Alaska Commission on Postsecondary Education met and voted to support a separate community college system, thereby reversing its long-standing opposition to dual systems. Toward the end of that month, the Community College Coalition and the Alaska Association of Community College Councils submitted an application to the state for an initiative petition to establish an independent community college system. Thus, even if legislative action failed, community college supporters were planning to put the issue before the voters in a referendum.

In April, the same two groups filed suit in state superior court against the board of regents, alleging breach of contract with local school districts, misappropriation of local funds intended for community colleges, violations of board policies concerning community college councils, denial of due process for students, and violations of the state's open-meetings law. The board greeted these actions sternly, passing a resolution reaffirming its actions and declaring its opposition to "any legislative proposal to divide the public higher education system as being contrary to sound educational and fiscal policy" (Meyers, 1988, p. 19).

The Process

Toward the end of that month, institutional restructuring advisory councils were appointed at each institution to oversee the implementation of restructuring, including the drafting of a revised mission for each of the "new" universities, the development of a new admissions policy to encompass the goals of both the university and the community colleges, a new rank and tenure system for faculty, plans for the operation of business and administrative systems, the sharing of resources, and many other issues related to merger. The restructuring councils, chaired by the chancellors, carried out their work through a number of sublevel task forces that included citizen representatives from community college regions as well as faculty and administrative representatives. The nonuniversity people may have helped broaden the viewpoints of university faculty, but they also added to the complexity of the task by becoming involved in issues that are traditionally the purview of the faculty. Over two hundred people at each of the larger institutions were intensely involved in this process from spring 1987 until spring 1988.

July 1, 1987, was set as the effective date for implementing the merger, to coincide with the new fiscal year and its reduced funding. Although not all issues had been resolved by that date, they were at least being dealt with by the restructuring councils. Throughout May and June 1987, a series of emergency regulations was passed by the board to effect a smooth transition. Despite the public, legislative, and legal battles of that spring, the legislature adjourned without acting on the separation bill, although it did add a number of "legislative intent" restrictions to the new budget. Many of these attempted to protect the community colleges, and one established a special legislative oversight committee to review the process and report to the 1988 legislature. Thus began another round of hearings.

Intense public and political pressure had been brought to bear on the board of regents. Its ability to resist was due in part to its constitutionally established status. The mandate for operating the university system clearly belonged to the regents and not the governor or the legislature. Besides, concepts such as a lean and efficient administration, reduced bureaucracy, and preservation of direct instructional services were difficult to oppose. Politicians realized that with revenues still falling, they were not about to appropriate the additional revenue necessary to keep the old system intact, thereby increasing the state's deficit. Their involvement would thus have put them in a no-win situation, and that tempered any desire they might have had to act. In addition, by filing a petition for a referendum while seeking legislative relief, the Community College Coalition in effect gave legislators the easy out of delaying any action until the public had voted.

Political pressure was beginning to take its toll on the new organizations, for in response to each criticism, the board of regents took a number of actions to try to shore up community college support. Unfortunately, these responses were frequently to the criticism of the moment without regard to how their actions would be integrated into each of the universities. For instance, in response to the criticism that vocational education would be lost, the board created a statewide coordinating office reporting to the central administration. Seven years later, there was strong consensus that it had done nothing, was not needed, and had in effect wasted more than $2 million. By the time consultants recommended its elimination, however, the office had taken on a political life of its own, and no action was taken.

In response to community service critics, the board modified intrauniversity administrative alignments, thereby disrupting internal relationships. To placate local control interests, the board adopted a policy permitting local communities that provided at least one-third of the annual support to maintain a separately accredited community college with semi-independent status. Only one college in the system could qualify under that provision, and it became a semi-independent part of the University of Alaska Anchorage.

Yet another accommodation provided instant rank and tenure in the restructured universities to community college faculty based on time employed and without peer review. Surprisingly, although this action constituted a major abridgment of the board's own academic policies and a substantial unfairness to university faculty who were being turned down in the review process, only University of Alaska, Fairbanks, administrators and some faculty raised objections.

The Community College Union Issue

Faculty issues became the most complex, longest-running, and most mishandled issues in the entire process. The statewide community college faculty had bargained collectively since 1974, and under their contract, although unranked and nontenured, they had strong employment security, including binding arbitration in cases of termination and nonrenewal of appointment. By contrast, the university faculties were not collectively organized and had systems of rank, tenure, and promotion that included peer review and annual evaluation. University faculty typically taught three courses per semester, ranging from lower division through graduate instruction, and had additional assignments in research and service, while community college faculty were required to teach four lower-division courses per semester and had a one-fifth-time service assignment. There were also major differences in the level and type of preparation required of the two faculties.

From the beginning, both the university system and the union recognized that certain issues would have to be bargained to permit complete restructuring, but the two parties could not agree on what those issues were. The university saw an obligation to bargain with the union over the *effects* of restructuring, but the union insisted that it had a right to bargain over the *decision to restructure*. The board asserted as its sole right the power to establish or disestablish colleges. In the absence of a common starting point, no negotiations occurred. Under the terms of the existing bargaining contract, the university could not require the bargaining unit members to become university faculty, but it could offer them transfer opportunities, which it did. The university reasoned that if community colleges no longer existed after July 1, 1987, that faculty's bargaining unit would no longer exist either. If faculty members refused the transfer opportunity, they would then be laid off.

In an attempt to minimize negative reactions from community college faculty, the system administration convinced itself that despite the existence of a contract that negated tenure, any community college faculty member who had been with the system at least seven years would be considered to hold tenure in the restructured universities. Those with less time would be given a full seven years before they would be required to stand for tenure, and many were offered multiyear contracts, which were not available to university faculty. Professorial rank was awarded to community college faculty on the basis of individual placement on the negotiated salary scale, although none was automatically given a full professorship, a minor acquiescence to university faculty concerns over these developments.

With the adoption of these rules in June 1987, the union filed a grievance alleging that the university had unilaterally altered its policies by eliminating the community college system and thereby negating all provisions of the collective bargaining agreement. Arbitration was scheduled, and in February 1988, the arbitrator ruled that the existence of a collective bargaining agreement did not negate the board's authority to eliminate the community colleges but that there might be a remaining community of interest that would perpetuate the bargaining unit in the new universities. Arguments on this issue could not be scheduled until much later, and in a strange twist of fate, the arbitrator failed to render his decision for more than two years.

When the case was finally decided, the union position largely prevailed. Although some changes had occurred, those who had previously been community college faculty were essentially performing the same teaching duties in the universities as they had in the community colleges. A third arbitration resulted in a settlement of more than $4 million to the union and its members. Almost five years after restructuring had been implemented, the bargaining unit and the union were reinstated. As a result, some faculty at each institution are now under collectively bargained agreements and others are not, even within the same academic departments. After five years of unrest, former community college faculty had added university rank, tenure, and promotion rights to all the protections of the union contract without ever having to bargain for these new provisions.

The Results of Restructuring

Assessment of Alaska's restructuring effort is difficult, for, as is so often the case, there are no clean "bottom lines" against which to measure success. One can observe what has happened, but it is more difficult to see what has been lost as a result of actions taken and what might have occurred under other plans. In nonmonetary terms, the restructuring contributed to a loss of forward momentum and continuing instability within the system.

Some Winners, Some Losers

By virtually all accounts, the most positive impact of restructuring was felt by the more traditional, baccalaureate-oriented students. There were no longer arguments over transferability of credit between community colleges and universities, for they were now one and the same. In Anchorage, which serves over half of the system's students, problems with class times and course numbering, which prior to restructuring did not always mesh between the university and the community college, disappeared.

During the five years immediately following restructuring, total enrollment grew by 10 percent while full-time-equivalent enrollment grew by 18 percent, reflecting a greater emphasis on the full-time student (more of a university value) than on the part-time student (more of a community college value). Although course offerings were actually fewer after restructuring, program emphasis appeared to be stronger. Part-time enrollment at the two larger universities saw virtually no increase during this time.

Many observers believe that the quality of lower-division offerings was substantially improved under the more rigorous standards exercised by the universities, providing greater added value for students.

Students enjoy better advising, and the ease of movement from a regional campus to a main campus of one of the universities has stimulated a stronger interest in baccalaureate programs. Articulation between associate and baccalaureate degrees improved, and new bachelor's degrees were developed to complement lower-division vocational programs.

Despite budget reductions, the number of courses offered in the evening and at off-campus sites remained fairly constant, while upper-division and graduate work on campus grew, particularly in the Anchorage area. In areas outside the larger population centers, bachelor's degree programs were extended in greater abundance as the universities undertook responsibility for serving a more distant population.

In some cases, the merged institutions became stronger while one or more of its parts might have been weakened. Even the most ardent community college supporters admit that the University of Alaska, Anchorage, is a stronger institution today, although they believe it was at the expense of the community college. At the University of Alaska Fairbanks, the Rural College became a much stronger combined entity because of its shared faculty and resources, although each of the campuses that comprise it may have been individually weakened. With major improvements in technology and the pooling of faculties in the jointly operated Center for Distance Delivery, the college has been able to expand its coursework across regions to more students, thereby reducing somewhat the cost of instruction. It seems that the whole was indeed stronger than the sum of its individual parts.

The loss of autonomy as freestanding, separately accredited institutions was very difficult for community college personnel and their public supporters. They had been proud of their own identity and feared that as part of a larger entity, they would be lost in the bureaucracy of the university and would not get a fair shake. Some of these fears seemed justified; others were more imagined than real. For instance, some campus directors point to the loss of certain direct budgetary line items that they once had but fail to acknowledge that they now receive a similar direct service support from the main campus without any charge. Some bemoan the loss of flexibility they once had and point out that the universities' academic processes fail to approve some part-time faculty they seek to hire. In almost the same breath, though, they virtually all admit that their academic offerings are much improved, much sounder, and of higher standards. A few, when pressed, begrudgingly admit that better academic approval processes have resulted in stronger faculty and courses.

Yet there was some real loss in flexibility, and it did become more cumbersome to do business across vast distances. On the main campuses, the people in charge of the more specialized community college functions felt that there was no opportunity to market their programs differently, to schedule flexibly outside the traditional semesters, or to offer self-support courses at a higher fee rate to increase responsiveness to public demand. They believed that associate degree programs had not been understood as adequately as baccalaureate programs and consequently were not sufficiently marketed. Ardent community college supporters see this as evidence of the erosion of the community college philosophy and mission.

What many people feel was one of the most significant setbacks of restructuring was the loss of a high-level advocate for community college functions, without whom, they reason, erosion of mission will continue. They feel strongly that the corporate cultures of community colleges and universities are different and that this has tempered how problems and issues are perceived and addressed. Some believe that restructuring moved in the direction it did because neither the president nor the board understood these cultural differences. This same viewpoint prevailed in the early seventies before the community colleges were separated from the universities.

In the first seven years following restructuring, the number of vocational education offerings in the system had decreased, although most experts believe that what might be called "hard" vocational-technical programs such as welding would have been reduced in rural Alaska even without restructuring due to limited employment opportunities. During those seven years, no new associate degree programs in vocational-technical fields were established, although two had been added in paraprofessional studies. Furthermore, since restructuring, community service programs are increasingly offered on a self-support basis, as perhaps they should have been all along.

Differentiated tuition rates between the community colleges and the universities disappeared, and from 1988 to 1994, tuition increased 65 percent for full-time students and 55 percent for part-time students, potentially jeopardizing the financial accessibility that community colleges have historically tried to ensure.

The merger of the faculties yielded mixed benefits. Small college faculties that had long functioned without much interaction with a broader group of colleagues could now explore their ideas and problems with other faculty who could provide different perspectives on an issue. Some main campus faculty became more attuned to the needs of working adults and cultural minorities, with whom the rural faculties were more familiar. Communication increased, but with it came a lot more acrimony among faculty as differing values surfaced. As the airing of differences increased, more confrontation and greater disharmony resulted. Former community college faculty again felt a sense of second-class status, particularly those from departments that did not fit within the university mainstream. Some university faculty developed a similar paranoia, believing that the board and its administration focused too much on community college and off-campus concerns and too little on traditional university issues. All of this took a toll on morale.

The unresolved union issue created an undercurrent of disruption and in some disciplines precluded the development of true colleague relationships. With the subsequent reemergence of the union, faculty differences surfaced. Collective bargaining unit members could not serve in the traditional role of department head because collective bargaining draws firm lines between administration and faculty for the purposes of unit definition. As new agreements are negotiated and differences become further highlighted, greater division and hostility may well occur.

Ultimately, the legal and political actions brought against the university were all resolved in its favor, with the important exception of the collective bargaining arbitrations. Whether it had acted wisely or not, the board of regents had acted legally within its constitutional powers. However, it erred in seeing the existence of the bargaining unit as tied to the existence of the community colleges rather than to the type of work the bargaining unit performed. As a result, it permitted the development of organizations and structures that are tenuous at best. At some time in the future, either the bargaining unit will have to be expanded to include those not yet represented, or its members will have to be organized into structures where their work can be differentiated from that of their colleagues.

In the referendum on the separation issue, Alaskans decided that the maintenance of a unified public higher education system outweighed the need for separate community colleges. Historically, they had always been part of the university. In Anchorage, the unification of the community college and the university actually had some very positive political consequences. For the first time, there was a single institution for the public to rally around, although a small minority still mourned the loss of the community college. It became easier for the legislative delegation from Anchorage to support a single institution than it was to deal with both the community college and the university when they competed for support. At the extended campuses, political support has been more variable, as the university is sometimes blamed for the problems and the local campus is praised for the successes.

Cost Savings

It is clear that restructuring saved some money. A legislative audit two years after the restructuring confirmed that $5.1 million in savings had been realized. Although falling short of projected savings, the actual reduction represented about 4 percent of the state's financing for the university system.

Some savings, however, were not permanent. Knowledgeable

system personnel believe that some 20 to 30 percent of the identified savings grew back in the first five years following restructuring.
An internal analysis of spending from fiscal years 1988 to 1992
showed a 14 percent increase in expenditures for institutional support. The cost of reimplementation of the collective bargaining
contract between the university and the union carried financial
damages of about $4 million, although these were onetime costs.
By all accounts, the estimated $2 million spent on the unneeded
Office of Vocational Education was wasted. An uncalculated cost
of restructuring remains the faculty workload of former community college faculty members whose instructional effort was
changed from eight courses per year to five or six. So while there
were savings, there were also added expenses, which were not calculated, that lowered the total amount of savings actually achieved.

Political Advantage

Some observers believe that the system gained intangible political
support by taking bold action at a time of major financial crisis in
the state. Consequently, they reason, the system was insulated from
further budget reductions over the next few years. Legislators
accepted the fact that "higher education had already given" and
thus seemed less inclined to extract a further pound of flesh, at
least for a while. However, this view is difficult to prove in the face
of other factors that undoubtedly had an impact, including the
election of a more supportive governor; oil price stabilization,
which eased demands for further budget reductions; and major
legal settlements that brought some windfall revenue to the state.
Comparisons of state agency appropriations from fiscal 1989
through fiscal 1993 suggest that higher education received no
more favorable consideration than other publicly supported entities; indeed, eleven of nineteen agencies received a higher percentage budget increase than the university did over that period
(Baggen and others, 1993, p. 7).

Continuing Instability

Ideally, the massive effort to restructure higher education in 1987–1988
would have been followed by a period of organizational stability during which changes could be fully integrated. Regrettably, this was not

the case as the board tinkered further, following a well-established history of using structural changes to solve perceived problems. For example, after merging the rural colleges in 1987 in response to political arguments, it separated them again in 1992, thus destabilizing them twice in four years. The board moved the only nationally accredited teacher education programs in the state from professional school status to that of a department within the College of Liberal Arts, thereby jeopardizing the future of this accreditation. Once again, the board responded to loud, shrill voices with their own political agendas instead of leaving organizational decisions to the administrators hired to operate the universities and confining their own attention to setting system policy and establishing expected outcomes.

In 1993, the board resurrected the idea of returning to a single-university model, failing to realize that this was the structure that had imploded around them some twenty years before. Some post-restructuring appointees to the regents harken back to a simpler time in Alaska's higher education chronicles, a time that has long since passed into history. Institutional memory is absent, and too few members understand the travails that the system has endured. Such board discussions reflect an unwillingness to build on what it created in 1987 and have stirred new anxieties among faculty and staff, which in turn inhibit momentum as creative energy is diverted from the important work of teaching and research to battle recycled issues.

What Might Have Been

Alaska's restructuring was rooted in financial crisis and prevailed in many ways because of it. It was clearly and broadly recognized that rapid response was critical, and new directions were thus taken without subjecting them to the scrutiny that would normally have been associated with an undertaking of such magnitude. The consequence of this haste was a failure to analyze the types of institutions that might best have served different parts of the state. Such an analysis might have suggested a community college in communities with substantial vocational employment opportunities and university extension centers in rural locations with limited enrollment and primarily professional employment opportunities.

Restructuring never really succeeded in narrowing institutional missions, although subsequent budget limitations did this to some extent. Weak programs with small enrollments and little documented need managed to perpetuate themselves despite high costs and questionable benefits. Although it would have been virtually impossible to eliminate any institution, certain high-cost, low-production programs within institutions could have been pruned without major consequences. However, political considerations prevailed, and even programs originally targeted for discontinuance were maintained.

A less stable and less diverse system may have been the major intangible consequences of restructuring. The fear of diverse institutions has always plagued the board of regents. It has never been able to accept that different types of institutions might be of greater benefit to more Alaskans in the long run and that one university does not have to be like another. Rarely has the board permitted variable policies for its universities and colleges, nor has it defined a clear, distinct purpose for each that meets different state needs. It has instead allowed missions to surface from what the institutions desire to be rather than from any clear vision of what Alaska needs and can afford. The basis was there for three really distinct institutions: the University of Alaska Fairbanks, with its traditional land-grant doctoral, research, and cross-cultural mission; the University of Alaska Anchorage, a large urban teaching university serving a commuting population; and the University of Alaska Juneau, tailored into a small, distinct undergraduate college for students who work best in such an environment. Instead, each university has been allowed to try to emulate the others, constantly broadening its mission while giving up nothing. Each aspires to grant doctorates, to be a major player in research, to be residential, and to serve the broadest possible array of students.

Lessons of Restructuring

For all the uniqueness of higher education in this largest state, Alaska's struggles over restructuring offer several lessons for others seeking to reorganize. A candid review of these lessons may also help Alaskans as they face an all but inevitable second round of organizational change.

1. *Match the new structure to the political, economic, and demographic realities of the state.* Public colleges and universities, whether they acknowledge it or not, are part of a powerful symbiotic relationship with their neighborhoods. For a rural community college, this neighborhood may be the town or village where it is located. A regional university has a larger bailiwick, and the state's land-grant university may lay claim to statewide and sometimes national and international allegiances. In Alaska, some citizens fail to see the land-grant university in Fairbanks as the statewide resource it is and look at it more as an asset to that former mining town near the Arctic Circle. Hence these individuals take a more parochial view of the campus than the regents, faculty, students, and administrators, who legitimately see it as a statewide university.

To achieve stability, it is essential to recognize these loyalties by ensuring that all units have sufficient voice in the new system and by allowing different institutions to develop programs and services that make sense to the people they serve. For example, it is important that the values and influence of the university in Fairbanks not be perceived to crowd out the priorities of Anchorage or the more rural institutions. Conversely, the important land-grant mission of the university in Fairbanks must be protected from regional politics.

Local needs are stubborn. They cannot be long ignored. The three-university model that the regents adopted appears to many people to represent the triumph of traditional, elitist academic interests, and many community college advocates hope that this triumph will be only temporary.

2. *Acknowledge the political clout, member loyalty, and legal rights of unions.* Restructuring might have been easier to accomplish without having to deal with unions, but ignoring their interests and rights can be damaging to long-term solutions. In fact, the threats, real or imagined, to faculty job security and seniority rights occasioned by restructuring help make unions even more powerful. In times of uncertainty due to structural change, individuals who fear for their livelihood turn to the one organization whose top priority is their job security, the union. The system administration, which may once have advocated in the legislature for faculty pay raises or defended faculty rights, is now seen as the enemy.

In this case, both parties agreed that there was a need to negotiate but could not find a mutual starting point. Both the regents and the union felt that their rights and powers were being infringed. What might have been an alternative? Instead of perpetuating the impasse into a series of binding arbitrations, voluntary mediation by both sides might have opened fruitful ground for practical negotiations that might, in the long run, have helped guide the formation of structures that saved money, protected board and union prerogatives, and ultimately smoothed the transition. Massive restructuring is not something that typical labor contracts anticipate, so extraordinary measures may be necessary to foster meaningful dialogue. Earlier involvement of the union leadership in the substance of restructuring might be a way to achieve this. Even more important, the people in charge of restructuring must acknowledge that organizations like unions have rights in addition to the individuals they represent. Though Alaska went the extra mile to protect the rights of individuals, policy makers did not acknowledge that the union had any substantive rights as an organization, and this proved to be wrong.

3.   *Acknowledge and accommodate different institutional cultures within a system.* Statewide systems that include a heterogeneous mix of institutions are more complex and often more expensive to administer than those comprised of, say, all community colleges or regional universities. Yet one has only to look to the states that have comprehensive systems and to such mature models as Wisconsin or North Carolina to conclude that they can be made to work successfully.

Broadly speaking, there seem to be two ways of accommodating disparate identities under one governing board. First, the administrative structure itself may be engineered so that each of the separate types of institutions comes under one executive. At one point, Alaska employed a chancellor for all the two-year institutions who had equal authority with the chancellors of the state's three universities. Second, which may make more sense, is to ensure that the interests of differing units are accommodated by distinct practices and policies. These systems must be administered by broad-minded individuals who understand the unique strengths and limitations of the different types of institutions under their charge. Board members also need to show respect for all their institutional children in equal measure. Despite their good intentions, the Alaska regents' use of the three-university model gives the appearance of subjugating the interest of two-year institutions to those of the universities. Subsequent administrators, however fair-minded, have not been able to extinguish the resulting sense of resentment.

Shifting Sands

Since the early 1970s, Alaska's structural foundations for the institutions and the system itself have been built on shifting sands. Programs and campuses have been added and deleted from each of the institutions with a high level of regularity as board members and administrations come and go. From 1975 to the restructuring in 1987, there were five major structural changes, each bringing a degree of turmoil, a change in focus, and a diversion of the collective energy of the faculty and administration from the task of building strong institutions. A particular direction gets charted, and after a few years, a major shift is made and the map is redrawn. The institution building from the first course is redirected when it moves to the second, and the inroads that had been begun are short-circuited as new and different priorities distract attention from the first. The system has been very unstable, and the board, with its all too frequent changes in structure, has failed to realize that enduring foundations are necessary to build strong institutions. Perhaps this commitment may yet be found.

References

Baggen, A., and others. *UA in Review.* Fairbanks: University of Alaska, 1993.

Cashen, W. P. *Farthest North College President.* Fairbanks: University of Alaska Press, 1972.

Meyers, D. *Restructuring: A Chronological Report.* Fairbanks: Board of Regents, University of Alaska, 1988.

Naske, C., and Rowinski, L. *Anchorage: A Pictorial History.* Norfolk, Va.: Donning, 1981.

O'Dowd, D. *Recommendations to the Board of Regents on the Implementation of Restructuring the University of Alaska.* Fairbanks: University of Alaska, 1987.

O'Rourke, P. "Universities and Community Colleges: The Changing Structure of Alaska Higher Education." Paper presented to the Northwest Association of Schools and Colleges, Anchorage, Alaska, Dec. 1987a.

O'Rourke, P. *University Restructuring.* Fairbanks: University of Alaska, Nov. 1987b.

Rogers, B., and Gaylord, T. "Restructuring the University of Alaska Statewide System of Higher Education." Paper presented at the Twenty-Third Annual International Conference of the Society for College and University Planning, Toronto, Canada, Aug. 1988.

Chapter Six

The Human Side of Restructuring: Minnesota

Terrence J. MacTaggart

Restructuring in Minnesota took the form of combining three disparate systems, each with its own board, executive, and bureaucracy, into one integrated organization. In 1991, the legislature passed and the governor signed a bill that would join the state universities, the community colleges, and the technical colleges into a new system called Minnesota State Colleges and Universities. Interestingly, the new board, to be known as the Higher Education Board, would not gain operating authority until the first day of July 1995, some fifty months after the original merger legislation had passed. The new system would inherit more than sixty campuses, serve some 160,000 students and employ about 20,000 faculty and staff. It would become the eighth largest employer in the state.

As chancellor of the state university system from 1991 until the eve of merger, I was a close observer and frequent participant in the planning and the politics that preceded the official transfer of authority. Because the eventual success or failure of this restructuring can only be determined well after the publication of these words, commentary on its public or educational benefits would be largely speculative. Instead, because the four-year gestation period provided plenty of opportunity for human emotions to emerge and display themselves and because the eventual effectiveness of this change, or any major organizational change, will rest on the skill with which leaders engage the hearts and minds of employees, I chose to concentrate on the human side of restructuring.

132

The subject of this chapter is the impact of merger on the emotional and professional lives of employees caught up in the shifting gears of organizational change. The insights presented here are based on extensive interviews with a variety of players, including dispossessed system heads, managers embraced by the new system as well as those spurned by it, upwardly mobile administrators and some in the final stages of their careers, persons whose careers were dramatically altered by the occasionally toxic emotional brew stirred up by restructuring, and the few who took advantage of the change to pursue a new life path. Interviewees included men and women of a variety of backgrounds in order to determine if gender or race affected one's response to the stress and opportunities posed by this change.

All of the professionals who contributed to this chapter by agreeing to be interviewed disclosed similar patterns of behavior and attitude. Some of these were predictable; others were surprising. The most important common reaction was the universal desire to play a role in the creation of the new order of things. Virtually every interviewee sought to be given the chance to contribute to reshaping public higher education. This appetite prevailed for those seeking a job in the new system, which is not surprising. But those who planned to retire or leave the system were also eager to be creatively engaged. And the single most important determinant of one's attitude toward merger was whether or not these overtures were reciprocated. Those whose offers of help were spurned were the most pessimistic of the new system's chances for success. This group exhibited various forms of exit behavior, from emotional disengagement to calculated sabotage. Whether altruistic or self-interested, this broad-based desire to contribute to the making of the new system is a critical resource for the leaders of change.

The interviews revealed four basic types of responses to the change. Winners, persons who had secured a new and higher position within the system, tended to feel positive about the change, while losers, some of them very sore losers, doubted that much good would come of it. The large majority of those affected might describe themselves, as one of them did in an interview, as "lunch bucket workers," individuals who bring a figurative lunch box to work each day and labor wherever they set it down. A smaller group has been labeled "pathfinders," Gail Sheehy's (1982) term for people who took advantage of a change to seek a new career path. Leaders who understand these basic types of responses will be able to manage change more successfully than those who wrongly assume that all workers respond in similar or identical ways.

The human response to restructuring included a grieving process that progressed over time through the now familiar stages from denial to anger to some form of acceptance. Some people moved through these phases in constructive ways, often working on planning the new system while still grieving over the loss of old relationships. Others failed to transcend anger and, in extreme cases, left their jobs with bitterness in their hearts. Those mired in anger tended to personalize it by criticizing the state senate majority leader, who wrote the merger bill, or the interim chancellor of the new system, among others.

Many were bound up in the change at a critical time in their personal development. Those engaged in what Dan Levinson (Levinson and others, 1978, p. 191) calls a midlife transition found their secure organizational homes dissolving around them at precisely the same time they were questioning their own accomplishments. This coincidence of external and internal change heightened their feelings of anxiety.

The drama of organizational change can be Shakespearean in its complexity and power. Strong emotions, held in check under the old social order, are unleashed as one set of superior-subordinate roles gives way to another, possibly its opposite. Not only do individuals react to the way they perceive they are being treated by the new regime, but they react to the fortunes of others as well. In at least one well-known instance, a senior academic officer who was ascending in the merged system felt driven from the state because of the anger of his current superior. The superior, by contrast, may have regarded the officer's good fortune as evidence of disloyalty.

Questions of loyalty, the sense of having a special attachment to an organization, its personnel, and often its leaders, came into play early in the transition process. Leaders in one of the preexisting systems declared it positively disloyal for top administrators to work for the new administration during the transition. One of the other systems took the opposite tack by encouraging its staff to assume influential positions in the process in part to ensure that its institutions would, in the words of its chancellor, "have friends in high places" when the new administration officially took charge. Several respondents reported feeling a sense of conflict and sometimes guilt over where their ultimate loyalty should reside. The organizations that supported their employees in finding a place in the new system and encouraged honest discussion of these conflicts preserved a high degree of organizational integrity up to the end. They also retained the loyalty of their staffs longer than those that regarded the new system as the enemy and anyone who might prosper in it as a traitor.

Managing the human side of a major restructuring effort requires not only knowledge of the conventional aspects of personnel management, such as staffing procedures, contract negotiation, and outplacement strategies, but also a deep understanding of how humans behave in the midst of change that affects their lives and careers. Following a summary of events that led to restructuring in Minnesota, this chapter focuses on the recurring patterns of behavior and attitude that any change of this magnitude elicits. It concludes with a discussion of ways in which leaders, those in charge of implementing the new order as well as those whose organizations or units are being absorbed, can make this sometimes painful and occasionally exhilarating process as creative as possible.

The Minnesota Context

To understand how restructuring came to be in Minnesota, it is necessary to appreciate the legendary "Minnesota Miracle." In 1971, the Minnesota legislature made a massive commitment of public monies to equalize school district funding at a high level across the state. This pledge grew out of the state's current prosperity and confidence in its future and its citizens' profound belief in the importance of education. Scandinavian farmers at the hard work of turning prairie flowers into corn and soybeans, miners digging ore from the deep pits on the northern iron range, and middle-class families in the Twin Cities shared an almost religious belief in the importance of education for their children and the prosperity of their state.

This willingness, even passion, to invest in the future extended to higher education as well. Consistent with the Minnesota Miracle, the legislature followed an unwritten policy that no citizen in a town of five thousand or more should have to travel more than thirty-five miles to a postsecondary institution. Thus a state that at the time had a population of less than four million committed itself to paying for an array of over sixty technical institutes (eventually to be named colleges), community colleges, and regional state colleges (later to become universities). These developed in addition to the venerable University of Minnesota, with its five coordinate campuses. To oversee the burgeoning higher education enterprise, the legislature established three system boards, each with its own executive, a chancellor, and staff. A fourth board, the Higher Education Coordinating Board (HECB), was to coordinate the efforts of the technical institutes, community colleges, and state universities as well as the University of Minnesota, under its own board of regents, and the private colleges. As a lobbyist who was on the scene when the Minnesota Miracle was enacted and some twenty years later at the time of the merger bill put it, "The miracle was that we thought we could pay for all this."

Over the twenty years that followed enactment of the Minnesota Miracle, higher education grew and prospered. Extraordinary capital expansion lagged only slightly behind enrollment growth in Minnesota's four large separate systems. The citizens of this high-effort state contributed a large share of their tax dollars to higher education. But a growing population and one of the nation's highest postsecondary participation rates among high school graduates led to a decline in funding per student. The systems complained bitterly about this trend but continued to grow their institutions and expand program offerings. Ten years before merger, Governor Rudy Perpich named a commission to review the state's commitment to higher education and, many observers believed, recommend ways to control its unbridled growth. Instead, the commission recommended still further expansion of access and programs. In light of this history of public and legislative support, few in the state's higher education establishment thought that the 1991 merger bill would pass.

But by the close of the 1991 legislative session, lawmakers passed on to the governor a bill that called for merging the state's technical colleges, its community colleges, and its seven state universities under a new higher education board. The new board, half of its members to be named by the governor and half by the three constituent boards, would have only a planning role for four years. On July 1, 1995, the three existing boards and their chancellors would yield governing authority to this new entity. By February 1993, the new board had hired an interim executive who began an active transition process involving literally hundreds of employees of the existing systems on more than a dozen task forces and committees. *Merger*, the shorthand term used to denote this massive undertaking, which would yield a system second only to New York State's in the number of institutions it contained, loomed large in the consciousness of the twenty-one thousand employees who were to become part of the new order of things.

There had been numerous attempts over the years to harness Minnesota's gargantuan higher education enterprise. The state's Higher Education Coordinating Board periodically received additional oversight authority from the legislature, but lacking fiscal control over the systems, it could do little of real worth to coordinate, much less regulate, their activities. The private colleges claimed virtual independence of the HECB, a stance never really contested by that agency. Legislative proposals to create a superboard that would exercise governing authority over all public higher education in the state, including the University of Minnesota, foundered largely because the university successfully asserted its constitutional autonomy. Facing the threat of loss of power, proponents of the three other systems argued that their distinctive identities would erode if they were combined under one board.

When it occurred, merger came about as the result of a contest of political will. Roger Moe, the steel-jawed senate majority leader, refused to allow the 1991 legislature to adjourn until it agreed to his merger language in the higher education appropriations bill. Lyndon Carlson, longtime chair of the education committee in the house and a devoted champion of education generally and of distinctive missions for the higher education systems, opposed merger. With great reluctance and in the vain belief that it could overturn the merger plan in a subsequent session, the Minnesota House of Representatives acquiesced. Various attempts to overturn the bill or dilute its provisions in later legislative sessions failed. By fall 1993, even its most ardent opponents in the legislature and among the systems accepted the inevitability of merger.

As a kind of epitaph to the era of growth, the chair of the

higher education committee in the Minnesota house during 1994 observed that the systems "wouldn't need to worry about merger if they had learned to work together twenty years ago. Credit transfer, duplication of effort, lack of cooperation, and budget sharing all joined to frustrate the legislature and the governor to the point of merger."

Key Features of Mergers in Minnesota

Four distinctive features of restructuring in Minnesota make it an interesting venue for the human drama that is the subject of this chapter. First, the merger process was singular in its lack of planning, discussion, or debate preceding its enactment into law. The merger bill itself contained only the most general set of goals. Merger was to improve quality, access, and transfer and enable higher education to become more "customer-friendly." But if the amount of discourse preceding the bill was minimal, there would be plenty of time after merger became law for discussion and planning.

The second distinguishing feature of the Minnesota experience was the four-year gestation period between the creation of the new board and its receipt of full authority. These fifty months provided ample opportunity for the early stages of the grieving process, denial and anger, to express themselves. Odd language in the bill called for one interim chancellor to do early planning and for a second interim chancellor to provide leadership up to the July 1995 date when the new board would assume full authority. Interestingly, the bill required a third search to begin after July 1995 for a more or less permanent chancellor. This confusion, coupled with lingering opposition in the legislature and especially among technical college proponents, meant that the new board could lay claim to effective serious planning only during the last two years of the premerger period.

The diversity of its components represents a third distinguishing, if not unique, feature. The three systems had developed radically different governance patterns and policies over the years. The community colleges, with twenty-one institutions ranging in size from a few hundred students to several thousand, had created a strong central administration that provided, among other things, most of the personnel management systems and decision making for the campuses. The state universities, by contrast, consisted of seven largely self-contained institutions with much discretion over academic and administrative policy. The technical colleges had until recently been governed partially by local school districts and partially by a central board. Excepting those in the central office, all technical college workers were employees of the local school districts, each with its own salary and benefits package. Employees in the new system would be represented by ten different bargaining units. The new board faced a daunting challenge in attempting to bring together three complex bureaucracies, each of which would cling tenaciously to its way of doing business.

A fourth distinguishing feature of the new system had less to do with enabling legislation or structure and more to do with early decisions on staffing. The new system pursued a staffing agenda that in piecemeal fashion selected some employees to begin work on a split schedule that included continuing assignments with their "home" system, while it informed others that they would have a position when funds became available in July 1995. All of this took place in sequential rounds of hiring so that no one was told that he or she would not have a job but merely that no job was available yet. For a time, people were told that they would have a position but not which position. In the case of student affairs and system advancement, the subordinate positions were filled before the senior posts, which would remain open until after the effective date of merger. All three of the existing systems loaned staff to work in the merger office. Some of these individuals became bona fide employees of the new system; others served as loaned executives.

Even though the legislature had made the ambiguous guarantee that no one would lose a job due to merger, it was unclear how the new system would preserve jobs while also achieving its goal of reducing the central staff by 20 percent. Finally, because the staffs in the existing systems had different pay scales for similar jobs and brought these differentials with them to the new system, the new administration faced such unenviable choices as freezing or reducing some salaries, instantly raising others in the interests of equity, or explaining to some new employees, frequently women, that they would have to be patient with their lower pay. This confusing approach to staffing contributed to the stress and uncertainty among professionals in the three systems.

The clerical staff, most of whom were represented in the three systems by the American Federation of State, County and Municipal Employees, found themselves in equally ambiguous circumstances. All of their positions in the old systems were eliminated. Clerical workers could bid on jobs in the new system. Those who were not rehired were offered various options, including early retirement for those over age fifty-five. Though the package ultimately available to these employees was generous by some corporate standards, too much time elapsed before workers knew what their futures would be. This period of uncertainty heightened anxiety and reduced productivity.

It is fair to say that most of the employees in the three systems were critical of merger. With a few exceptions, the prevailing opinion was that the legislators' concerns could have been resolved with a more focused bill. Still, once the reality of merger set in, virtually all wanted to play an active role in its planning and implementation.

Need for Engagement

"If you want to achieve anything positive as a result of merger, you cannot be a casual observer. You have to commit in some way." This conclusion came from a program director who felt, at times, bitterly disappointed by the lack of initiatives to increase opportunities for minorities within the new regime. Still, like virtually all of the people interviewed, he wanted to be engaged with the new system and expressed a personal need for a constructive role. Maslow's well-known analysis of human needs seems to apply here. Once people's most basic wants for the wherewithal to provide food and shelter were satisfied, there remained a strong desire to play a role in and make the merger meaningful personally as well as for the students and the state. Readers who find the latter observation naive may recall that Minnesota is a midwestern state where service to the community, defined in a variety of ways, is a strong feature of the culture.

The response to this near-universal desire to play a constructive role was the key decision in determining one's attitude toward merger. As Figure 6.1 outlines, the people who received a positive response to their offers to help were relatively more upbeat about the prospects for the new system, took a future orientation in their thinking, progressed through the stages of grief fairly rapidly, and developed loyalty to the new system. Interestingly, they also felt more guilt over apparent disloyalty to their old employers and colleagues. At best, these were the winners both in the sense that they were awarded good jobs in the new system and in the sense that they felt that they had personally come out ahead after facing one of life's challenges. At the very least, these were successful "lunch bucket workers" who worked diligently for the new system.

The staff of the old systems who did not receive a role in the new system or who felt diminished in the role given them took a much darker view of the new regime and its leaders. Skeptical about the chances of success for the system, these individuals pursued various forms of exit behavior. Some began to look for work elsewhere. Others distanced themselves psychologically. A few engaged in deliberate acts of sabotage directed at merger itself but more often at the interim chancellor. The saboteurs tended to display anger, sometimes amounting to rage, at what they regarded as the unfairness of it all. If they accepted the inevitability of merger itself, they set about damaging its interim leader with a vengeance.

Of course, many who lost in the game of reorganization did not become saboteurs. Some remained good soldiers until their time of discharge or retirement. Among those who did not find satisfying options within the merged system were a fascinating small

Figure 6.1. Results of Engagement in the New Order.

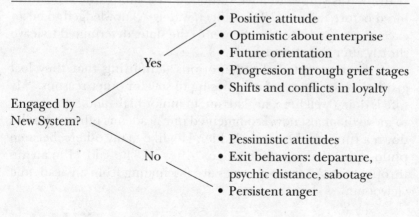

group whose decisions led them to new paths. These people took advantage of events to chart an alternative more challenging and more rewarding course for their lives and careers. Gail Sheehy has chronicled this type in *Pathfinders* (1982).

Winners, Losers, and Lunch Bucket Workers

"Sometimes I refer to myself as 'His Accidency,' the last one left standing. I came out a winner personally and professionally, but I feel some anxiety along with that." Winners came by their new positions along a variety of routes. Some were chosen, especially in the fiscal affairs area, through a meritocratic process. Others got their jobs because of an unwritten rule to achieve balance in hiring among the three systems. Still others, as in the case of this interviewee, got their jobs almost accidently when the manager originally hired left to take a position elsewhere. Though pleased that their economic futures were secure and generally more optimistic about the future of the restructuring, most of the winners were far from smug about their good fortune.

An interviewee who did not find the role he desired in the new system was fond of quoting a star football player who was supposed to have said that it doesn't matter if you win or lose—until you lose. The losers, both those without a job in the new system and the larger group who suffered a demotion in the transition, were angry. A senior officer in one of the older systems was told that he could have a second-level job in the new one and apply for a job at his former level when it was authorized. He rejected it out of hand: "I think it is stupid to have someone in a subordinate position hired before the boss." This officer, widely acknowledged to be an exceptionally talented newcomer to the state, determined to leave shortly after this episode.

Others accepted the demotions, admitting that they lost ground in the process but choosing to stay for other reasons. "My wife is doing well here, my kids are in junior high, and I don't want to move them just now," commented one academic officer who slid down a rung on the career ladder. He, like many others, became philosophical about the change. "After all," he said, "I'm an anthropologist. All these changes are fascinating from an academic viewpoint."

The status of winner or loser is often temporary. As we shall see, at least two talented administrators who had won high-level positions in the system eventually left, one driven out by the hostility of a superior in his old system and the other, in part, by the enmity of those who had competed for his job and lost. Both of these individuals went on to find satisfying and more remunerative jobs elsewhere. The wheel of fortune spins quickly in times of restructuring.

The unfortunate and confusing scheme used to transfer employees from the existing systems to the new alienated more workers than it rewarded. As mentioned earlier, one of the distinctive features of Minnesota's restructuring was a personnel process that often told employees that they would have a new position in the system without telling them which one. An administrator who received one of these ambiguous appointments put it this way: "This 'cattle call' approach diminishes all of us. I'm a professional. I'll take a job equal to my training, but I don't want a voucher for some job yet to be defined." This individual, like several others, took what was offered by the new system but felt little sense of commitment to the job or the system.

By far the majority of those who migrated from the old system to the new were not clear-cut winners or losers but "lunch bucket workers." These people were prepared to offer the proverbial honest day's work for an honest day's pay. As one of them put it, "I learned a great deal about work and responsibility when I was in the military. You're given an assignment, you take your orders, say 'yes, sir,' and do it." Another said that he felt that this example of restructuring offered a model of "how not to do it" but went on to affirm, nevertheless, that "it's my job to make it work." If they lack the emotional passion of the happiest winners and the sorest losers, lunch bucket workers are a critical resource for the new order. With good communication, direction, and support from top management, these pragmatic workers will make solid contributions every day on the job.

Pathfinders

Sheehy (1982) describes pathfinders as those who escape the "ruts into which most lives eventually fall" (p. 2) by pursuing a "critical passage in an expanding, self-renewing way" (p. 3). It is tempting to cast the pathfinders in a romantic mold as those who dared to leave the security of a job to pursue a bold new career or an alternative way of life. But the decision to leave the well-trodden path is full of ambivalence. The journey of the pathfinder is one of missteps, retraced paths, and uncertainty. Perhaps pathfinders would be less heroic if they were not doubly challenged by ambiguities in the external world and ambivalence within.

One individual, the senior employee relations executive in the new system, an attorney, had accumulated over twenty years of experience in service with the state. Having risen to the top of his profession, he became acutely aware that the actual task of negotiating and then managing the multiple union contracts did not hold great appeal. The job really amounted to a continuation of what he had been doing for some years. It was also apt to be a thankless task. The union representing the state university faculty that had won for its members the highest salaries and the lowest teaching load would seek to stay ahead of the other unions, which themselves would strive to reduce the pay and workload gap. Some of the new board members had substantial experience in the politics and techniques of human resource management in the public sector and would be helpful in labor relations. Others with much less experience also wanted to set labor policy.

From a personal point of view, this professional had long held a desire to test himself in what he regarded as the more challenging arena of private practice. He had rejected offers from various law firms over the years but now decided to change course. "I began to feel that I was on a treadmill," he said, "and my life was turning into a marathon just to keep up." In his late forties, this pathfinder left the relative security of state employment and joined an aggressive law firm in the Twin Cities.

Asked why he forsook the security of state service and a high-status position, he replied, "It was probably fifty-fifty, push-pull. Had it not been for merger, I would have been content to stay in place. But the new environment, the political infighting, and the fact that I was not learning anything new didn't appeal to me. Moving to the private sector was a healthy choice."

This individual sought a new path outside of the merged system. Another pathfinder chose to remain within public higher education but in a new antiestablishment role. This community college president had recently immigrated to Minnesota because, as he put it, "I was attracted by merger. I thought this was a chance to lead in creating a master plan for Minnesota like California's in the time of Clark Kerr." After six months of experience with the new system, this person disagreed with the interim chancellor over the direction of restructuring. Well credentialed, this person was highly employable outside of the system. Yet he chose to become a leader in what he described as the "loyal opposition, not opposed to merger but to its direction and loyal to the idea of using change to improve access."

This leader of the opposition pursued an activist agenda, including writing a widely distributed newsletter, op-ed contributions to regional newspapers, and frequent presentations to the new board. He was also roundly criticized, not only by the leadership of the new system, but also by many of his colleagues, for not being a team player. The Community College Board was sufficiently impressed, however, that it made him its chancellor for the last six months before merger, when the incumbent left for another position. A risk taker, this person was also realistic about the consequences of his new role as self-appointed critic. He felt that he would be fired if his opponents came to power in the new system. The payoff, however, was personal. "I'm intellectually quite engaged. I'm learning state politics at a different level. It's tremendously stimulating to lead with ideas."

Stages of Grief and Stages of Development

Thanks to the popularity of the work of Elizabeth Kübler-Ross (1969) and others, virtually all of the players in merger were familiar with the stages in the grieving process. They recognized that these emotions and behaviors occur when familiar work relationships are substantially altered or removed, just as one grieves the loss of a loved one. Because of the four-year period between the passage of the merger law and its effect, there was plenty of time for the various stages to be expressed. The interim chancellor, whose unhappy task it was to lead many where they did not want to go, became the object of much undeserved anger.

That little worthwhile merger planning was accomplished during the first two years of the gestation period may be explained in part as the result of denial and anger. Opponents of merger could have also logically concluded that each of the legislative sessions during those years afforded the opportunity to reverse the merger bill. By the time those attempts failed, most participants had moved to some level of acceptance. Political realities played hand in hand with the stages in the grieving process.

Ultimately, most of the participants, winners and losers alike, came to accept the new order of things as inevitable. Winners did so more quickly than losers. A shorter gestation period and more efficient hiring practices would have led most to the acceptance stage sooner. The few who remained mired in one of the middle stages were the least productive. Those who could not forsake anger either left their jobs or withdrew from an active role in the merger process.

Though all of the people interviewed went through the grieving process to one extent or another, their private dramas often reflected their stage in adult development. Most of the participants were white men between forty and fifty. Those at the lower end of that range were caught up in what Daniel Levinson describes as that period of midlife transition during which a man may experience a developmental crisis, an "overwhelming feeling that he cannot accomplish the tasks of becoming One's Own Man: he cannot advance sufficiently on his chosen ladder; he cannot gain the affirmation, independence and seniority he wants" (Levinson and others, 1978, p. 191). An acute illustration of this crisis affected an administrator who had moved from a secure position in another state in order to advance himself in one of the Minnesota systems. With merger and the possibility of needing to change jobs again, this person felt traumatized: "I was preoccupied at home. It was hard to focus on my wife and marriage. I was sitting in a daze when I should have been with my kid." The threat of job loss creates stress in its own right, but the anxiety is reinforced if it coincides with a time in life when one feels especially vulnerable.

Older and perhaps more mature workers, those in their mid and late forties, have largely worked through the crisis of self-confidence of the earlier years and now, according to Levinson, seek a greater sense of structure in their work and family life (Levinson and others, 1978, p. 178). Whereas restructuring in the workplace may impede this quest for greater definition, for some people it also occurred at a very convenient time. One interviewee who felt that he was able to make a worthwhile contribution to the new order had this to say: "Merger came along at an opportune time for me. I was bored with what I was doing and needed a change. I can see myself working on this project for the next ten years of my life."

There is a cadre of administrators in their mid forties who have substantial experience and who, due to of commitments to family, comfort with their current quality of life, and lack of opportunity elsewhere, are not particularly mobile. Those in the stage of middle adulthood may become an especially valuable resource as the new system's need to define itself corresponds with their personal need to achieve greater definition and structure as well.

Women and Minorities

Do women as a group and minorities as a group respond in distinctive ways to the changes posed by restructuring? In her work on communication between men and women, Deborah Tannen (1990) argues that women tend to seek connectedness and relationships whereas men are more likely to be motivated by the desire for power and status (pp. 29–30). Tannen's work is intriguing, but the largely successful, career-oriented, powerful women interviewed for this chapter did not reveal (or I failed to perceive) a predisposition to be connected rather than influential in the new order.

What women clearly sought, however, was equal pay for what they regarded as equal work and the opportunity to compete for the top jobs in the new system. The apparent ascendancy of men in compensation and status was not readily accepted by women and minorities during the transition. For example, the chief academic officer in the technical college system, a woman holding a master's degree, came into the new system with the same title as the chief academic officer from the state universities, but at a substantially lower salary. The leaders of the new system were prepared to make an equity adjustment in her salary but not to close the gap entirely due to the fear that the costly adjustments would anger the legislature. Not surprisingly, this was not a satisfactory response to the many women who had grown weary of being told to be patient.

The lack of women at the highest levels in the new order contrasted sharply with the case in the older systems, where women

held several senior positions, including two of the three chancel-
lorships. The Minnesota Women's Consortium, an influential Twin
Cities advocacy group, called attention to this discrepancy in its
newsletter. The interim chancellor felt compelled to defend himself before the group's executive committee. Eventually, a woman
was hired to replace a departing senior executive, but the lethargy
in finding qualified women for leadership roles left lingering
doubts about the new system's commitment to equal opportunity.

Members of minority groups interviewed for this chapter
shared a sense of disappointment over what they regarded as the
low priority given to diversity. Each of the existing systems had
long-standing programs aimed at increasing participation and
graduation rates among people of color and other minorities.
Many hoped that the glass ceiling keeping numbers of minorities
in the two-year institutions would be shattered as merger brought
about closer ties between the two- and four-year systems. Others
felt that the presence of the state universities, with their relatively
restrictive admissions policies, would move the new system in an
elitist direction. As a Native American administrator put it, "Throw-
ing the state universities into this mix means that a lot of the academic policies will be driven by graduate and baccalaureate needs.
This removes opportunity from the disadvantaged." He felt that
explicit policies would need to be put in place to ensure that the
community and technical colleges remained open-door.

To these people and others, the failure of the new system to
establish a minority advisory committee or to push forward with a
plan to capitalize on the new structure to improve access was a
major disappointment. In fact, the interim chancellor and the new
board did make efforts to respond to minority concerns. The
interim chancellor met more than once with one of the system's
advisory committees, although he did not immediately name one
of his own. The board, over the objections of some members,
agreed to add a tribally controlled community college to its roster
of state institutions and thus positioned it to receive added public
funding. These actions, however, failed to dispel the widely held
view that the historical commitment to diversity would diminish
under the new regime.

Women and minorities, whether they regarded themselves as
winners or losers in the restructuring process, did not reveal a pre-

disposition toward the change that could be traced to their gender or race. Of course, it was not the intent of the interviews to elicit gender- or race-based differences; more probing with that goal in mind might have yielded some differences of attitude. Women and members of minority groups did share a serious concern that policy, or lack of policy, in planning the new system would work to their disadvantage. In retrospect, it is clear that the leaders of the new system would have been well advised to display their personal commitment to equal opportunity and diversity in more visible ways.

Loyalty and Self-Interest

Loyalty is a potent concept. It summons up such basic virtues as honor, integrity, fidelity, and trust. Yet restructuring involves destruction of existing relationships and new demands of fealty. The question of loyalty becomes problematic. Loyal to whom? To my old boss or the new? To the organization that hired me or the one where I'll spend the future? To myself? To my responsibility to support my family? There are few clear answers.

Paul Hirsch (1987) tells corporate executives that in a time of mergers and restructuring, they should pack their own parachute and not trust anyone in the organization to look out after their welfare. In the best discussion available of the changes in corporate culture brought about by mergers, acquisitions, and downsizing, Rosabeth Moss Kanter (1989) has this to say about shifting loyalties: "If a person cannot trust the employer, the only locus of trust is in oneself, in one's own skills and goals" (p. 336). She goes on to say that "a positive side of the new loyalty is that those who keep their jobs will be loyal to the best interests of the enterprise, not the hierarchy" (pp. 338–339).

Though a strong sense of alienation exists during restructuring in higher education, it is mitigated by the fact that few people actually become unemployed as a result of the change. Individuals feel intensely anxious and adrift during the time when the old bureaucracy is clearly destined for destruction but the new organization has not been fully created and one's place in it remains uncertain. Several of the interviewees reported that they actively sought positions elsewhere during this interval. Their searching ended, however, once they were notified that they had a secure place in the new system. Then conflicts over loyalty to the new organization and the old became stronger. "Some weeks, I feel that the community college system is still my system and I should support its agenda," reported one woman who held positions simultaneously in both systems, "but other times, I feel that my responsibility is to support different policies, which are those of the new organization. I don't see a clear-cut answer."

Albert Hirschman's study (1970) of loyalty in corporations argues that it exists in relation to voice—the opportunity to influence the course of events—and the possibility of exit—the option to leave the organization (pp. 76–77). He defines loyalty as a special attachment to the enterprise and its leaders that is maintained so long as the individual feels that he can influence the decision-making process, even though his opinion may not be decisive (p. 37). Exit, the choice to forsake loyalty, comes into play when there is no opportunity for voice or the expressions of voice are consistently ignored (pp. 82–83). A striking illustration of the general truth in Hirschman's analysis came in this bit of dialogue with a talented administrator who planned to exit the system: in the existing system, he reported, "I feel very, very free to disagree. If I was told to do something and I objected to it, I would try to talk the chancellor out of it. Once I'm told it needs to be done, I'll do it. There is not much freedom to disagree over there [in the new system]. The way the situation is shaping up, I'm not planning to be here much longer."

Others felt that they had substantial opportunity to express themselves in the new administration, and these may have felt stronger conflicts in loyalty. One man commented that he felt torn by "an emotional commitment to the old job and the people I work with now while I am developing a commitment and a loyalty to the new one, which is my future." The same individual, who had experienced a significant restructuring in another state, went on to make this observation: "Call it loyalty or call it tribalism, it will continue for a long while after the start of the new system."

As the power of the existing systems to protect employees and to govern their behavior diminishes, their ability to command loyalty erodes. Although the impact of merger on faculty and students was not a major focus of this study, it is interesting to note that their unions and organizations became more important to them as the old systems waned. The community college faculty union leader, an instructor in philosophy who had long been active in policy debates within the state, pursued a public role in the merger process that at times eclipsed that of the system's chancellor. The state university student association, which had enjoyed effective and stable leadership over the years, became an even more important voice for such student priorities as affordable tuition and more financial aid. Of course, faculty and student loyalty had long been divided among their systems, their advocacy groups, and a number of other causes and interests. Yet with restructuring, many faculty and students felt, accurately enough, that their unions or advocacy groups could do more to represent their interests than either the old administrative order or the new. Leaders of the new system will have to contend with the enhanced power of the unions and student organizations into the foreseeable future.

Lessons for Leaders

Leading the people who will do the hard work of designing and implementing the restructured system is the most important task of the executive in charge. It is widely estimated that 70 to 80 percent of attempts at reengineering in the corporate world fail not because of technical lapses but because leaders do not recognize the importance of human culture in the change process. The lessons from restructuring in other states suggest that failure is due less to design flaws in the new structure and more to human frailty. There are plenty of ways to fail in the tough business of restructuring, but the surest way is to ignore the need to lead people. Chapter Nine comments on leadership generally in restructuring. Here the focus is on what leaders must know and do with respect to the human side of their enterprise.

1. *Respond to the need to be engaged.* Everyone wants to be on the team, and no one wants to be the last chosen. The Minnesota experience suggests that participation helps employees get beyond their resentments and move toward a more positive and optimistic attitude. The task of the leader is to place as many people as possible in meaningful roles in the planning and implementation of

restructuring. One of the strengths of the Minnesota approach was the creation of more than a dozen task forces to hammer out and recommend policy. Though unwieldy at times, this effort led to the active involvement of literally hundreds of different employees, most of whom developed a greater stake in the outcome.

The goal is to have as many staff as possible, from the top to the bottom of the organization, feel that they are emerging as winners in the transition. Leaders should give special attention to the group of pragmatic workers who dutifully show up for work each day. By reaching out to this large segment through regular communication and expressions of concern, the leader can help this type move from a kind of stoic exercise of responsibility to real commitment. Leaders in the old order, whether or not they will have a place in the new over the long run, need to be given at least symbolically important roles in the transition process. Their experience and credibility may well be useful to the new administration, and by being given responsibility for some piece of the action, they will have less freedom to complain about changes in the status quo.

Losers in the game of musical chairs should be helped to move on to the next stage in their life as soon as practicable. Those who feel that they have been seriously diminished by the change process will add nothing to it and are likely to try to thwart the effort. It is important not to mistake weakness for compassion. Retaining those who play no constructive role in making restructuring work invites mischief from some and merely delays the inevitable movement to the next job for others. Early retirements, transfers, and aggressive outplacement initiatives are all in order.

2.   *Create and communicate meaning.* In describing restructuring in Minnesota, one able university president quipped: "This is a merger in search of meaning." For the hundreds of staff members caught up in the change, and for the thousands of faculty and other employees who would be affected less immediately, making sense of the change is very important. In the best of circumstances, the legislature or the board will give a broad direction for change. It is the leader who must define and communicate a vision that at once inspires employees and underpins specific decisions.

The "vision thing" has come in for increasing criticism of late, partly because it is confused with being a visionary. Actually, a vision is a very practical tool for communicating goals and securing endorsement of them. One fair critique of the Minnesota merger is that it had too many goals (over a hundred at one count) and too little vision. Virtually every person interviewed for this chapter lamented the lack of vision because they all felt it led to a lack of sense of direction.

In the absence of a vision clearly defined or regularly communicated in the early days, others, especially newspaper editorial writers, imposed their own expectations. Thus the new administration found itself explaining why the new system would not save vast amounts of money instead of pointing out all the good it would do for the people of the state.

What might the vision have been? In my opinion, it could have been as simple as creating a system in which students would progress as far as their talents would take them, a system that would be a national model for linking technical and liberal learning, one that would substantially reduce administrative costs in order to invest more in educational activities. Any number of other formulations that reflected the desires of stakeholders for giving greater priority to students as customers, for emphasizing technology and technological training and reducing noneducational costs, would have done as well. In fact, these ideas were all expressed in various system documents, but they lay buried amid too many other good ideas, and none stood out as the defining goals of the change.

3. *Expect anger, anxiety, and distrust.* Anger is a near-universal phase in the grieving over the loss of the relationships and familiar ways of work. That anger will be directed at the nearest agents of the change, most often its leaders. In some cultural milieus, it will be acted out in dramatic ways. In Minnesota, where the expression "Minnesota nice" refers to the high level of public courtesy displayed even among adversaries, the anger was less visible but no less real. The capacity to achieve true emotional distance or at least to appear to have done so in the face of rage is a valuable leadership asset.

Loyalty is a two-edged sword. Good persons, by some definitions very good persons, who accept positions with the new system remain loyal to the old, at least for a time. They may make special efforts to serve the interests of former co-workers, to divulge confidential information that will benefit one institution over another, or otherwise show less than unqualified devotion to the new administration. Most often, loyalties will be divided between the old and the new with a gradual tilt to the latter.

With the exception of serious breaches of confidence, the new leader would be well advised to exercise patience while waiting for the tides of fidelity to shift. Leaders of the old order should take the same advice. In the one instance where coercive power was applied in an attempt, one supposes, to retain loyalty, it failed miserably. Leaders who acknowledged and openly discussed these ineluctable transfers of loyalty actually retained the respect and the friendship of their staffs far longer.

Anger is a widespread and usually temporary phase—but not always. For some personalities who have lost in the change, feelings of being wronged or diminished will grow into rage and be acted out as a personal vendetta against the leader of the change. Clytemnestra, Iago, and Lady Macbeth sometimes leap off the stage to join everyday life. Often the unfortunates who fall prey to their emotional demons do so transparently. These people become increasingly isolated and unable to do seriously harm to the enterprise. Those better equipped to mask their passions may sabotage the new effort and its leaders in a variety of clandestine ways. Leaders do not need to become paranoid to believe that there are people who really are out to get them. After setting aside *The Prince*, leaders of change would be well advised to pick up Aeschylus or Shakespeare.

4.   *Champion good causes.* One of the dangers in large-scale restructuring is that the exceedingly complex technical work necessary to merge mature bureaucracies may drive out the larger educational and social agenda. In Minnesota, for example, the need to create a new financial management system to "insure that every employee gets a paycheck" threatened to eclipse other priorities, especially because of a forceful and effective chief financial officer. This preoccupation with the strictly management side of the transition may have caused the leaders to be blind to the need to march at the front of a few well-chosen parades.

There was no shortage of good causes. With declining participation rates among low-income Minnesotans, many of whom are minorities, the new system could have fulfilled its mission of strengthening access by being outspoken on the diversity front. The good sense in advocating for equal employment opportunity and equitable pay is obvious. Students and their parents would have welcomed a champion of affordable tuition or improvements in the way financial aid was allocated in the state. The faculty and the state's employers would have responded well to the clarion call for strengthened quality across the board.

By choosing to champion a few good causes, the leader builds an ethos that contributes not only to his or her personal influence but to the credibility of the new enterprise as well. It also makes practical sense. It is far better to be hailed as the active patron of noble ideals than to have to explain to interest groups and the press why you failed to make high access, say, or fair compensation a priority. And after all, the community has a right to expect advocacy for just causes from those who would be called its leaders.

5. *Renew yourself.* Bringing about a new order of things makes extraordinary demands on leaders. There are too few resources with which to buy compliance. Expectations of important stakeholders may be at odds. In the emotional turbulence that surrounds restructuring, leaders are always the objects of anger and sometimes its victims. The human beings who are being asked to work to make the changes occur have little time and often less inclination to nurture their leaders. Besides, that is not their job.

In this environment, there is no substitute for emotional maturity. Leaders must be wise and patient and distant enough to understand the pressures on the people they oversee. They should also possess a high level of understanding of themselves. Leaders must be teachable. They will most often learn by doing, by reflecting on their mistakes and victories. The critical internal resource is the ability to learn, grow, deepen, and restore optimism for oneself. Leaders with the capacity to renew themselves will possess the energy and insight to inspire the hundreds, even thousands, of human beings whose working lives are centered on making restructuring succeed.

References

Hirsch, P. *Pack Your Own Parachute: How to Survive Mergers, Takeovers, and Other Corporate Disasters.* Reading, Mass.: Addison-Wesley, 1987.

Hirschman, A. O. *Exit, Voice and Loyalty: Responses to Decline in Firms, Organizations and States.* Cambridge, Mass.: Harvard University Press, 1970.

Kanter, R. M. *When Giants Learn to Dance: Mastering the Challenges of Strategy, Management, and Careers in the 1990s.* New York: Simon & Schuster, 1989.

Kübler-Ross, E. *On Death and Dying: What the Dying Have to Teach Doctors, Nurses, Clergy, and Their Own Families.* New York: Macmillan, 1969.

Levinson, D. J., and others. *The Seasons of a Man's Life.* New York: Ballantine, 1978.

Sheehy, G. *Pathfinders.* New York: Bantam Books, 1982.

Tannen, D. *You Just Don't Understand: Women and Men in Conversation.* New York: Ballantine, 1990.

Chapter Seven

Restructuring and Its Aftermath: Maryland

Robert Berdahl and Frank A. Schmidtlein

In 1987, a new governor, William Donald Schaefer, took office in Maryland. In his inaugural address, he announced four priorities for his administration: education, economic development, transportation, and helping people in need. In the section devoted to higher education, the governor said, "We must devote our energies to creating a coordinated, unified system of higher education with first-class centers of learning. We must implement an aggressive program to develop our universities, colleges, and community colleges into renowned centers of research and high technology."

However, after considering the complexity of the issues and the time required to resolve them, Governor Schaefer delayed submitting legislation on higher education until the 1988 legislative session. He then placed higher education at the top of his legislative agenda, proposing a major restructuring of the state's higher education system to provide greater operating efficiency and fiscal and academic accountability. Following a year of public debate, lengthy legislative hearings, political maneuvering in the general assembly, intense lobbying, and a conference committee that completed its work just hours before the end of the legislative session, a lengthy, complex restructuring bill was enacted.

The Maryland Context

This chapter describes factors that created the impetus for restructuring Maryland's higher education system, events during development of the restructuring plan and its enactment into law, issues involved in implementing the restructuring, and state and university officials' assessment of the new structure and its future prospects. The information in this chapter was obtained largely from off-the-record interviews with thirty-three state and institutional officials and from various documents and correspondence dealing with the restructuring. Before describing events leading up to the bill's passage, however, some context is provided by briefly describing Maryland's government, the state's political character, and the history of its higher education system restructuring.

Government and Politics in Maryland

Maryland's governors are among the most powerful in the fifty states. The executive budget system gives them great control over state agencies and political and economic priorities. The state's constitution "restricts the actions that the legislature may take with respect to the budget. The governor's budget proposals may not be increased or rearranged between categories. The legislature may only reduce the amounts proposed in the budget" (Boyd, 1987).

The Maryland legislative body, the general assembly, through the 1970s was relatively weak. It did not meet annually until the 1950s and did not create a bureaucracy to support its work until the 1960s (Calcott, 1985). However, it now has a large, professional, nonpartisan, full-time staff, and its committees meet year round. It is composed of two houses: the house of delegates and the senate. It meets annually, for ninety days, but most members now list their occupation as "full-time legislator." The legislature by the 1980s had become a significant and substantive player in policy development.

Despite recommendations throughout the years by various commissions, Maryland did not have a statewide higher education agency until 1963, when the Advisory Council for Higher Education was created. Statewide coordination was provided largely by the governor and the general assembly as part of the budget process. The somewhat stronger Maryland Council for Higher Education supplanted the advisory council in 1968, and the State Board for Higher Education, with substantially increased authority, was created in 1976, only to be succeeded in 1988 by the Maryland Higher Education Commission, possessing even greater authority.

A number of the state's political characteristics have influenced its policies toward higher education. Maryland, as a border state, represents a blending of northern and southern traditions. As in the northeastern states, until after World War II, independent institutions were viewed as having the primary role for providing higher education in Maryland. The state has had a long history of providing financial support for these institutions, and they remain politically potent. As in the South, segregation was enforced by law and custom in Maryland until the 1950s, and the state has four historically black institutions: Morgan State University, Bowie State University, Coppin State College, and the University of Maryland, Eastern Shore.

The state is made up of what Calcott (1985) refers to as its "four cultures." Baltimore until the middle of the twentieth century dominated the state politically, economically, culturally, and educationally (Arnold, 1976). Its population was composed of ethnic minorities who lived in distinctive neighborhoods. Recently, however, its influence has declined with the "flight to the suburbs" and population increases in the parts of Maryland surrounding Washington, D.C. Politically, the city has traditionally been liberal.

The Eastern Shore and Southern Maryland make up the second region. This part of the state is more southern and very conservative. Even though the "Shore" has been somewhat isolated from the rest of the state by the Chesapeake Bay, before the one-man, one-vote decision it provided a disproportionate number of the state's political leaders. The third region, Western Maryland, extends into Appalachia and, unlike the rest of the state, is politically moderate, electing candidates from both parties. The fourth region is the suburbs around Washington and Baltimore. These are the state's fastest-growing areas. The Baltimore region and the Washington suburbs contend for political influence. Baltimore and its suburbs do not view Washington suburban institutions, including the state's major public graduate and research university at College Park, as serving their area. For over two decades, the *Baltimore Sun* newspaper has conducted a major editorial campaign to create a comprehensive graduate and research university in Baltimore. The political rivalries among these four regions have had a substantial influence on state higher education policy.

History of Restructuring in Maryland Higher Education

Lawrence (1990), in her history of three Maryland higher education commissions, notes that Governor Schaefer's "decision to use governance and structural change as the primary vehicles to achieve his goals of improving the quality and stature of Maryland's colleges and universities is just the most recent development in the long history of the expanding state role in higher education" (p. 3). Statewide higher education planning and restructuring in Maryland has been carried out largely by a series of temporary commissions appointed by various governors and named after their chairpersons (Lawrence, 1990; State Board for Higher Education, 1978). Between 1924 and 1985, ten gubernatorial commissions have studied Maryland higher education at intervals ranging from two to ten years apart. The recommendations of these commissions, though often not directly implemented, appear to have shaped subsequent debates over higher education's structure and policies and no doubt contributed to the character of later restructurings. (Details of these gubernatorial commissions are available directly from the authors.)

General assembly committees began a series of studies of higher education in the late 1970s, and these culminated in Governor Hughes's establishing the Commission on Excellence in Higher Education, known as the Hoblitzell Commission, in 1985. This commission proposed a major restructuring of Maryland's higher education that will be discussed in detail later in this chapter.

The Impetus for the 1988 Reorganization

State Structures in 1988

The structures to be reformed consisted of the five-campus University of Maryland system (UMS), governed by a board of regents; the six-campus state college system, governed by a board of trustees; two single-campus four-year public institutions with their own boards; seventeen community colleges (with nineteen campuses), twenty-four private institutions; and the State Board for Higher Education (SBHE), with a mandate to coordinate the entire system (see Figure 7.1). The State Board for Community Colleges (SBCC) coordinated those institutions and in turn reported to the SBHE.

With the exception of the two four-year institutions, with their individual governing boards (St. Mary's and Morgan State were originally independent and had been taken over by the state), the Maryland pattern resembled the tripartite public system present in many states (with university, state college, and community college segments). The SBHE was a fairly typical coordinating board with regulatory powers to approve new academic programs for public sector institutions and to make recommendations regarding independent institutions' new or significantly amended programs. Eligible independent institutions received significant state tax dollars, both directly as a percentage of the amount appropriated per student to designated public four-year colleges and indirectly through state student aid programs. They also sometimes received up to 50 percent matching state grants for qualified (nonsectarian) capital projects.

What was wrong with this structure? From the standpoint of the institutions, nothing that increased state funding and decreased state controls could not fix. In a letter to the Hoblitzell Commission, dated December 5, 1985, Allen Schwait, the chair of the University of Maryland board of regents, observed, "Maryland's existing tripartite system of governance does not, in our view, require modification. . . . Appropriate forms of institutional cooperation are feasible under the present organization and already exist. . . . In our judgment, the State can make good use of all the present institutions by appropriate cooperation and by strengthening and modifying programs under the existing system of governance. Within that system, we believe that the Commission can help all the institutions by identifying procedural obstacles to the best use of resources."

In support of its request for improved state funding, the letter included four charts comparing Maryland's efforts with seven other "peer" states (California, North Carolina, Texas, Virginia, Illinois,

Figure 7.1. Organization of Postsecondary Education in Maryland as of 1987.

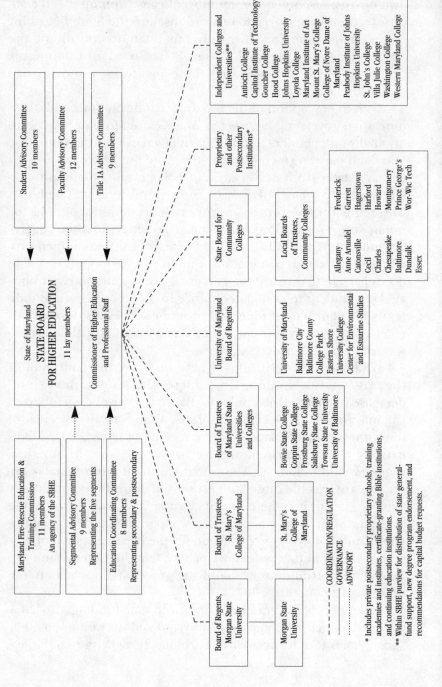

Wisconsin, and Michigan) along the following dimensions: state appropriations per full-time-equivalent student, public higher education appropriations as a percentage of tax revenue, state appropriations for higher education per $1,000 in personal income, and higher education appropriations compared to potential ability to pay. The peer states had reputations for having excellent systems of public higher education; Maryland never ranked in the top half on any dimension. In a separate chart on tuition and fees, however, Maryland ranked third from the top, indicating that its citizens were being asked to make up, via tuition and fees, at least some of what the state failed to appropriate in tax dollars.

From the state point of view, in contrast, the reform concerns were less about finances and more about issues of efficiency, duplication of programs, quality and excellence, and accountability. Seen from the state capitol, the institutions portrayed in Figure 7.1 seemed to need some tightening of controls in order to serve better the public interest. Thirteen institutions were governed by four separate and competing governing bodies, a structure that did not appear to provide effective coordination. All institutions seemed to be trying to be all things to all people.

Some key players at both the institutional and state levels shared concerns about three long-standing issues: enhancement of the role of the University of Maryland, College Park (UMCP), as the so-called flagship campus of the public sector; some effort to rationalize what the *Baltimore Sun* had long editorialized about: "the mess in Baltimore"; and genuinely mixed feelings about what to do to improve the state's four predominantly black public institutions.

On the first issue, there had been some tensions created between the College Park campus and the system headquarters over the system's alleged refusal to single out UMCP for "enhancement" as the state's major public graduate and research institution when the SBHE was urging, in the light of apparently limited state resources, that it be given special status.

On the second issue, the *Baltimore Sun* criticized the existence of multiple public sector institutions in the Baltimore area that might be merged to create the beginnings of a second comprehensive research university to serve the needs of the state's most populated urban region (the flagship campus at College Park is thirty-five miles to the south but is regarded by at least some in Baltimore as "belonging to Washington, D.C.").

On the third issue, opinions differed as to whether the best way to help the predominantly black institutions was to merge some of them to achieve a higher critical mass or to try to increase state resources going to all four. Given the power of the black caucus in the state legislature and its opposition to any mergers, that issue became moot.

Higher Education Studies in the 1980s

We have already referred to the historical state pattern of commissioning numerous study plans. That practice continued into the 1980s. First, the University of Maryland itself in 1981 published the report of a long-range planning study directed by Dr. Malcolm Moos, *The Post–Land Grant University*. The report, among many other recommendations, proposed a merger of the University of Maryland at Baltimore (UMAB), with its professional schools, with the University of Maryland, Baltimore County (UMBC), and, from the state college segment, with the upper-division University of Baltimore (U of B), with its law and business schools. For reasons more connected to Baltimore politics than to state-level concerns, this recommendation went nowhere (although UMAB and UMBC later merged their graduate schools).

Governor Hughes also launched three study commissions: one, the Civiletti Commission, successfully recommended substantial additional state support for elementary and secondary education; another, the Curran Commission, successfully recommended decreased state procedural controls over higher education; and the third, the Hoblitzell Commission, recommended with mixed success a breakup of the six-campus state college system into individual governing boards (failed), an enhancement of UMCP through reduction of its undergraduate enrollment by 20 percent with the prospect that its budget would not be reduced as a consequence (partial success), and a strengthening of the State Board of Higher Education (with a new name) to ensure stronger accountability mechanisms (delayed success).

However, by the time the Hoblitzell Commission reported, Governor Hughes's term of office was coming to a close, and his successor, Governor Schaefer, felt no obligation to implement its recommendations (although initially he considered doing so).

The Debate over the Character of the New Structure

One person closely involved in numerous issues involving Maryland higher education in the 1980s observed that had Schaefer not been elected governor, concerns about the state's higher education structure would have continued to stew for the next four years. Schaefer universally was described as a "hands-on, do-it-now" governor who wanted to "push one button" to get results and who had little patience for delays and indecision. The press regularly reported on his calls to state agencies giving them short deadlines to repair road-side signs or remedy problems he observed in his travels.

The Governor's Decision to Submit a Legislative Proposal

Before the 1986 election, Schaefer, in his campaign for governor, had many meetings with advisers on issues of importance to the state. The speaker of the house of delegates and senior members of the house, who had been examining higher education for a decade, urged him to make higher education a top priority. A campaign aide also prepared a position paper on higher education giving it high priority. Schaefer did not have many specific notions of what he wanted to do but was convinced that some action was needed. The structure reportedly did not mean a great deal to him, but he did want to have someone he could call to get things done. In fact, one state official suggested that the proposed reorganization had more to do with getting higher education on the agenda than it did with structural issues. One of the governor's aides remarked that in the end, the momentum to make higher education an important issue was so great that doing something became necessary.

After the election, Hoblitzell met with Schaefer and briefed him on his commission's report. He believed that Maryland needed a higher education board "with teeth." He perceived the institutions as "looking at the SBHE and then doing what they pleased" and believed that a strong state-level board was better than a strong board of regents. The governor was reportedly "sold" on the broad objectives of the commission report and asked one of his legislative aides to draft a legislative proposal. The aide, however, believed that there was not enough time to prepare legislation for 1987 and sought a delay until the governor's second-year legislative program. Schaefer's political advisers concurred, and a higher education bill was not submitted until 1988.

Development of the Governor's Legislative Proposal

As soon as the 1987 legislative session ended, two of the governor's staff members began working with Lieutenant Governor Melvin Steinberg on the legislative proposal. The staff members interviewed presidents of the four-year public campuses, encountering many negative reactions to the Hoblitzell Commission recommendations. One reported that the primary issues they discovered were these: prospects of institutional mergers; two institutions' desire to retain their own boards; the balance of power between a statewide coordinating board and institutional boards; some distrust of President John Toll, of the UMS; the extent of state-level program review and oversight; and the roles of the community colleges and proprietary schools (although these were minor issues).

Discovering the lack of support for the Hoblitzell recommendations (or for any other set of recommendations), the governor called a meeting with the chancellors and presidents of the public four-year institutions and announced that he planned to reorganize higher education and asked for their participation. He left a clear impression that a restructuring would be followed by increased appropriations. The governor wanted a single chain of command, according to one state official, and John Toll, the president of the multicampus University of Maryland, saw himself as that person. Toll had come to the University of Maryland as its president in 1978. He had made its becoming one of the top ten public universities in the nation his goal and was widely credited with greatly increasing its quality. He saw in the governor's request an opportunity to do further good for the university and for the state. He sought and got a commitment from the governor to get more funds for higher education if he could bring about a more streamlined structure.

Following the governor's meeting with the chancellors and presidents of the four-year institutions, Toll immediately set about consulting with them to obtain their agreement on a plan. One president reported that this group was far from passive in making suggestions on the nature of the merger. Toll sought to unite all of the state's four-year public institutions under the University of Maryland's regents and to replace the State Board for Higher Education with an advisory group made up of himself and the leaders of the other segments of higher education (the community colleges and the independent institutions). This group would deal with intersector issues and advise the governor and the legislature on higher education policy. President Toll sought support for his plan by pointing out that the governor's lack of confidence in the current structure would continue the fiscal neglect of higher education, whereas his proposed structure would create conditions necessary to increase state appropriations.

President Toll obtained support from the regents for his plan, despite some opposition from the chair. One legislative leader believed that he "kept the regents in the dark" and made it difficult for outsiders to get good information on reactions to his plan. After getting the support of the regents, Toll asked the campus chancellors and the presidents of the other four-year public institutions for their formal endorsement. Except for the presidents of Morgan State and St. Mary's College, all endorsed the plan, some reportedly under considerable duress.

After the Toll Plan was unveiled, both state and institutional officials began to examine structures in other states to assess their effectiveness and to obtain evidence to support their views. Toll pointed to the University of North Carolina (UNC) system as highly successful and one that Maryland should emulate. A meeting arranged for the governor with a former UNC president, Bill Friday, convinced the governor to support the Toll Plan and make it the basis for his legislative proposal.

Reactions to the Toll Plan

The Toll Plan encountered heavy opposition as soon as it was announced. The opposition came from certain institutional officials and faculty members, some key legislators, the association representing independent institutions, and members and staff of the existing State Board for Higher Education. In the face of this criticism, the governor's staff, as they were developing the governor's legislative proposal, described the Toll Plan as influential but less decisive than many people presumed. The governor's staff considered it just one of many competing proposals. In fact, several key persons would have preferred no bill to the Toll Plan. People were also going to key senators expressing concerns about the plan. In addition, as Toll began vigorous promotion of his plan, his single-mindedness and tenacity in the face of major political opposition was reported to have alienated some state political figures.

The various positions taken on the proposed restructuring are illustrated by the brief summaries concerning certain of the key constituencies. (Again, fuller details are available directly from the authors.)

Legislative Black Caucus

The Legislative Black Caucus opposed the Toll Plan on several grounds. Foremost, it did not want Morgan State University, a historically black institution, to be under the proposed consolidated governing board. But it also favored more decentralization within the merged system and more accountability of the merged system to a strong statewide board than was provided in the Toll Plan.

President of the Senate

The president of the state senate was from the Washington suburbs and was not on good political terms with the governor, a former mayor of Baltimore. One observer suggested that he did not want to hand the governor a major political triumph by passing the governor's bill. Perhaps more important, he agreed with complaints from the University's College Park campus, located in his county, that the bill would result in a "leveling down" of its quality and sought a solution that would allay these concerns.

State Board for Higher Education

Part of the impetus for reorganization was the presumed impotence of the State Board for Higher Education. The governor came to office having heard negative things about that agency and was not supportive of the commissioner. There were differing perspectives on the role of the board. Not surprisingly, the commissioner and the board favored a system with a strong coordinating agency. Consequently, the SBHE proposed an alternative structure to that in the Toll Plan that included strengthening its role and giving institutions their own boards. The SBHE's influence on the legislation appeared to be relatively modest.

UMS Officials

Toll viewed the governor's challenge to come up with a reorganization plan as a chance to give Maryland more resources and to break out of the existing system's restrictions. In addition, he was having difficult relations with some regents, and several observers believed that he viewed a reorganization as a way out of that dilemma. The regents reportedly were not entirely enthusiastic about a reorganization. His persuading the regents to support the plan, despite their prospective demise, was crucial to bringing the merger about. Throughout his tenure, Toll had viewed the University of Maryland as one indivisible institution, with campuses in various places serving various state needs. This contrasted with another vision of having a set of relatively autonomous institutions receiving policy guidance and general direction from a modestly staffed system office. He believed that campus chief executives had to report directly to him if he was to direct the university effectively. Consequently, he reportedly strongly objected to the use of the term *system* for the new structure and argued for several weeks to exclude that term from the bill. Toll also did not want a state-level coordinating board but finally went along with the notion of a weak one. He was totally opposed to the state coordinating agency's having budget authority.

UMCP Officials

The strongest institutional opposition to the Toll Plan came from the College Park campus. Although Chancellor John Slaughter believed he was compelled to follow the lead of Toll and the regents, he had serious reservations about the consequences of the plan for the campus. The campus had a history of resenting the University of Maryland's highly centralized decision-making structure and saw no relief in the plan. UMCP, with Slaughter signing on to the president's plan and then opposing it *sub rosa*, played a very risky game.

The deans played a highly significant role in opposing the plan. They were greatly upset that it had been developed with no consultation because of time constraints. They prepared a paper opposing the plan that they sent to Toll and circulated in the state capitol. The *Sun* quoted it, making them a political power in the debate.

Other UM Campuses

Other campuses of the university also opposed the "Plan" despite their official endorsements; although University College, the University's non-traditional and distance learning campus, viewed a consolidated governing board as a means to gain faculty salary equity with the College Park campus. The Baltimore City campus was reported to be very "skittish" about the new structure for many of the same reasons it was opposed by College Park. The Baltimore County campus also saw the new structure as potentially "leveling down" their status but wanted to be seen as "team players."

Trustees of the State Universities and Colleges

The members of the Board of Trustees of the State Universities and Colleges (BOTSUC), which would go out of existence if the Toll Plan were enacted, were concerned about its implications but largely took a neutral stance. Their executive director, like Toll, was opposed to a strong statewide coordinating agency. However, the trustees were assured by campus presidents and their executive director that if they became part of the University of Maryland, they would get "wrangling over higher education" behind them, and they would have brighter prospects. However, they saw the reorganization as a merger of equals, not a takeover by the university, and were very concerned about their staff's being treated fairly in the transition.

The BOTSUC Campuses

In the beginning, the presidents of the six board-of-trustees institutions sought to have individual campus boards but changed their position after opposition from the governor. Heavy arm twisting was reported to have taken place, and Toll was reportedly "persuasive" in picking the presidents off one by one. However, by and large, they saw themselves gaining from their association with the University of Maryland campuses and being "at the table" when decisions affecting the university were made. The real battle for them was to be certain that the legislation protected their considerable degree of autonomy and their roles as equal partners in the reorganized system. There was some concern among them that "Toll did not know how to brag about teaching institutions."

Morgan State University and St. Mary's College

Both of these institutions had once been private and had been taken over by the state as a means of surviving and of enhancing quality. Except for a brief period in which Morgan State had been part of the State University and College Board, both had been granted their individual governing boards, and both were reluctant to give up that status. Morgan State insisted on maintaining its separate board and, with the strong support of the Legislative Black Caucus, had ample political strength to do so. One observer stated that the black caucus could veto almost any bill. Morgan State's president wanted a board that had that campus as its sole concern and believed that such a board would be more influential in helping it get resources it needed to fulfill its publicly mandated mission as an urban university with programs through the doctorate. He wanted direct access to the governor and the legislature.

Since Morgan State did not want its separate status to be viewed as racial politics and knowing that St. Mary's College also wanted to maintain its own board, Morgan State proposed a joint effort to remain outside the proposed system. St. Mary's also had strong political supporters and had a unique mission as a four-year baccalaureate-granting public liberal arts institution. Several observers believed that these institutions, by staying out of the consolidated governing board, greatly strengthened the case for establishing a stronger statewide coordinating agency.

Independent Institutions

Perhaps the most influential opposition to the Toll Plan came from the independent institutions. The Maryland Independent College and University Association (MICUA) made it clear that it did not take a position on the merger of the public sector institutions but that it strongly believed there was a continuing need for an effective statewide coordinating board to handle cross-segment issues. The independent institutions in Maryland get state financial support, and some observers saw this support threatened by having all of the public four-year institutions under a powerful consolidated governing board.

Community Colleges

The community colleges played a rather peripheral role during development of the legislation. The chair of the SBCC early on asked not to be a part of any reorganization plan. The community colleges generally favored a strong coordinating agency and had some fears about the potentially negative effects that could come from competing for resources with a powerful consolidated governing board. The community college presidents' major concern, but not one they sought to have addressed at that time, was that the State Board for Community Colleges was too intrusive.

Drafting the Bill

A political split between Lieutenant Governor Steinberg and Governor Schaefer at the end of 1987 complicated drafting the bill because it had been largely handled by Steinberg, and Schaefer did not have a detailed knowledge of the issues concerning higher education. Lieutenant Governor Steinberg reportedly wanted a weaker merged board and a strong role for the independent institutions, whereas the governor did not see a conflict between a strong board of regents and a strong role for the independents through a state coordinating agency.

One of the governor's aides reported that he, personally, favored a strong coordinating board and individual institutional boards, but another favored a stronger board of regents and a weaker coordinating board. He also believed that the independent institutions were getting considerable state funds but were not accountable. He advocated more accountability for these institutions but was unable to get such provisions incorporated in the governor's bill because of strong political opposition from MICUA and member presidents.

Legislative Consideration of the Bill

The governor's higher education bill was introduced into the house of delegates and the senate simultaneously. It then languished in both chambers for a considerable portion of the 1988 session because of the opposition just noted and policy differences among legislators. In the house, several influential delegates had come to favor a consolidated governing board for the four-year institutions but not the Toll concept of "a single institution with campuses in various locations." One reported that the more the concept of individual campus boards was aired, the less delegates liked the idea. They reportedly were tired of system heads quarreling with the State Board of Higher Education but also wanted to give individual campuses flexibility. They saw the "pulling apart" of the Washington and Baltimore regions and believed that a strong consolidated governing board could combat this politicization of higher education. In addition, they envisioned such a board as more effectively coordinating institutions in the Baltimore region. Although key members of the house had been examining higher education for some years and had played a key role in placing higher education on the governor's agenda, given the senate president's public criticism of the bill, the house took the position that it would not act on the bill until it came over from the senate.

Key senators, particularly the president of the senate, were less enthusiastic about restructuring the higher education system and did not favor a consolidated governing board. As noted earlier, the governor's relationship with the senate was different from that with the house, where he was reported to have helped elect the speaker, who came from the Eastern Shore. In fact, without consulting the governor, the senate had angered him by dividing his bill into four separate bills. The governor had sought an omnibus bill to simplify its monitoring and steering.

Two key senators, however, viewing the criticisms of the higher education system and the legislative impasse, thought it would be a mistake to lose all of the momentum behind higher education reform and got agreement to have the senate take the lead on rewriting the governor's bill. To get agreement on a bill, a senior senator suggested to the senate president that he select a group of the senators most interested in education to see what was "salvageable" in the governor's bill. Despite Senate President Mike Miller's distrust of the governor's intentions and his dislike of provisions in the bill, he observed that efforts to oppose restructuring were like "stopping a freight train" and decided to support the senator's efforts to develop a modified bill. He sought to make the best of the bill by increasing higher education funding "to make it work," providing flagship status to the University of Maryland, College Park, and increasing institutional autonomy within the system. He viewed Morgan State and St. Mary's as having been successful, and because "you don't mess with success," he supported retaining their separate boards.

The senators rewriting the bill met for several days without staff, except for the sitting commissioner of higher education, Sheldon Knorr, who was on friendly terms with at least one of the senators, and prepared a draft. A participating senator described the governor's staff as being flexible during redrafting of the bill because they realized that the "votes were not there for a centralized system." Perhaps the most crucial event in writing the bill came when Lieutenant Governor Steinberg, frustrated by lingering conflicts over the bill's provisions that were continuing to stall its progress in the senate, held an evening meeting with senators, with Chinese food brought in, to resolve differences. He reportedly kept the food outside the meeting room while they met so that participants could smell it, keeping them in the room until they came to a consensus. A staff member outside reported hearing cursing and screaming in the room! By the meeting's conclusion, provisions of a bill were agreed on. The agreement weakened the board of regents, gave additional powers to the individual campuses, and limited some of the powers of the coordinating agency in contrast to the governor's bill. Nearly all of the persons interviewed described this dinner meeting as the most important event in getting a viable bill. Without the agreements developed during this evening's discussion, it is unlikely that significant changes would have been made in the higher education structure for at least several more years.

On receiving the revised senate bill, house members worked closely with the governor's aides to modify provisions they did not like and to move it closer to the governor's version. Toll was not included in these deliberations, a delegate noting that by this time, "they were out of love." Delegates sought a system with a strong chief executive but also strong campus chief executives, to have "a creative tension." The delegates were not enthused by the senate's proposal for lay institutional advisory boards, and they also did not believe that the funding commitments made by the senate were appropriate. They saw additional funds coming from efficiencies brought about by the reorganization, especially in the Baltimore area. This set the stage for the conference committee, made up of members of the house and the senate, who struck a compromise between the two versions to create the bill that was then passed by both houses in the dying hours of the legislative session and was signed reluctantly by the governor. He was not inclined to sign the bill, which he viewed as not his bill, but was persuaded that it accomplished much of what he wanted and was the best the legislature could produce.

The Structure Implemented

The current structure of Maryland higher education, with minor exceptions, is the pattern established by the 1988 legislation and is shown in Figure 7.2. Following the 1988 restructuring, in 1991, the State Board for Community Colleges (SBCC) was phased out over one year, and some of its functions were transferred to the Maryland Higher Education Commission (MHEC). The state also, in an unusual step for Maryland, took over responsibility for the Community College of Baltimore, which had been experiencing financial and management problems. Moreover, an additional community college was created in a county served previously by a college in another county. After the SBCC was dissolved, the presidents of the community colleges, in 1992, established the Maryland Association of Community Colleges (MACC) to represent their interests to state government and to undertake cooperative activities. The MHEC has tended to use the MACC to deal collectively with the community colleges.

Eleven of the thirteen four-year public universities and colleges are under the board of regents, whose chief executive officer is designated the chancellor. This terminology was reversed from the former University of Maryland, where the campus executives were

Figure 7.2. Organization of Postsecondary Education in Maryland After 1988.

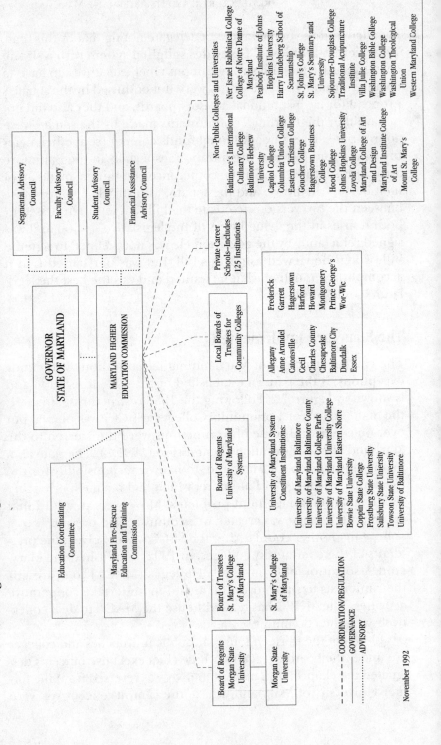

termed chancellors. Three of the eleven institutions under the regents are graduate and research universities. The remaining eight are comprehensive universities. Morgan State and St. Mary's each has its own board. There are seventeen county-based public community colleges. The community colleges each are governed by local county boards, two counties have more than one campus under their boards, and two colleges serve more than one county. Independent higher education continues to be represented at the state level by the Maryland Independent Colleges and Universities Association. The state also has approximately 125 proprietary and other postsecondary institutions, many of them represented by the Maryland Association of Private Career Schools. All of these segments of postsecondary education are coordinated or regulated by the MHEC. This commission is composed of eleven lay members appointed by the governor, with a support staff directed by a secretary of higher education, who is also appointed by the governor and serves as a member of his cabinet. The principal changes brought about by the new law were these:

1. The secretary of higher education is appointed by the governor from a list of three nominees provided by the twelve-member MHEC rather than solely by the MHEC.
2. The State Scholarship Board is now a part of the MHEC.
3. The MHEC has more explicit authority than the SBHE did to require institutional mission plans, accountability reports, and assessment plans.
4. The five former University of Maryland campuses are combined with the six former board-of-trustees campuses under the board of regents.
5. UMCP is designated the system's flagship campus, and the campuses formerly under the central administration of the UMS (see Figure 7.2) are given greater powers of self-government through legally prescribed decentralization.
6. The former BOTSUC institutions receive, through the merger, more procedural autonomy from state controls.

In addition to these structural changes, the 1988 legislation sets forth a "charter" for Maryland higher education and contains numerous other less significant language changes from the 1976 law.

Implementation of the Reorganization Legislation

In this section, two sets of relationships are examined: those between the merged board of regents (BOR) and the Maryland Higher Education Commission (MHEC) and those between the merged BOR and its eleven-campus constituent institutions.

MHEC-BOR Relations

Once the legislation was passed, the governor's first task was to appoint the two new bodies, the Maryland Higher Education Commission and the UMS board of regents. In many states, a governor who faces similar tasks finds that the most influential citizens tend to prefer appointment to the state university board more than to the state coordinating body. Governing real campuses with their school spirit, their prestigious alumni, their athletic teams, and their students somehow often seems more appealing than joining a state agency with no direct campus links. Yet Governor Schaefer evidently departed somewhat from this pattern. Several respondents said that members of the board of regents were more or less handpicked by a prominent political supporter and close friend of the governor's, Peter O'Malley, whom he had selected as its chair. Some persons speculated that most were nominated more for their ability to be good team players under O'Malley's leadership than for their individual reputations as persons experienced in issues of governing higher education institutions. In contrast, at least several gubernatorial appointments to the Maryland Higher Education Commission consisted of persons with reputations for having strong personalities, and one of them, Henry Butta, was designated as chair of the MHEC.

Developments after the initial appointments to the two bodies were to distinguish them even further. It was an open secret that there were disagreements between John Toll, chancellor of the UMS, and O'Malley, the board of regents chair, about the degree of centralization appropriate to an eleven-campus merged system. In fact, there were rumors that the reason that O'Malley had earlier resigned as chair of the former board of regents was disagreements with Toll over the way the university was administered. The 1988 legislation required the UMS to develop an academic plan, and it was a harbinger of things to follow that early on, two separate planning processes were begun, one led by Toll and the other by the chair of the BOR Education Policy Committee. It was not a total surprise, then, when Toll subsequently "resigned" and was replaced by an acting chancellor, Dolph Norton, while a search for a successor was organized.

What *was* a total surprise, however, was the resignation a short time later of O'Malley, the BOR chair. Apparently, when meeting a Harvard physician who had just been appointed president of the University of Maryland at Baltimore (the campus with law, medicine, and several other professional schools), O'Malley mentioned a plan to move the UMAB law school to Bowie State University, a predominantly black institution formerly in the state college system. The doctor, who happened to be black, evidently disapproved of the lack of prior consultation, withdrew his name, and returned to Harvard. O'Malley evidently took personal responsibility for this development and resigned from the board. "O'Malley's Muldoons" (as one legislator dubbed the board of regents) were left without either a chair or a permanent chancellor, and their general lack of experience allegedly became more apparent as they struggled to establish the corporate identity of this new system.

Under the guidance of the new board chair, George McGowan, and Acting Chancellor Norton, the BOR began to address some of its most pressing matters. Twenty-four task forces were established, tackling problems ranging from coordinating higher education in the Baltimore region to enhancing the predominantly black institutions. Some observers believed that these task forces bore little fruit, possibly because of continuing conflicts over the degree of decentralization in the new system. In contrast, responding to heavy legislative pressure, the acting chancellor hired a consultant whose report was used to reduce the two previous systems' combined staff from 230 positions to 150. The remaining staff continued the enormous job of merging the 376 policies, covering academic and administrative affairs, inherited from the combined systems into an even hundred UMS policies that reconciled conflicting concepts of the role of the system.

Following the reorganization, the system produced the legislatively mandated strategic plan. However, that plan was developed in the context of a time when "the state was pouring new resources into the system in accordance with its commitment to support the objectives of the 1988 legislation." The "cost containment" actions that had to be undertaken in 1990 in response to declining state revenue estimates made that plan, in part, obsolete. Therefore, the chancellor initiated a second process to "map out a new strategic vision for the system that would be more compatible with the current realities, producing a plan, *Achieving the Vision in Hard Times I* (1992), and a later version, *Achieving the Vision in Hard Times II* (1992). This plan proposed reallocations totaling about $25 million from program closures and reductions throughout the system. These funds were to be targeted to system priorities:

- Enhancement of the flagship campus, the historically black institutions, Baltimore area research and graduate and professional education, and undergraduate education
- Faculty salary increments
- Facilities construction and renewal
- Telecommunications infrastructure

The BOR also developed two sets of mission statements for each of its constituent units, a process involving considerable negotiations with the MHEC. The chancellor reported that the first set reflected the optimistic and expansive climate immediately after the reorganization and that the second set, with more sharply focused mission statements, reflected current and anticipated future realities. The board also began work on a performance accountability process.

By the summer of 1990, a new UMS chancellor had been named, Donald Langenberg, a physicist who had been chancellor of the University of Illinois, Chicago. Langenberg was to find the Maryland state political climate quite different from what he had previously experienced.

In the meantime, the new MHEC, as provided in the 1988 legislation, nominated to the governor three candidates for the position of secretary of higher education, who would be the executive officer of MHEC but also a member of the governor's Cabinet. Governor Schaefer took immediately to Shaila Aery, a state higher education executive officer from Missouri, and she was appointed. Among Aery's qualifications were a reputation for toughness and political skills of a high order. These abilities, in combination with the aggressive approach of Butta as MHEC chair and his close relationship with the governor, led to the commission's quickly picking up momentum. With these developments, the governor began to seek action from MHEC rather than the UM chancellor who had originally been portrayed as the person the governor would call to seek action.

The MHEC interpreted its charge from the state as ensuring the following:

- That campuses are held accountable for the quality of education they provide and for how they spend state funds
- That public colleges and universities remain affordable and accessible to all Marylanders, regardless of where they live
- That every public campus has clear goals and an educational mission that distinguishes it from other campuses and provides the context for its programmatic and budgetary decisions

In the interest of quality, access and choice, and accountability, the MHEC undertook a variety of actions, including a major reform of state student financial aid programs, assumption of functions of the State Board for Community Colleges, extended negotiations concerning mission statements for all public four-year and two-year institutions, a catalytic role in promoting student transfer and articulation, and guidelines for assessment of student learning outcomes, comprehensive financial plans, and cost containment procedures.

Senator John Cade of the Maryland state senate made a memorable remark at the time of the passage of the legislation, cited by three respondents: "In establishing both a strong coordinating board and a strong board of regents, we have created two five-hundred-pound gorillas and put them in the same cage" (the respondents' remembered weights differed, but the image remains the same!). Senator Cade obviously anticipated that the two strong systems would seek to occupy the same space and therefore clash from time to time. In fact that did happen, but in the early years the interactions were much influenced by the accidents of personalities and by the departures of Toll and O'Malley and the arrivals of Aery and Butta. The gorillas were no longer an equal match, and the preponderance of strength in the early disagreements went to the MHEC. Both boards were assigned functions in planning, role and mission assignments, budget review, program review, desegregation, articulation and transfer, accountability patterns, and capital planning. Presumably, the major difference was that the BOR's activities were to be primarily *intrasystem*, whereas the MHEC's perspectives were to be *statewide*. But such a homely division of labor did not seem to prevent frequent policy differences from emerging between the two boards.

Even in an ideal relationship, it would have taken time to sort out which board would apply which perspectives to which functions. But it was *not* an ideal relationship, for not only were the leadership issues complicated by the changes described, but the governor's promised increase in state appropriations following the merger lasted only two years before nose-diving in the face of a state fiscal crisis. Table 7.1 shows that the funds were enhanced during 1990 and 1991 but also that they receded thereafter. For example, general-fund support for the UMS declined from 1990 to 1992 by $123 million in real dollars, or 19 percent; when adjusted for inflation and workload, they declined by $166 million, or 25.7 percent. Initially, $649 million was appropriated for fiscal 1991 but only $593 million was received after mid-year funding cuts. However, it should be noted that overall funding for the UMS went from $444,044,395 in fiscal 1988 to $553,198,889 in fiscal 1995, an increase of 24.6 percent in real dollars over the eight years. During this period, state authorizations for capital projects at the university totaled $589.6 million.

There are no problems like budget problems to overload the processes of governance: all issues are viewed as threatening, turf protection becomes the rule of the day, and disagreements that normally would be handled with modest friction may get inflamed reactions. Stories from each side illustrated the sensitivity of the relationship. Allegedly, one or more meetings of chief officers from the two boards were sometimes canceled by one of the parties. Allegedly, a joint meeting of the two boards that one side thought was going to be a quiet constructive session turned out instead to be held in the presence of the press—with disastrous results. A much revered "elder statesman" from Baltimore who had become chair of the MHEC was reported to have resigned in part because of his unease at the degree to which MHEC-BOR relations had become so confrontational.

Table 7.1. General-Fund Support of Maryland Higher Education.

	FY 1988	FY 1989	FY 1990	FY 1991	FY 1992	FY 1993	Working Appropriation FY 1994	Allowance FY 1995
UM—Baltimore City	91,615,739	102,746,498	121,050,072	111,392,568	98,826,616	97,835,869	96,859,089	102,086,109
UM—College Park	165,328,054	191,988,090	224,850,223	221,554,862	199,584,530	202,989,227	200,885,521	212,075,911
Bowie State	11,486,568	13,404,806	14,412,101	17,732,388	15,762,883	14,960,509	14,876,424	15,492,097
Towson State	35,397,139	40,198,381	50,087,064	49,012,966	43,383,671	42,474,368	42,487,815	44,697,918
UM—Eastern Shore	11,212,586	13,222,745	14,986,140	15,927,175	14,126,448	14,380,042	14,392,114	15,484,940
Frostburg State	15,555,493	17,581,623	19,452,090	20,160,931	17,940,720	17,812,760	17,705,817	18,800,640
Coppin State	10,327,819	12,272,751	13,627,915	13,983,317	12,367,513	12,222,083	11,995,499	12,551,109
University of Baltimore	12,735,756	14,507,822	18,338,814	19,105,832	16,338,456	16,349,107	16,451,535	18,086,583
Salisbury State	13,114,253	16,414,037	18,997,510	19,124,793	16,998,234	18,077,241	18,199,403	19,092,985
UM—University College	0	1,500,000	3,829,442	3,548,656	3,193,543	0	0	0
UM—Baltimore County	34,214,566	39,708,257	46,386,991	45,095,349	40,595,681	41,914,519	41,865,544	44,517,997
Agri Experiment St (1)	10,256,244	11,206,973	13,518,867	13,776,975	6,401,784	24,534,812	24,235,257	25,212,963
Coop Extension Service (1)	12,657,215	14,243,258	17,029,749	17,254,702	15,758,748	0	0	0
Center Enviro & Estuarine	6,329,606	7,106,833	8,512,874	8,531,309	7,787,612	7,308,472	7,230,179	8,098,788
Biotech Institute/SG	0	5,811,301	8,080,438	8,102,266	7,321,821	7,735,297	7,627,490	10,790,254
System Administration (2)	13,813,357	14,646,394	15,553,863	8,586,974	7,913,012	7,304,117	5,963,504	6,210,595
UMS Total:	444,044,395	516,559,769	508,714,153	592,891,061	524,301,272	525,898,423	520,776,191	553,198,889
St. Mary's College	6,814,393	7,874,940	8,918,321	10,404,208	9,252,715	10,380,489	10,647,584	11,073,356
Morgan State	24,173,255	28,730,773	32,411,803	31,672,272	28,655,245	31,741,238	31,200,723	32,641,278
Baltimore City CC (3)	0	0	0	16,441,041	15,156,231	15,988,943	15,692,726	16,641,288
Community Colleges (4)	98,807,632	104,314,269	117,368,940	105,507,803	86,678,723	113,284,179	109,160,442	108,495,385
Public Subtotal:	129,795,281	140,919,982	158,699,064	164,025,324	139,742,914	171,394,849	165,701,475	168,851,307
State Board for Com. Col.	755,994	807,182	941,463	1,040,925	563,783	0	0	0
MD Higher Ed Comm (5)	7,836,632	6,440,663	10,520,139	10,403,965	8,234,256	7,244,876	6,070,796	6,210,514
Scholarships	10,042,608	16,329,890	19,600,300	21,140,647	22,328,701	25,533,572	29,351,375	32,327,051
Aid to Independents	17,007,490	19,131,987	23,237,520	25,554,250	21,286,430	22,096,642	25,789,684	26,220,280
All HE Total:	603,482,400	700,189,473	821,712,639	815,056,172	716,457,356	752,168,362	748,699,521	786,808,041

(1) AES and CES, formally known as MIANR, are a part of College Park's budget.
(2) A portion of the reduction is a result of functions transferred to the campus level.
(3) Baltimore City Community College was an entity of Baltimore City until state assumption in FY 1991.
(4) Aid to community colleges includes BCCC while it was a city entity in FY 1988, FY 1989, and FY 1990.
(5) The Commission budget includes educational grants and administration.
(6) FY 1993 onward, $7.0 million at UMAB & $3,036,719 at UMCP will be special-funded with a corresponding reduction in general funds.

Source: Executive Budget Books, FY 1990 through FY 1995.

Whether the just-mentioned resignation sent a strong signal or whether the approaching end of Governor Schaefer's second and final term raised the question of his successor's considering a new secretary of higher education or whether the gradual learning of the new UMS chancellor and his relatively new board of regents meant that the UMS team was becoming politically more astute—whatever the reasons, parties associated with both sides, and some legislators, reported that interboard relations have started to improve.

BOR–Constituent Campus Relations

According to one member of the board of regents, a senior member of the state attorney general's office remarked soon after the passage of the 1988 legislation that, in law, the merged system resembled the former Board of Trustees of the State Universities and Colleges (BOTSUC) legal structure more than that of the former University of Maryland. This is because written into the law are requirements to decentralize to the campus level significant powers held by the former BOR, a practice more in keeping with BOTSUC precedents than those experienced earlier in the UM five-campus system.

As though to confirm this observation, a current president who heads one of the former BOTSUC institutions remarked that their institutions changed the UM campuses more than vice versa. By this he meant that the BOTSUC institutions used their negotiating position during the legislative process to ensure that the results would be a true merger featuring major decentralization and not a takeover by a fairly centralized university. Consequently, built into the legislation were numerous provisions for powers to be exercised at the campus level, and the UMS board of regents reflected this in its *Report . . . Regarding the Organization of the University of Maryland System* of July 1990, which showed how policies covering sixteen major delegations had been undertaken. Among the basic functional assignment and distribution principles adopted were the following two (p. 16):

The Chancellor's Office provides broad direction, oversees, monitors, assists, assesses and audits the activities carried on by the constituent institutions. Only in emergency circumstances and for very limited periods does it engage in any form of direct institution management.

The Chancellor's Office does not provide overhead services to units directly except in a very limited number of areas (e.g. capital planning), although it does maintain a small staff of expert coordinators, who may also serve as consultants in each basic administrative and academic topic area. Expert consulting services are available to institutions upon request; their use is not mandated.

This is clearly not the language of a heavy-handed central system administration. There has been, nevertheless, some of the inevitable "back-and-forthing" between central and the campuses over a variety of matters that have to be worked out following a merger of two mature systems—for example, whether alumni relations and fundraising would be handled centrally or by the campuses (some functions were decentralized). However, a former state college official ruefully noted that although they might have won the decentralization battle, it had not gone unnoticed that after the drastic staff reductions of the combined systems' staff, only two members of the BOTSUC staff had survived in the central office.

Several respondents also commented on the fact that an MHEC newsletter called *Currents* (July 1994, p. 2) included a chart showing that St. Mary's College and Morgan State University, the two four-year public institutions that had stayed out of the merger, seemed to be getting a higher percentage of their unrestricted operating budgets from state support than the average institution in the eleven-campus merged system. The implication was that an institution obtained larger budget increases outside the system than inside it. But more careful inspection of the charts showed that the system average cloaked a wide variety of institutional percentages and that in fact Coppin State did better than either of the two outside institutions and Bowie State did better than St. Mary's. The real significance of the chart is that it shows a higher-percentage state investment in the predominantly black institutions, whether inside or outside the system.

One further issue, which will be more fully discussed in the concluding section, is whether the flagship campus at College Park is receiving the distinctive treatment envisaged by the language of the 1988 legislation. Clearly, the state's fiscal crisis has slowed down the ambitious enhancement recorded in 1989–1991. But when an institution generating about 40 percent of the total system enrollment finds that it must sit around the Council of Presidents' table as merely one vote among many, and when its access to the governor's office must normally be routed through the system chancellor, there is an understandable concern over the long-run dangers of "leveling down." Ironically, with a different cast of characters, one finds something of a replay of the premerger tension wherein the commissioner of the old SBHE was seen to be urging Dr. Toll, of the former central administration, to give more preferential treatment to the College Park campus.

Today one hears stories that the current secretary of higher education similarly has urged the chancellor of the UM system to give more preferential treatment to College Park. Even though the board of regents can point to a number of ways in which this has been done, the feeling remains among some state officials that not enough has been done. For example, the legislature has mandated that the board of regents report officially on the extent to which the 1988 legislative language concerning the flagship "mission" has been implemented. And an element in the legislation allowing local "boards of visitors" to be appointed at each campus has just been invoked to create such a board for College Park, with the charge for it to report annually on UMCP's development. Whether these developments will suffice to keep the College Park campus, and its fairly strong support in the state capital, content to stay in the system remains to be seen.

This section, however, should not end on a negative note, because nearly all of the people interviewed, representing many different constituencies, revealed a fairly widespread feeling that whatever the problems and the frictions of the past six years, things seemed definitely to be getting better. Not only were the board of regents and the chancellor gaining additional political skills and learning how to live better with the MHEC, but also reportedly units inside the merged system were learning better how to live and cooperate with one another and to work more closely with the system administration.

Critique of the New Structure and Prospects for Further Change

It is now six years since the reorganization legislation; what can be said about it? This question was posed to nearly all interviewees, and the answers received defy easy generalizations. In the interests of brevity, they are combined under relatively few headings, and this chapter then ends with speculation on what the future may bring.

The Role of Restructuring in Reforming Higher Education

This is not the place to open a debate as to whether an emphasis on moving from single-campus governance to systems and from smaller systems to larger systems flies in the face of current efforts, such as reinventing government and total quality management, to put maximum powers as close to operating units as possible. Suffice it to recognize that "thirty-seven states have chosen to govern some or all of their public baccalaureate and doctoral degree-granting colleges and universities through multi-campus college and university systems. . . . Fifty-two such systems, each comprising [from] two to more than sixty constituent colleges and universities, enroll in the aggregate some four and one-half million students" (Johnstone, 1993, p. 1).

Thus multicampus systems seem here to stay—although Pat Callan (1994), rebutted by Johnstone (1994), recently asked whether the multicampus emperor was really wearing clothes!—and it remains to ask whether it seems to make much difference for the quality, cost, and accessibility of state higher education if the institutions are in one multicampus configuration or another.

Aims McGuinness (1991), from his earlier base at the Education Commission of the States, has often observed the propensity for state policy makers to try to solve long-standing higher education problems through structural reforms. Rarely, he notes, are their hopes realized, as the interplay of structures, personalities, policies, and funds seems so complex that well-intentioned changes often fail to produce desired results.

Ambiguity over Results

In Maryland, what were those desired results? Governor Schaefer had wanted to centralize responsibility in the *governance* system. But instead of Dr. Toll as chancellor of the merged system on the other end of the "red phone," it turned out to be Dr. Aery, the secretary of the MHEC, a *coordinating board*. How did this come about? First, the governor found important elements left out of the merged system: Morgan State, St. Mary's, all the public community colleges, and obviously the whole independent sector. In contrast, the MHEC had umbrella jurisdiction over all the constituencies. Second, while the CEO of the merged board of regents was chosen by the regents themselves, the governor chose the secretary of higher education from a list of three names submitted by the MHEC, and furthermore, this person, once selected, sat in the governor's cabinet. Thus the accountability pattern that emerged led more often than not from the governor's office through the secretary and the MHEC to the various governing boards of relevant institutions.

Desired results for most public institutions would have been more state funds and fewer state controls. The increased state funding that the institutions had been led to believe would follow the restructuring did appear in fiscal years 1990 and 1991 but quickly receded in the face of the major state fiscal crisis that followed. Nor did the institutions get fewer state controls. The former state colleges did receive more procedural operating freedoms from state government after the merger, and the University of Maryland campuses received greater autonomy from the university system, but all public institutions were ultimately subjected to the enhanced authority of the MHEC. Ironically, one of the institutions' motivations for supporting a reorganization was to reduce the authority of the coordinating agency! The original Toll-Schaefer plan, based on a trip to examine the North Carolina model, had called for eliminating the SBHE and replacing it with a small council of segment heads meeting with the governor. However, the bill in its final form not only retained a statewide board but also materially strengthened its powers. Earlier sections of this chapter have explained how the Maryland Independent College and University Association, the State Board for Community Colleges, and several powerful legislators had all favored keeping a strong state coordinating board. We found that some key legislators continue to favor a strong state board, but quite a few of the institutional figures have developed mixed feelings about the MHEC. How much of this antipathy is based on the commission's extensive powers and how much on the current personalities is hard to determine.

The legislation implementing the restructuring included enhancement of the flagship campus, more coordinated public higher education in the Baltimore area, special care of predominantly black institutions, improvement of undergraduate education, less program duplication, greater efficiency, and greater accountability. The results from the reformed structure were very mixed:

1.   The flagship campus issue has not gone away. Although UMCP budgets for 1990 and 1991 reflected major increases, the subsequent reductions were large and caused the campus to initiate its own retrenchment, closing seven departments and one college. In terms of its ongoing relationship with the central administration of the UM system and with the MHEC, a mild irony prevails. In the "old days," tension had existed between John Toll, president of the five-campus University of Maryland, and Sheldon Knorr, commissioner of the State Board of Higher Education, over the issue of singling out UMCP for preferential treatment within the five-campus system. Toll had been reluctant to do so, arguing that the university was a single institution with various campuses. Knorr countered with the statement that higher education was not receiving sufficient state resources to bring the whole university system along at the same pace and that College Park's role was so crucial that it merited preference. Though Toll and Knorr are no longer on the scene, traces of the same dispute over priorities linger among the new cast of personalities at UMS headquarters and at the MHEC. However, several respondents noted that the position of College Park within the merged system had improved somewhat over its former status, both because UMCP supporters were able to get explicit protective language about flagship status into the reform bill and because the new chancellor, Donald Langenberg, while confessing some uncertainty about the meaning of flagship status, has nevertheless been less resistant than Toll to the legislative call for special treatment.

2.   Concerning what the *Baltimore Sun* described as "the mess in Baltimore," neither the merged board of regents nor the strengthened MHEC has been able to alter the basic dimensions of the problem. Institutions simply do not want to merge with other institutions and so lose their identity, and they receive strong community support in that struggle. Even the Joint Graduate School of UMAB and UMBC has not opened its ranks to qualified faculty from the other institutions in the area, as anticipated by some of the parties to the merger. If there was one problem that the system merger seemed designed to improve, it was this one in Baltimore, so resistant to major change. At the same time, however, several respondents said that cooperative relations between institutions in the merged system had definitely improved, and not only in the Baltimore area.

3.   Of the predominantly black institutions, three found themselves inside the merged system and one, Morgan State, outside. Though all four received the highest percentages of their unrestricted operating budgets from state general-fund appropriations, the consensus among respondents was that Morgan State had profited most from its position outside the merger. This had allowed its leadership direct access to the governor's office in ways not usually encouraged from within the UM system.

4.   The purposes of efficiency were apparently served by the MHEC's taking over the functions of both the State Scholarship Board and, somewhat later, the State Board of Community Colleges. In the former case, most respondents believed that the takeover not only saved money but also made programmatic sense, in that the MHEC could combine its interests in tuition levels and admission standards with its new jurisdiction over student aid.

Greater efficiency and reduced program duplication were also presumably achieved through the merged board of regents process, described in *Achieving the Vision in Hard Times I* and *II* (University of Maryland, 1992). The broader jurisdiction of the merged board allowed a wider swath for its retrenchment efforts.

5.   Finally both boards undertook programs to increase institutional accountability and to improve undergraduate education and assessment of student learning. Respondents were generally

unable to judge whether the merger and restructuring had seriously affected the nature of the results. St. Mary's College, however, was in no doubt that its freedom outside the merger had been a major factor in the improvement of its mission as a public "honors college." In exchange for an agreement to receive increases in state funding tied only to inflation, the college received what it calls the "maximum autonomy" granted to any public institution in the country, including the right to set its own tuition and exemption from most state procedural controls. The college also agreed to increase its student aid funding so that low-income students would not be precluded from attendance by the higher tuition.

Several persons noted that it is still too soon to be able to judge the fruits of the merger. They stressed how enormously complex and time-consuming it is to blend the detailed policies of two large preexisting systems. The costs alone, they point out, should give anyone pause before attempting such an extensive restructuring.

Additional good marks were given to the merged board of regents for its work in developing instructional technology, in improving procurement procedures, in student articulation within the enlarged system, and in terms of capital development.

The nearly unanswerable question that must be posed is, How much of the results achieved could have been achieved equally or better under the premerger structures? Obviously, no one can prove one's answer to everyone's satisfaction; there are too many variables involved to be able to demonstrate that a given structure did or did not lead to given results. Instead, we suggest, as sheer speculation, that probably *most* of the postmerger developments could have emerged from premerger structures, but we see four possible exceptions:

1.   The merged structure caused the issue of decentralization *within* the enlarged structure to be legally recast greatly in the direction of more campus autonomy for the former UM campuses. It is possible but unlikely that such decentralization would have occurred inside the premerger University of Maryland five-campus system (the BOTSUC system was relatively decentralized prior to the merger).

2.   The merged structure caused the issue of increased autonomy from *state* procedural controls to be legally recast in terms of
more campus autonomy for the former BOTSUC institutions. It is
possible but unlikely that such autonomy would have been granted
in the absence of the reform process (the premerger UM system
already had considerable procedural autonomy from the state).

3.   By casting the policy issue as "more funds under a reformed structure," the governor's office was probably more willing
to make substantial increases in funding for higher education than
it would have been had the reform not taken place. The fact that
such enhanced funding was soon terminated by the state fiscal crisis should not prevent recognition of the unusual increase or of
the benefits of the prior increases when cuts became necessary.

4.   By accepting the policy package as "more funds under a
reformed structure," the institutional presidents and chancellors
bought into a process that produced, among many unintended
consequences from their perspectives, a strengthened statewide
coordinating board. Whereas earlier state reform efforts had
resulted in strengthened state boards and whereas some observers
believed that the MHEC's stronger powers were more a function
of personalities than of laws, it seems to us unlikely (but possible)
that such a strengthening would have occurred in the absence of
the reform process.

Structures, Money, and Personalities

From the accounts in the preceding pages it should by now be
obvious that the interplay of reformed structures in Maryland was
heavily influenced by the presence of a major state fiscal crisis and
by the "accident" of the passing personalities. But one cannot
"rewind the tape" to see how the structures and personalities would
have interacted if there had been more state funds available as a
lubricant to lessen the friction or if there had been different personalities in key positions. One can speculate on what the early
departure of John Toll and Peter O'Malley or the early arrival of
Shaila Aery and Henry Butta might have meant to the course of
BOR-MHEC relations. Surely, however, this Maryland case study

reinforces the argument that personalities and funds are often as important as structures in influencing public policy outcomes.

As a case in point we cite the numerous references to the importance of the North Carolina model in persuading Governor Schaefer and President Toll that consolidating the governance of all public four-year institutions was the best way to achieve excellence, efficiency, and accountability (the single telephone call again!). Evidently, a trip to North Carolina and a conversation with former UNC President William Friday, among other people, provided all the convincing necessary.

But the intention to apply the North Carolina model to the Maryland scene can be faulted in at least two significant ways. First, there was a failure to appreciate the extent to which Friday's own strong personality had played a major role in the success widely attributed to the North Carolina system. It is part of "conventional wisdom" among specialists examining state systems of higher education that the presence of a major actor like President Friday can make a serious difference in the ability of a given system to tackle its problems.

Another element from the North Carolina scene that seems not to have been well understood by most of its Maryland observers is the fact that most consolidated boards, even those originally created with increasing accountability in mind, ultimately move toward acting more as an institutional advocate and less as an arm of state accountability. This is because they are legally responsible for the governance of these institutions and consequently regard protection of these institutions as their primary function.

In contrast, a coordinating board, which does not govern any of the public institutions, is potentially in a better position to look to the broader public interest and to recommend state policies more evenhandedly across the segments (public four-year and two-year, private, and even proprietary institutions). That is why the Maryland private institutions and public community colleges favored the retention of a state coordinating board even in the face of (and, one might guess, especially because of) the prospect of one merged board for most of the public four-year colleges.

Another lesson that can be drawn from the Maryland experience is the mixed results that may emerge from having the state higher education executive officer (SHEEO) not only chosen by the governor (from a list of three nominated by the MHEC) but also subsequently serving both as the MHEC's executive officer and as the governor's secretary of higher education, sitting in the governor's cabinet. Some persons reported that in the short run in Maryland, the dual role of the SHEEO had acted to the benefit of higher education, as the secretary had been privy to cabinet budget discussions about severe state cutbacks and, in that capacity, had been able to lessen the severity of the cuts to higher education. Furthermore, because the SHEEO was secretary of a commission to which all of the initial members had been appointed by the same governor, there was less danger, again in the short run, that the SHEEO would be pulled in two opposite directions. Nevertheless, the possibility exists for a sharp clash of interests, and this fact must be recognized.

Theoretical Explanations of the Restructuring

Political and organizational theories shed some light on the struggles over the structure of Maryland's higher education system. Three theoretical constructs are described briefly. Then the Maryland restructuring is examined from the perspective of these theories.

First, reorganization can be viewed as a redistribution of power among affected parties, and one then can examine perceptions of, and reactions to, the consequences of particular redistributions of power. Redford (1969) notes:

> Decisions on administrative organization reflect the expectation that certain kinds of interest will be promoted by the kind of organization chosen. Specifically, decisions on whether to have a commission or a single-headed agency for economic regulation, or on qualifications of heads of agencies, reflect the choices of decision makers on interests to be promoted. Every forum of decision ultimately comes to represent in its purpose, in the rules and policies it follows, and in the roles of its personnel, some combination of interests. There is not such thing as a neutral decision on these matters—even the decision to have a presumably neutral agency is a decision that certain interests shall prevail [pp. 29–30].

From this perspective, the conflict over the design of Maryland's higher education system can be viewed as an attempt to reconcile differing views on which structure and distribution of responsibilities best allocates decision-making power among the various parties. The notion of what is "best" rests on the various parties' conflicting assumptions about what interests should be promoted by decision makers.

Second, another theory (Meisinger, 1976) suggests that the participants were seeking to reduce uncertainty in dealing with their environment by gaining as much autonomy (or power) as possible so they can adapt quickly to emerging circumstances. They sought to avoid as many external constraints on their discretion as possible. Professor Frederick Balderston at the University of California, Berkeley, once expressed this desire. He remarked that there is a "universal law" of organizational behavior that applies to every unit at every level: "Persons at all levels in organizations seek the maximum degree of autonomy from those above them in the organizational hierarchy and seek maximum obedience from those below them" (personal communication, 1972). Furthermore, Meisinger (1976, p. 185) suggests that uncertainty increases when there is a breakdown in consensus on appropriate roles among those in an organizational structure, a good description of circumstances in Maryland in 1988.

Third, there is a body of theory (Olson, 1971) that deals with conflicts between collective (state) and individual (institutional) interests. From this perspective, the struggle over restructuring can be viewed as an attempt by the state to "rationalize" the higher education system by countering institutions' suboptimizing behaviors. In the state's view, unfettered institutional autonomy is unlikely to result in the most effective mix of institutions and programs, the pre-1988 system being viewed as an example. Without intervention, the strong can continue to get stronger at the expense of the weaker regardless of the merits of the outcome. From the institutions' perspective, however, state intervention is costly and time-consuming and hinders their ability to respond flexibly to emerging conditions. There was little agreement on the trade-offs between these two legitimate concerns in Maryland.

These theoretical perspectives suggest that the search for a new organizational structure was motivated by a desire to reduce the uncertainty created by the breakdown in consensus over the previously existing roles and powers of the various parties. In this environment, all parties sought to obtain or maintain as much control as possible over their circumstances. For the institutions, this meant having their own boards and as much autonomy from state-level and multicampus systems intervention as possible, except in the few cases where these agencies' interests were seen as consistent with campus interests. For the governor and legislators, it meant having power allocated within the structure in a way that would facilitate accomplishing state objectives, that is, giving considerable power to a statewide higher education agency or consolidated governing board. The public institutions feared the power of a statewide agency over which they would have little control, and many state political leaders feared the consequences of unregulated competition among public four-year institutions.

These competing views of the appropriate distribution of power and its effects on their levels of uncertainty led to the long stalemate over the form a new structure should take and created the need for compromise if a change was to occur. The institutions, some more reluctantly than others, preferred a consolidated governing board to a powerful state coordinating agency. They presumably viewed a governing board, representing institutions, as more sensitive and responsive to their concerns. Some of the "comprehensive universities" also saw a governing board as an ally in protecting them from the politically powerful graduate and research campuses. Former University of Maryland campuses saw advantages in sharp mission differentiation to protect their graduate research role, while former board-of-trustees campuses saw advantages in their gaining greater equity in funding and programs by blurring missions. Some state legislators believed that a governing board would have more power to ensure attention to state priorities than a coordinating agency (an expectation that most scholars of higher education characterize as naive), while others believed that state interests would be better served by a powerful coordinating board. The independent and community college segments also viewed a strong coordinating board as a means to control the ambitions of the public four-year institutions.

In the end, the desire to reduce the uncertainty generated by the general lack of confidence in the existing structure exceeded participants' uncertainty over the consequences of restructuring. The compromise was brought about by giving the former University of Maryland campuses more autonomy from the governing board than they had previously enjoyed and the former board-of-trustees institutions more autonomy from state agencies. The politicians who sought a consolidated governing board got a partial one (two four-year institutions retaining their own boards), but with somewhat lesser powers than they wished, and those favoring a strong coordinating agency got one, but not as powerful a one as some would have preferred (its role in budgeting is quite weak).

Because none of the parties saw the restructuring as an ideal reallocation of powers that would enable them to gain fuller control over their uncertainties, the basis for further restructuring and conflict inevitably remains. Future restructuring will most likely depend on whether the perceived liabilities of continuing struggles to balance greater "obedience" with greater "autonomy" will create more uncertainty than the conflicts and upheavals resulting from further restructuring. There may be an optimum balance between autonomy and control, but the debate over where it lies is unlikely ever to end.

Maryland higher education currently (and historically) does not have an informal setting wherein the various parties can come together and interact informally over their common concerns. If such a setting could be devised, it might serve as a vehicle for creating the trust and confidence among the various parties necessary for them to deal productively with the tensions in their relationships. The fundamental tensions would remain, but the parties might be able to come to view one another as having legitimate concerns rather than merely as self-serving and ill-intentioned.

What Does the Future Hold?

As Governor Schaefer's second and final term drew to a close, a new governor was elected, and there may be a new secretary of higher education. The close relationship between the governor and Shaila Aery probably precludes her staying on very long with his successor. If that came to pass, it would raise the question as to whether it might also be a propitious time to reexamine the current structure. Certain respondents believed that legal clarification of the BOR-MHEC relationship would be desirable. However, others suggested that a change in personalities might be sufficient to improve the rocky relationship and that it was wiser not to reopen the legislative process on this issue.

Another source of temptation to alter the current structure is speculation about whether College Park, like Morgan State and St. Mary's, would be better off outside the system. It is too early to tell what effects the recent creation of the UMCP's own local board of visitors will have on this issue. Suffice it to say that very different reactions to it were found among the many respondents. One legislator wryly noted, "You can't be a flagship without other boats in the bathtub!"

Both authors must struggle with the basic problem that we are from College Park and opposed the original merger proposal. However, reaching as deeply for objectivity as possible, we suggest that because of the great divisiveness engendered by apparently threatening structural reforms, the enormous amount of time and resources needed administratively to "sweep up" after the reform process, and the fact that the present merged system is showing signs of "settling in" a bit, all parties should for the time being work together to make the present system more effective rather than risk opening again the Pandora's box of legislative reform, the ultimate unintended consequences of which no one can be sure.

That our sense of caution is grounded in more than personal reactions to passing problems is shown, perhaps, by a quote from the ancient Romans:

> We trained hard, we performed well, . . . but it seemed that every time we were beginning to form into teams and become reasonably proficient, we would be reorganized. I was to learn later in life that we tend to meet any new situation by reorganizing . . . and a wonderful method it can be for creating the illusion of progress while producing confusion, inefficiency, and demoralization.

> —Petronius Arbiter, 210 B.C.

References

Arnold, J. "The Last of the Good Old Boys: Politics in Baltimore, 1920–1950." *Maryland Historical Magazine,* 1976, *71*(3), 443–448.

Boyd, L. *Maryland Government and Politics.* Centreville, Md.: Tidewater Publications, 1987.

Calcott, G. *Maryland and America, 1940 to 1980.* Baltimore, Md.: Johns Hopkins University Press, 1985.

Callan, P. M. "The Gauntlet for Multicampus Systems." *Trusteeship,* 1994, *2*(3), 16–19.

Commission on Excellence in Higher Education (Hoblitzell Commission). *Higher Education: An Investment in Excellence.* Annapolis, Md.: Commission on Excellence in Higher Education, 1987.

Johnstone, D. B. "Public Multi-Campus College and University Systems: Structures, Functions, and Rationale." *National Association of System Heads Issues and Answers for Public Multi-Campus Systems,* 1993, *1*(2), 1–10.

Johnstone, D. B. "Does This Gauntlet Need to be Picked Up?" *Trusteeship,* 1994, *2*(3), 20.

Lawrence, J. F. "Gubernatorial Commissions and Maryland Higher Education, 1946–1987." Unpublished doctoral dissertation, University of Maryland, College Park, 1990.

McGuinness, A. C., Jr. "State Coordination and Governance of Higher Education, 1991." In *State Postsecondary Education Profiles Handbook.* Denver, Colo.: Education Commission of the States, 1991.

Maryland Higher Education Commission. *Currents.* Annapolis, Md.: Maryland Higher Education Commission, 1994.

Meisinger, R. J., Jr. *State Budgeting for Higher Education: The Uses of Formulas.* Berkeley: Center for Research and Development in Higher Education, University of California, 1976.

Olson, M., Jr. *The Logic of Collective Action: Public Goods and the Theory of Groups.* (Rev. ed.) New York: Schocken, 1971.

Redford, E. S. *Democracy in the Administrative State.* New York: Oxford University Press, 1969.

State Board for Higher Education. *Maryland Statewide Plan for Postsecondary Education.* Annapolis, Md.: State Board for Higher Education, 1978.

University of Maryland. *The Post–Land Grant University: The University of Maryland Report.* Adelphi: University of Maryland, 1981.

University of Maryland. *Report of the Board of Regents to the Governor and General Assembly of Maryland Regarding the Organization of the University of Maryland System.* Adelphi: University of Maryland, 1990.

University of Maryland. *Achieving the Vision in Hard Times,* Vols. 1 and 2. Adelphi: University of Maryland, 1992.

Lessons of Restructuring

Chapter Eight

A Model for Successful Restructuring

Aims C. McGuinness, Jr.

Debates about centralization versus decentralization and the impact of central control on campus autonomy are as old as higher education itself. The United States has seen a half-century movement toward more and more elaborate structures beyond the single public college or university campus. Writing in 1991, Clark Kerr noted that "the freestanding campus with its own board, its one and only president, its identifiable alumni, its faculty and student body, all in a single location with no coordinating council above it, is now the exception whereas in 1945 it was the rule" (p. 257). At that time, 40 percent of all students attended schools that were parts of multicampus institutions (Kerr, 1971). By 1994, that proportion had increased to 65 percent.

Only in the past decade, however, have serious proposals been advanced for reversing this trend. Again, it was Clark Kerr, writing in 1984 about the condition of the presidency of American colleges and universities, who identified the multicampus system as one of the "sore points in American higher education; a few systems seem to exist on the verge of explosion" (Commission on Strengthening Presidential Leadership, 1984, p. 71). He identified the tendency of systems not to appoint and support strong campus leaders, ambiguities in responsibilities of campus and system chief executives, and ineffective performance of both system boards and their chief executives. He elaborated on these concerns in a subsequent study of governing boards (Kerr and Gade, 1989).

The intent of this chapter is to make a realistic assessment of the future of multicampus systems and to provide a concrete example of how systems might change to meet the demands of the next decade. The underlying point is that systems are likely to be more, rather than less, a feature of American higher education a decade from now. If this is true, the relevant issue is not the abstract question of whether systems should exist but rather how systems should be designed and structured so that they stimulate, support, and sustain an outstanding, highly diverse, and responsive higher education enterprise.

Perspectives on Systems

What is emerging is a debate with at least three perspectives, each moving in a different direction.

Defense of Systems and Practical Suggestions for Improvement

Several respected leaders are emphasizing that systems are likely to continue to be a dominant dimension of the American higher education landscape and therefore focus on practical ideas about "what works" in system organization and leadership. Examples include a report by D. Bruce Johnstone, former chancellor of the State University of New York, titled *Central Administrations of Public Multi-Campus College and University Systems* (1992); a report for the American Association of State Colleges and Universities titled *Shared Visions of Public Higher Education Governance: Structures and Leadership Styles That Work* (Schick, Novak, Norton, and Elam, 1992); and a report by Marian L. Gade for the Association of Governing Boards, *Four Multicampus Systems: Some Policies and Practices That Work* (1993). Though each of these authors would acknowledge the need for periodic evaluation and change, none argues for fundamental restructuring of multicampus systems (Johnstone, 1994).

Calls for Reinventing Government

Political leaders at the state and federal level are using the rhetoric of "reinventing government," "restructuring," or "reengineering" to suggest that large, bureaucratic, hierarchical systems such as multicampus universities should be undertaking major changes to increase flexibility and responsiveness to external demands and constraints. Commentaries from outside higher education, such as David Osborne and Ted Gaebler's *Reinventing Government: How the Entrepreneurial Spirit Is Transforming the Public Sector* (1992), are used to bolster these arguments. Although higher education systems may be implementing changes that reflect this thinking (primarily spurred by severe economic conditions), none appears to be applying them in a comprehensive manner. Only a few attempts have been made to think through how these ideas might be applied to radically different conceptions of higher education systems (see Armajani, Heydinger, and Hutchinson, 1994).

Suggestions for Elimination or Restructuring

This perspective is best illustrated by the recent challenge by Patrick M. Callan, director of the California Higher Education Policy Center. Callan's perspective is shaped by what he perceives as a lack of appropriate response to the state's economic realities of the two large public systems: the University of California, with eight campuses, and the California State University, with twenty-three campuses. In a recent article, Callan called systems "vestiges of past and possibly obsolete models and concepts. . . . Governing and coordinating structures and processes will either change with their social environment or become redundant" (1994, p. 17). He then continued by listing six questions about systems:

1. Are multicampus systems the product of earlier organizational models that relied, quite reasonably at the time, on economies of scale, centralization, standardization, and process-oriented accountability?
2. What are the real costs of multicampus system governance— not just central staff salaries and support, but also the costs to the campuses in such systems?
3. How effective are multicampus systems against undue political intervention?
4. Have multicampus systems been successful advocates for their campuses?
5. Have multicampus systems strengthened or weakened campus leadership?
6. Does the multicampus system of governance endanger the role of lay governance? [pp. 18–19].

Recent analysis of the role of systems in improving under-graduate education found a number of systems that are severely constrained by sheer size and the inertia that comes with the accumulation of policies and procedures over the decades. Not all of these constraints were identified in the policies and practices within the systems themselves. Many were embedded in policies of state governments outside the systems (McGuinness, 1994). Five common problems emerge most clearly from among those identified.

One problem is that systems are driven by inwardly directed faculty priorities related to disciplines and professions and defined in terms of resource needs and constraints. Such agendas were perceived as disconnected from the broader economic and social forces affecting the states in which the systems were located. Systems tended to push aside basic questions such as access and affordability that were on the public's mind as they were preoccupied with internal demands to maintain quality by reducing workload and increasing student tuition and fees.

A second problem is one of systems' failing to reinforce mission differentiation among the system campuses in financing policies, policies on faculty promotion and tenure, and incentives for undergraduate teaching.

The tendency of systems and external state government policies to become "one size fits all" solutions is a third problem. Such an approach inevitably imposes the values of research and disciplinary focus on campuses where undergraduate teaching is the primary mission.

Fourth, faculty pressures for "shared governance" that tend to elevate campus issues to the system level pose problems. As a result, the system-level consultative, consensus-building processes tend to impose the values of one unit on another. In many systems, intractable issues involving collective bargaining constitute significant barriers to differentiation and decentralization.

A final common problem is one of systems' lacking clear definitions of the roles that they could play in reinforcing campus initiatives on undergraduate education. Examples include promoting mission differentiation, providing special financial incentives, convening systemwide faculty development functions, providing technical assistance on assessment and other topics, and advancing the use of technology in both educational and services and administrative arenas (McGuinness, 1994).

In contrast to some of the complicated and esoteric schemes for "restructuring" and "reinventing" systems, political leaders seem poised to slash centralized structures to respond to the public's demands for smaller government. This is a core message from the 1994 midterm congressional elections. It is a worldwide phenomenon. In 1992, a newly elected conservative government in Sweden eliminated the nation's highly centralized higher education policy structure. The changes decentralized university governance and streamlined financing and accountability policies (Swedish Ministry of Education and Science, 1992). Even with the return of the Social Democrats to power in 1994, many of these changes will be retained. In a strikingly similar move, New Jersey Governor Christine Todd Whitman in 1994 eliminated the State Board of Higher Education and the Department of Higher Education, decentralized institutional governance, and established a new, much smaller state planning and coordinating structure.

Systems: A Likely Continuing Feature of the Higher Education Landscape

In all likelihood, time will prove wrong both observers who are predicting only marginal change and those who are advocating that systems be "blown up." Despite all the challenges and a few successful, radical changes, multicampus systems are likely to be even more a characteristic of American public higher education in 2015 as they are in 1995. What will change most dramatically is what constitutes a "system"; changes will be made in how systems are led and how they function, both internally and in relationship to multiple external stakeholders.

Intractable Centralizing Forces

There are four essentially negative reasons why systems will be exceptionally difficult to eliminate and, in fact, may be even more in demand in the next decade.

1. *States will continue to turn to systems as means to manage regional economic and political imbalance and to sustain political coalitions.* Beyond questions of sound education policy, three realities lie behind the development of systems and statewide coordinating

agencies. First, the politics of virtually every American state is dominated by regional struggles as some areas decline and others grow in political and economic strength. In some cases, these disparities are complicated by dimensions of race, ethnicity, and wealth. The second reality is that regions (or other significant economic and political blocs) inevitably see colleges and universities as the keys to economic standing, prestige, and political influence. And third, multicampus systems were often constructed purposely to create coalitions among regions in order to compete in the state political process.

The interplay of these three realities lies behind virtually every multicampus or consolidated system. Much of this can be traced to the location of land-grant universities in rural areas, reflecting the agricultural focus of the economy in the late nineteenth century, whereas the major developments in the twentieth century have been in urban centers. As new urban areas developed (among them Portland, Oregon, and Portland, Maine; Los Angeles, Las Vegas, Denver, and Miami; Chicago, Springfield, and other Illinois urban centers; Miami and South Florida), appeals were made for new branch campuses, new engineering programs, new high-cost graduate and professional programs, and inevitably, freestanding "university campus" status. Rather than see competing universities develop in these centers, the older institutions reached out—first with extension centers, later with branch campuses, and finally with largely autonomous university campuses. From a political perspective, the ability of the older institutions to sustain state support depended on their ability to develop political coalitions across the state, especially in the major urban centers.

In the 1960s, during the "golden years" of expansion of public higher education, governors and legislators, frustrated either by the political fallout from these battles or by their inability to say no to growing areas, turned to statewide coordination and consolidated governance to achieve what many observers characterize as "more rational allocation of public resources." Only in rare cases did these entities prevent development of new or expanded higher education programs. In the best of circumstances, they contributed to more orderly development and a better match of new initiatives to state and regional educational and economic needs. In other cases, they amounted to little more than what Texas Higher Education Commissioner Kenneth Ashworth once called "speed bumps" on the road to the inevitable.

Even after the dramatic expansion of the 1960s, regional conflicts continued to dominate higher education policy debates throughout the nation as regions of growth and decline continued to shift. One can trace virtually every state controversy related to higher education governance over the past twenty years to these shifts and the resulting competition for new higher education institutions or programs. In fact, pressures for centralization—that is, for stronger statewide coordination or consolidated governance— can be related directly to the degree of imbalance among a state's major economic centers in their access to higher education. In most instances, this means access within commuting distance of a public institution with "university status" and graduate and professional programs and, almost always, engineering programs.

A few states have achieved this balance or equilibrium, but often by largely uncoordinated developments over the past quarter century in every urban center. They now face the challenge of higher education systems that are top-heavy in high-cost programs and largely beyond the reach of statewide efforts at "rationalization." But a surprising number of states still face the classic pressures from growing urban centers.

In a broader sense, the issue is not simply among regions but among elements within a state's population who vary in their access to the educational and economic benefits that colleges and universities offer. This point is most graphically illustrated by the political and legal struggles of the Hispanic population to gain greater state support for higher education in South Texas and in the continuing legal battles regarding desegregation and the role of historically black universities in southeastern states.

It is with these realities as background that one must consider the consequences of breaking up multicampus systems. Theoretically, it may be desirable for each campus to have its own governing board or, going one step further, to be freed from a system and given autonomous status. But if this will mean that long-standing regional political and economic balances will be upset and new regional battles will erupt in state capitals, governors and state legislators can be expected to demand that central coordinating and governing authority be reasserted.

As a corollary to this point, it may be in those states that are now "built-out"—already having developed university centers in each major urban center and achieved a degree of equilibrium among these centers in the state's political process—that decentralization can be tolerated.

A more likely reality is that the multicampus or consolidated system configurations formed to deal with regional conflicts or political realities a decade or more ago may not fit states' circumstances today. The regional imbalances are different. The coalitions necessary to gain state political and economic support may have shifted. These changes may lead states to reconfigure the institutional compositions of their systems. In other cases, large systems may be subdivided. In any event, changes will be made to maintain a degree of equilibrium among a state's major economic and political centers. It is highly unlikely, then, that systems will be abandoned in favor of freestanding, competing entities.

2.   *Legal issues, pressure for "shared governance" at the system level, and collective bargaining will make disaggregation of systems exceptionally difficult.* The people seeking the greatest leverage on the system tend to focus their attention on the highest hierarchical point. In virtually all systems, this means the system board and chief executive officer.

The complexity and actual or potential cost of legal issues to individual campuses requires them to seek legal assistance from the system beyond what they can afford. There are few signs across the United States that these pressures for centralization are abating; if anything, they are intensifying.

In a slow yet profound manner, the historic concept of lay governance is being replaced by "representative" governance in the nation's public multicampus systems. Faculty and student expectations for "shared governance" have led a number of systems to elevate to the system level the processes of consultation and consensus building that used to be primarily features of campus governance. Most system boards now have student members serving in at least an ex officio, nonvoting capacity. Fewer systems have faculty as members, but faculty are involved directly in deliberations of board committees. Most systems now consult systemwide faculty and student bodies before taking action on key academic and financing policies. To be effective, this involvement must make clear distinctions between system and campus issues. A blurring of these distinctions will inevitably lead to the values of one or two campuses (usually those with high-prestige research missions) overwhelming those of other campuses (usually those with strong undergraduate or nontraditional missions). It can also have the effect of undercutting incentives and support for effective campus governance.

Faculty collective bargaining, under which the system is the single bargaining unit for all campuses, is now a core feature of many of the nation's multicampus systems. From both the system and the union perspectives, this has advantages. Theoretically, it can provide the framework for negotiating the conditions appropriate to campus differentiation. But in reality, such differentiation is exceptionally difficult to achieve. The pressures are overwhelmingly in favor of equal treatment without regard to important mission differences. Frontal assaults by political leaders on collective bargaining in the name of promoting greater differentiation are more likely to "freeze" centralized and confrontational policies. Nevertheless, in the severe economic conditions of the past few years, not many systems have been able to develop the climate of mutual respect and trust necessary to achieve agreement on greater differentiation and decentralization.

3. *Worldwide pressures are accelerating to merge nonuniversity sectors with university sectors.* Despite concerns about the "drift" of institutional missions away from undergraduate teaching, workforce preparation, and public service, nations—and some American states—are still acting to merge or consolidate university and nonuniversity sectors. Examples include Australia's merger of the colleges of advanced education with the universities beginning in 1988, the Dutch government's move to consolidate smaller vocational institutes to create larger institutions with missions strikingly similar to those of the universities, and the United Kingdom's recent abolition of the binary system through the merger of the funding councils for universities and polytechnics (Goedegebuure, 1994). Ironically, while government leaders often advance these mergers as means to manage great differentiation, the natural bureaucratic processes (extensive consultation and effort devoted

to formulating systemwide coordinated, consistent and often unified policies) result in exactly the opposite. In fact, bureaucracy
transmits academic values (such as the high-prestige values of the
research university) across a system perhaps better than any other
means of coordination (Clark, 1983).

4.   *In difficult economic times, political leaders can be expected to
resort (or revert) to traditional alternatives aimed at increasing expenditure
controls, eliminating duplication, and centralizing in an effort to achieve
economies of scale.* Despite much talk about "reinventing government," basic state administrative and fiscal control practices change
very slowly. Concerns about unnecessary program duplication and
administrative costs associated with the operation of highly decentralized services are always high on legislative agendas, especially
in difficult economic times. Some academicians might argue the
benefits of numerous separately governed public colleges and universities, but from the state government perspective, this may
look like an excessively wasteful duplication of administration and
dispersion of accountability. As Kerr and Gade observed, "State
authorities . . . find it helpful to hold one board and one chief
executive officer accountable. They prefer to have to place or
receive only one phone call rather than to have to deal with several or many competitive and combative institutions, their representatives, and supporters" (1989, p. 118). This reality is reflected
in the perennial proposals for "superboards" in states with com-
paratively decentralized higher education governance.

Reasons Why Systems May Be Preferred

Beyond these negative reasons for the persistence of systems, there
are at least three reasons why systems may be essential for the
strength of colleges and universities over the next decade.

1.   *Systems may help meet the need for stability, continuity, and long-
term perspective in an increasingly turbulent political environment.* Such
trends as term limits, the spread of "direct democracy" through initiatives and referenda, and the kind of anti-incumbent sentiment
that transformed legislatures in the November 1994 elections are
dramatically changing state-level higher education politics. In times

past, public higher education could be confident that a core of state legislators on key committees had a sense of the history and values that should undergird effective relationships between a state and its colleges and universities. Now, as one university official recently commented, communicating with the state legislature will be like "making a speech to a parade." Short time spans for legislative initiatives, often lasting no more than a single budget cycle, have been an increasing problem, and in the future, the pace of change may become even faster and the life of initiatives shorter still. States will enact new initiatives before those enacted in the past legislative session have even been implemented.

Complicating the state role further will be pressures to downsize state agencies, including state higher education bodies. The state agency capacity to undertake long-range planning and careful implementation of new policies will be severely limited.

The arena for policy making may, in fact, shift away from the state capitol as major changes in state policies for revenue and expenditures affecting higher education are decided through statewide initiatives and referenda. Both this trend and the high rate of legislative turnover will mean a shift in accountability strategies. Attention may move away from traditional bureaucratic accountability to state agencies and legislative committees, broader communication through the statewide media, and more local and personal communication with voters throughout the state.

In these circumstances, multicampus systems may be a critical means to provide for long-term, consistent attention to a public agenda that connects higher education to states' major social and economic challenges, and they may be the only means to develop and implement long-term policies that will stimulate and support institutional responses to these public concerns. Such policy leadership is unlikely from the state agencies that are directly dependent on and accountable to an increasingly unstable state political leadership.

2. *Systems may provide the means to respond to the increasing demands of the clientele for statewide consistency in quality and accessibility of higher education services and in credit transfer.* Students and other clients will increasingly demand common standards and access to university services throughout the state, regardless of the campus

that is their primary or initial contact. In an age of branch banking, automated teller machines, the Internet, and a host of other technology-related mechanisms, the public has come to expect the same assurances of quality, accuracy of information, and record transfer regardless of their physical location. Pressures for hassle-free credit transfer, one of the most enduring sources of legislative annoyance, can be expected to intensify. This will mean that systemwide, consumer-oriented information systems, common policies, and other mechanisms to conform services across the state to the same quality standards will become more important. All these points run directly counter to the traditional higher education value placed on institutional autonomy and mission differentiation. Breaking up systems in ways that will undermine these systemwide client advantages would be directly contrary to what is happening in the rest of the economy and society. Yet multicampus systems that fail to respond to these demands may be replaced by others that do.

3.   *In a more market-oriented environment, intense pressures for cost containment and technological advances are likely to lead to the same kinds of mergers and consolidations now under way in health care.* The age of the freestanding general hospital has long passed. Although the changes in higher education will of course be different, the same pressures are likely to force more systemic thinking about the ways in which colleges and universities can join together to provide higher-quality services at lower cost. Multicampus systems could be the catalysts for these new relationships. But many alliances will be with entities *outside* the formal confines of current systems: with the private sector, across state and national boundaries, and so on. Systems that are seen as barriers to these changes will be restructured or eliminated. But they will be replaced by other systems. The free-standing institution—especially in the public sector—is likely to be an anomaly.

Principles for Future Systems

Assuming that systems will be a major feature of American higher education in the next century, how might they be designed, led, and managed to counter some of their potentially negative effects?

The following list is certainly not definitive but suggests some of the points that should be considered with respect to existing systems.

1.   *The system should have explicit objectives that relate to both external state and societal priorities and internal system priorities.* The system mission should be distinct from, but complementary to, that of the individual campuses. Systems can easily drift into a "middle muddling through" position in which they are neither providing policy and educational leadership on behalf of the state and broader society nor fostering diverse, well-managed campuses. Both roles are important. Compromising one at the expense of the other will not work.

2.   *The system should maintain a distinct balance between its role in representing the public interest to the academy and its role in representing the academy to the public.* In other words, advocacy must be a two-way street. Too many systems become captives of internal constituents and fail to serve as appropriate advocates of society's priorities.

3.   *The system should have a legal standing (in the state constitution, if appropriate) that will enable it to provide sustained, consistent, long-term policy leadership in the face of increasing turnover and turbulence in state political leadership.* Whether states grant this independence will depend directly on the extent to which the system demonstrates its commitment to the public agenda and public accountability. In some states, it may be possible to organize the system board and leadership as a public corporation with a legal status independent of state government and with a largely self-sustaining governing board. Having some (perhaps one-third) of the board members appointed by the governor and confirmed by the state senate would ensure that the state's political leadership has a seat at the table. In states in which the public corporation model is not feasible, changing the board membership to two-thirds self-sustaining and one-third governor-appointed might increase stability yet retain an important degree of responsiveness to state leaders' priorities.

4.   *The presumption should always be in favor of decentralization to the individual campuses or units.* In other words, the system should have to justify (through periodic external review, if feasible) each of its functions in terms of these kinds of questions:

Is this a function that cannot be undertaken more effectively and efficiently by the individual campuses?

Is this a function that addresses system and public interest questions that individual campuses cannot address?

Does this function add value to the sum of the contribution of the individual campuses?

In the case of services, is this a service that campuses could not purchase from another source other than the system at lower cost and the same or higher quality?

5. *Before adding a system-level operational or service function, systems should explore all other alternatives.* For example, they might assign system responsibility for the function to one of the campuses (establishing a lead campus), contract out the function to a nonstate entity, or operate the function as an independent, self-sustaining entity that must compete with other potential vendors in terms of the quality, responsiveness, and cost of services to the campuses.

6. *The system should seek to break bureaucratic links between and among campuses and academic units with significantly different missions.* It should challenge the inevitable upward pressure for consultation and consensus building at the system level—especially to the extent that these system processes undercut or undermine consultation, teamwork, and group responsibility at the campus or subcampus levels. This means that systems should consider at least three alternatives.

One is the creation of campuses as corporate entities separate and distinct from the system but still within the system framework (in other words, perhaps the campuses could be "franchised" by the system).

Another is the decentralization of all personnel policy and related decisions to the individual campuses. The key is that the system should seek every means to make units other than the system the final point of appeal. The system, then, can retain an important role in providing legal and technical assistance to the decentralized units but can avoid being encumbered by legal issues that are more appropriately handled at the campus level.

A third option is the decentralization of collective bargaining to the campus level, as it is the campus that is the legal entity responsible for personnel decisions. For the reasons suggested earlier, this may be one of the biggest challenges systems face. They must seek a balance between assurances of fairness and due process across the system's diversity and the need to foster highly differentiated campus communities and cultures. Precipitous actions that devastate trust will freeze centralized structures and policies. Step-by-step changes, negotiated in a climate of trust and respect, are likely to lead to the most productive and most lasting changes.

7.   *The system should deliberately foster or create smaller academic units (for five to ten thousand students) whose principal mission is undergraduate education.* Preferably these units should be legally and bureaucratically separated from other system units. It should be the system's role to guard against the inevitable "creep" of intercampus consultative processes that will undermine any unit's distinctiveness.

8.   *The system should provide for new pilot or demonstration sites to be established within the system that are separate, and preferably isolated from, other units so as to increase the chances for innovation and improvement.* Again, the emphasis should be on smaller units, legally and bureaucratically separated from other units (especially those with different missions and faculty reward systems).

9.   *The system should use financing policy to influence, through incentives and other means, the willingness of institutions to respond to major public priorities and to undertake their own internal renewal and restructuring.* Specifically, systems should reserve approximately 10 percent of the total state appropriation for allocation according to public ends in one or more categories. These might include incentives for each institution to improve performance effectiveness and efficiency in accordance with its mission (for example, matching funding contingent on the institution's identifying savings through internal restructuring); competitive funding to stimulate and support new and more cost-effective delivery systems (freestanding, between and among existing institutions, in collaboration with other entities, public and private, in-state and out-of-state); and incentives for institutions to address state issues through applied research and technology and other means.

10.   *The system should consider establishing freestanding, noninstitutionally based assessment centers where students can demonstrate that*

they have met general education requirements applicable to any baccalaureate degree awarded by an institution in the state.

11.   *The system should retain sufficient authority to use financing policy and other tools to curb unnecessary program duplication, counter "mission creep," and resolve inevitable disputes among regions and interest groups.*

12.   *The system should be open in the sense that it deliberately fosters collaboration with entities (public and private, in-state and out-of-state) beyond the formal state bounds.* As just suggested, the system should provide financial incentives for institutions to establish these alliances when it is in the public interest to do so.

Illustration of Possible Changes

To provide a sense of realism as to how an existing system might change to meet the principles just outlined, let us examine how a hypothetical state might move from a consolidated multicampus system to a redesigned system (McGuinness, 1992). This case is intended to illustrate some of the changes that states and systems might consider. Such changes must be worked out state by state, taking specific economic, demographic, cultural, and historical circumstances into consideration. Transposing one state's solutions on another's very different problems—a common practice in higher education policy—is a serious error.

Current Situation

The characteristics of the hypothetical state can be described as follows.

Economy and Demography

Enrollment is projected to increase by 10 to 15 percent by 2010 in populations and regions different from current patterns: more urban, more ethnically diverse, and more adult, focused on upgrading and retraining.

Growth in the state economy is projected to be less than 2 percent per year, in a strong antitax climate. Demands and mandates in other areas will mean likely declining support for higher education, support that will fail to keep up with currently projected increases in demand and costs.

For both educational and workforce purposes, the state is concerned about the 75 percent of all middle school students who never gain a postsecondary education or training certificate at a time when the number of jobs that do not require this level of education is rapidly declining.

Postsecondary Education System

About 15 percent of enrollment is in the private, nonprofit sector, especially site-bound adults in proprietary programs operated by out-of-state institutions, some of which make extensive use of technology and telecommunications.

All institutions except postsecondary technical institutes are under the central governing authority of a single statewide board. The board was created in the 1970s through the merger of the state land-grant university and its branches, the state comprehensive universities, and the state-funded community colleges. The technical institutes are under the supervision of the state department of education.

The state land-grant university campus is located away from the state's major urban areas.

Two of the other state university campuses are in urban areas and have been seeking additional authority to develop graduate and professional programs, especially in engineering.

In virtually every region, two or three publicly funded institutions are competing to provide less-than-baccalaureate-level occupational programs. These include some of the state universities, state-funded community colleges, public university branch campuses, and state technical institutes. The university system was created in part to solve this problem, but little progress has been made in the past fifteen years.

Governing Structure

The system functions as a single corporate entity.

The state university system board is composed of fifteen members appointed by the governor and confirmed by the senate. A nonvoting student member serves ex officio.

The system chancellor is the chief executive officer. Campus presidents are appointed by the board but report to the board through the chancellor.

Faculty and student members, elected by systemwide councils, serve as members of board committees.

The principal board committees (academic affairs, fiscal affairs, student affairs) are staffed by system vice chancellors who in turn work with systemwide councils of their peer vice presidents.

The chancellor works closely with a statewide council of presidents; few items are placed on the board agenda on which there is not consensus among the presidents.

Reflecting the chancellor's commitment to "shared governance," a systemwide faculty council, elected by the faculty senates of each campus, is extensively involved in policy development and implementation at the system level.

The chancellor and board attempt to project a public image of one university with many units, but each campus functions as a separate academic unit. Faculty receive campus-specific appointments, and promotion and tenure decisions are campus-specific.

Each campus has extensive advisory mechanisms, but the system board has opposed formation of formal campus boards for fear that this would spawn regional conflicts and undermine the system.

Year by year, board agendas and central staff resources are becoming increasingly dominated by legal issues that come to the system board because it is the final legal authority and point of appeal for all campuses.

Financing and Budget Process

All state appropriations are made to the system board and then allocated to individual campuses. Budgets are developed on an incremental basis. The system does not use a formula either for developing the budgets or for allocating state revenue.

Tuition and fee policies as well as per-campus tuition and fees are set at the system level and approved by the board. Rates vary by campus, but the system board has maintained tight control to ensure a degree of consistency across the system. Campuses may not retain any tuition revenue.

Collective Bargaining

The system has a single statewide bargaining unit. All four-year institution faculty are represented by one union, the community college faculty by another.

In recent years, the faculty unions have been arguing for parity in workloads and salaries among the four-year campuses. Efforts at further differentiation based on mission are strongly opposed.

State Government Culture

There is a strong tradition of detailed procedural controls by state purchasing and personnel departments. These have been relaxed in the past decade, but only to the extent that the university system has been willing to maintain its own central controls.

All legislators who played a role in forming the university system have now left office. In fact, only one-third of the legislators have been in office more than one term. Furthermore, both houses just changed party leadership for the first time in a decade.

Proposed Redesigned System

The newly elected governor, in concert with the university board, announced a major redesign of the statewide leadership, financing, and governance of the state's postsecondary education enterprise. Although some steps are to be taken immediately, the plan is to be carried out over a five-year period. Core elements of the plan call for the following:

- Decentralizing campus or unit governance, with strong emphasis on campus responsibility and accountability for performance and on flexibility and innovation. Deliberate incentives will be included for forming new, competitive, and cost-effective units and delivery systems.
- Redefining the system's responsibilities to emphasize policy leadership on strategic public priorities, public communication, standards and accountability, and financial incentives for institutional renewal, change, new partnerships, and new delivery systems.

- Committing the state to a long-term, strategic investment funding system that will fund higher education at a rate not less than the current base, adjusted annually for the increase in the consumer price index plus an allowance for enrollment growth, and allocate not less than 10 percent of all state appropriations on the basis of strategic investment and performance criteria developed by the new university board.
- Moving toward an open, more market-driven concept of a system that provides incentives for institutions to be more consumer-driven and for the development of alternative, perhaps nonpublic, educational delivery systems. Such a system would also use a state subsidy to enter the market (through the underlying incentives in the financing system) in order to ensure that institutions respond to major public priorities, develop partnerships between formal units within the system and entities outside the system (schools, employers, nonpublic institutions, institutions in other states and nations), and transform accountability from internal bureaucratic reporting to the state to external reporting to the general public, clients, and major system stakeholders.

At the end of a five-year phase-in period, the broad outlines of the system would be as follows:

Campus or Unit Governance

Each campus would be established as a separate public corporate entity distinct from the system. Ownership of all property would be transferred to the campuses. Campuses would have autonomy with respect to all personnel matters, including collective bargaining agreements, setting tuition and fees, and using tuition and fee revenues.

The basic corporate charter and mission of any campus or unit to receive state funding through the new structure, or any change thereto, would be subject to approval of the new system board (to be described shortly). In other words, no campus or unit could be established or change its status without approval of the new system board. As the new system of decentralization is implemented, each campus would submit its proposed corporate charter and mission to the system board for initial approval.

Each campus would have its own lay governing board. Initially, all members would be appointed by the governor and confirmed by the senate. The governor has established an independent nominating commission charged with screening and recommending persons for board appointments. Board members may be from out-of-state. In time, as initial terms expire, two-thirds of each board would be appointed by the board itself on a self-perpetuating basis. One-third would continue to be appointed by the governor. Campus presidents would be appointed by and serve at the pleasure of the campus board.

Each campus would be required to develop and report publicly according to a set of performance indicators. The indicators would include information that is campus-specific and reports on institutional performance on major public priorities as defined by the system board. Campus performance indicators would be subject to approval by the system board and would serve as the basis for allocating a portion of state funding to the campus.

System Board

The system would be changed from a statewide governing board to a statewide higher education policy and service corporation. To ensure long-term stability and continuity, the new board and its basic charter would be given a legal basis in the state constitution.

The new board and corporation would be explicitly prohibited from governing or operating an educational institution or program, except that the board would have authority to assume governing responsibility for a campus on an emergency basis of no more than two years if the institution fails to meet system performance and accountability requirements. The board would also have the authority to initiate a new campus, program, or educational delivery system on a pilot basis for not more than five years, provided there is an explicit plan to transfer responsibility to a separate corporation by the end of that period.

The system board would be responsible for approval of the basic corporate charters and missions of each campus or unit (or any changes thereto) that would receive state funding through the new system. In other words, under the state constitution, public institutions could be established or their missions changed only if approved by the new system board.

The core mission of the system board would be to develop and maintain a long-term (five- to ten-year) public agenda to link the state's postsecondary education enterprise to the major strategic social, economic, and educational issues of concern to the state. The board would develop and revise the public agenda annually with direct involvement of the governor and legislative leadership.

This agenda would shape the board's public accountability system and would be linked directly to the state funding of higher education. Further, the system would make an annual "state of the system" report to a joint session of the state legislature.

Financing

All state appropriations for higher education, including student assistance, would be made to the system board. The board would develop and recommend to the governor and legislature a single budget and appropriations request for all higher education. This request would be presented in a multiyear format to make the long-term investment and change strategy clear and would be linked directly to the public agenda developed jointly with the governor and the state legislature.

The budget and appropriations request and the subsequent allocation to the system board would have five core elements. First, it would include a base budget adjusted for inflation and workload. Second, it would be funded for targeted enrollment growth linked directly to state priorities defined in the public agenda. Third, it would include special-purpose funding of not less than 10 percent of the total appropriation (excluding capital) for at least three separate purposes: (a) performance funding for each institution allocated on the basis of the extent to which each institution met its own performance expectations and state priorities and keyed to institutional matching based on internal reallocation; (b) competitive funding for two or more institutions to join together (or with other entities such as private institutions or employers) to develop and implement new, more cost-effective delivery systems that would be judged in part on how they related to the system board's public agenda; and (c) incentive or matching funding to encourage institutions offering one- and two-year less-than-baccalaureate programs in the same catchment or geographical area to coordinate program delivery (including merger or consolidation).

The fourth element would be state-funded student grants, with not less than 25 percent of the funding to be allocated on a income-sensitive basis to provide incentives for students to complete either degree requirements or the state's new alternative degree standards expeditiously.

Finally, the request would include a special appropriation for competitive grants to institutions for applied research and technology related to major state priorities.

Each institutional governing board would be fully responsible for tuition and fees related to that unit—with two exceptions. The system board would be authorized to provide incentives through the allocation of state appropriations for institutions to constrain tuition and fee increases and to achieve productivity improvements through internal resource reallocation. In addition, each campus would be required to hold public hearings on proposed increases and report to the public, using comparative data as appropriate, on how tuition increases relate to improvements in the quality of teaching and learning, productivity improvements, indicators of the student population's "ability to pay," and the availability of student financial assistance. These reporting requirements would be set by the system board and subject to its approval.

System Board Structure and Functions

The principal functions (and most likely the principal organizational units) would number at least seven. One would be managing the public agenda, financing policy, and resource allocation. This would comprise the key policy and substantive leadership function of the new entity. The new board's agenda should be focused primarily on these issues.

A second function would be to provide system and institutional public communication, information, and accountability systems. This function would place a high priority on clear, direct communication at every level of the system, in every community, and with all stakeholders about how the system and its units are responding to the needs of individual students, regions, and the state as a whole. Specific tasks would include the review and approval of institutional corporate charters and missions; development and approval of institutional reporting according to performance indicators; and maintenance of essential "system-level" data that emphasize system performance in relation to the state's major education, economic, and societal priorities. In total, this function would contribute to system accountability related to the public agenda.

A third function would be provision of special-purpose funding designed to stimulate restructuring within existing campuses; collaboration, if not consolidation, leading to new and more effective program delivery between and among campuses or other entities; and the use of technology or other means to develop entirely new delivery systems independent from existing campuses. (This might be organized as a state-level foundation with authority to seek nonpublic funds to supplement state appropriations for these purposes.)

A fourth function would involve the development and implementation of a new state-authorized, competence-based baccalaureate degree program and related independent assessment centers. Through such a program, students would be able to demonstrate at a regional, system-chartered assessment center mastery of required competences through prior learning, enrollment in state or nonstate institutions, or telecommunicated learning. Degree requirements and related assessments would be developed with extensive involvement of campus faculties. In order that the system would be a viable, competitive force related to on-campus programs, a portion of available student assistance funds would be available to provide support, on an income-sensitive basis, to students seeking to meet degree requirements through this new independent means.

A fifth responsibility of the new system would be to provide statewide student assistance programs. To the maximum extent feasible, the system board should delegate or subcontract out the actual administration of student assistance programs. The system board's focus should be on policies governing the allocation of assistance to students to address major priorities in the public agenda (minority access and achievement, for example), incentives to students for expeditious degree completion, and incentives to institutions to contain tuition and fee increases.

Sixth, the new system should make self-sustaining services available to institutions. Most of the previous system functions related to such areas as legal services, facilities planning, personnel, and payroll should be transferred to a subsidiary service corporation. Campuses should be free to contract with this service corporation or any other entity, depending on which can demonstrate that it can deliver required services at a competitive price. The system board would contract with this service entity for services needed to perform system responsibilities (legal services, for example).

Finally, competitive funding for applied research and technology related directly to major state priorities defined in the public agenda would be offered by the system. As in the case of the incentive funds mentioned earlier, this function could be organized as a state-chartered foundation authorized to seek nonpublic funds to supplement state appropriations.

Implementation

The changes just outlined would be implemented on a phased basis over a five-year period. Absolutely clear from the outset must be the purposes or ends to be served by the changes and the basic principles or values used to guide the means to these ends (for example, focus on public purposes, decentralization, greater reliance on market mechanisms, or sustained commitment of state support for strategic investment).

The first steps would involve gaining public support for the new constitutional board. Developing and phasing in the new funding and accountability systems would follow. Rather than immediately decentralizing the governance of each institution, the new system board might negotiate new charters on a campus-by-campus basis. This would allow necessary planning for the transfer of responsibilities. It would also allow time for delicate negotiations related to the transfer of responsibilities for issues such as collective bargaining.

As suggested earlier, precipitous change that undermines trust and freezes confrontational relationships will make decentralization difficult, if not impossible. It may be that systems with collective bargaining have more of a chance of developing these changes than those without this formal framework. The keys are most likely a systemwide framework to ensure fairness and protection of basic rights to due process, faculty leadership that recognizes and supports the benefits for faculty culture and working conditions that could result from a more decentralized system, and a high level of trust among faculty, campus, and system leaders. If these conditions are not met, decentralization will occur under confrontational circumstances, with long-term negative consequences. It is in the interest of all concerned—faculty, campus presidents, and systems—to avoid this "ultimate" alternative.

Conclusion

The forces that led to establishment of multicampus systems over the past century remain strong. Despite the moves toward decentralization in corporations and government, the pressures for centralization within higher education are likely to continue. Given these realities, the challenge is to shape new modes of state and system leadership that will counter the potentially negative consequences of large, bureaucratic entities. Some theorists may argue that multicampus systems should be dismantled—or "blown up." Those who make such proposals may be ignoring some of the practical reasons why systems were formed. They may also not be considering the important, positive roles that well-designed and well-led systems can play in an increasingly turbulent political and economic environment. I hope in this chapter to have found a middle road between those who would preserve the status quo and those who would blow things up. The principles and illustrations presented are intended not to be copied but rather to stimulate thinking about constructive alternatives for the future.

References

Armajani, B., Heydinger, R., and Hutchinson, P. *A Model for the Reinvented Higher Education System.* Denver, Colo.: Education Commission of the States, 1994.

Callan, P. M. "The Gauntlet for Multicampus Systems." *Trusteeship,* 1994, 2(3), 16–19.

Clark, B. R. *The Higher Education System.* Berkeley: University of California Press, 1983.

Commission on Strengthening Presidential Leadership. *Presidents Make a Difference: Strengthening Leadership in Colleges and Universities.* Washington, D.C.: Association of Governing Boards of Universities and Colleges, 1984.

Gade, M. L. *Four Multicampus Systems: Some Policies and Practices That Work.* Washington, D.C.: Association of Governing Boards of Universities and Colleges, 1993.

Goedegebuure, L.C.J. *Mergers in Higher Education: A Comparative Perspective.* Enschede, Netherlands: Center for Higher Education Policy Studies, 1994.

Johnstone, D. B. *Central Administrations of Public Multi-Campus College and University Systems: Core Functions and Cost Pressures, with Reference to the Central Administration of the State University of New York.* Albany: State University of New York, 1992.

Johnstone, D. B. "Does This Gauntlet Need to be Picked Up?", *Trusteeship,* 1994, *2*(3), 20.

Kerr, C. "Foreword." In E. C. Lee and F. M. Bowen, *The Multicampus University: A Study of Academic Governance.* New York: McGraw-Hill, 1971.

Kerr, C. *The Great Transformation in Higher Education, 1960–1980.* Albany: State University of New York Press, 1991.

Kerr, C., and Gade, M. L. *The Guardians: Boards of Trustees of American Colleges and Universities.* Washington, D.C.: Association of Governing Boards of Universities and Colleges, 1989.

McGuinness, A. C., Jr. "Redesigning the State's Higher Education System for the Twenty-First Century: A Hypothetical Governor's Proposal for Fundamental Change in a State's Higher Education Policies." Paper presented at the National Forum and Annual Meeting of the Education Commission of the States, Cincinnati, Ohio, Aug. 7, 1992.

McGuinness, A. C., Jr. *A Framework for Evaluating State Policy Roles in Improving Undergraduate Education.* Denver, Colo.: Education Commission of the States, 1994.

Osborne, D., and Gaebler, T. *Reinventing Government: How the Entrepreneurial Spirit Is Transforming the Public Sector.* Reading, Mass.: Addison-Wesley, 1992.

Schick, E. B., Novak, R. J., Norton, J. A., and Elam, H. G. *Shared Visions of Public Higher Education Governance: Structures and Leadership Styles That Work.* Washington, D.C.: American Association of State Colleges and Universities, 1992.

Swedish Ministry of Education and Science. *Universities and University Colleges: Quality Through Freedom.* Stockholm: Swedish Ministry of Education and Science, 1992.

Chapter Nine

Lessons for Leaders

Terrence J. MacTaggart

Well, does governance restructuring work? It depends. With reasonably clear goals; with a thoughtful and inclusive planning process; with cooperation from the governor, the legislature, and powerful internal constituencies; and with skilled leadership at all levels, governance restructuring can help bring about very positive change. Unfortunately, these conditions are seldom present, at least all at once. It is no revelation to say that unfocused, ill-managed change will produce few good effects.

This chapter presents the lessons that leaders ought to heed before plunging ahead with governance restructuring. The first section offers guidance to policy makers—governors, legislators, key staff, heads of coordinating and regulating agencies—in the form of general insights on how restructuring actually works and what can be expected from it. The second section offers practical advice to leaders who are charged with implementing new systems of governance. Students of public policy and organizational change, especially those intrigued by the problem of implementing what seem to be good ideas, should find both sections of interest.

Lessons for Policy Makers

Higher education policy makers should keep the following eight points in mind when making policy decisions.

1. *By itself, governance restructuring doesn't improve anything.* At its core, governance restructuring means changing the answer to

the question, Who is in charge? Restructuring takes a variety of forms, including creating new governing boards with new authority over more institutions, establishing new regulatory offices or transferring authority from existing agencies and boards to new ones, instituting new executive offices in which greater authority is vested in a chancellor or secretary of education, and transferring authority back to colleges and universities from various agencies, boards, and executives. But other than altering careers and reconfiguring organizational charts, these changes do not in themselves improve the quality of education or make the allotment of resources more efficient or accomplish any other noble purpose. The altered power equation may create the possibility of improvement by removing territorial barriers, setting new levels of accountability and expectations for performance, and installing fresh leaders, but restructuring itself is only a first step.

This point may seem obvious, but it is worth emphasizing in light of the frustration expressed by governors and legislators over the slow pace of reform following restructuring. As Aims McGuinness points out, reorganization is a means, not an end (1994, p. 38). The underlying forces that cause unhappiness with higher education in the first place, in particular its celebrated resistance to change and to productivity improvements, persist oblivious to the upper levels of the organization. The governance restructuring discussed in this book should not be confused with reengineering in the corporate sector, which, as described by Hammer and Champy (1993), for example, seeks to alter the scope of work of employees, their relations with customers, and their discretion in making decisions. The change described here is more akin to putting in place a new board of directors and a new chief executive officer. Expected good results may come from the actions these people take but not merely from their installation.

2. *Cheaper and less dramatic alternatives to restructuring should be considered first.* Large-scale governance restructuring is expensive and time-consuming, and its probability of achieving intended outcomes is by no means assured. Policy makers have an arsenal of more focused alternatives that may better serve their ends. Specific legislation, for example, that requires colleges to offer courses in an underserved area or increase transfer between two- and four-year

institutions may meet resistance but is more likely to result in change more quickly than governance restructuring. Granting greater authority to coordinating boards or other state agencies to review and discontinue programs, approve budgets, and evaluate performance may achieve changes in accountability more quickly than restructuring. Use of the budget to punish, reward, and otherwise alter the behavior of institutions and systems is an ancient and sometimes effective way of securing change. The power of governors to select board members and at least influence the choice and responsibilities of new executives should not be underestimated, even though board members and executives, once appointed, are often insulated (and properly so) from direct gubernatorial control. Other ways of encouraging reform involve the use of such strategies as forming prestigious commissions to study and recommend solutions to serious problems in higher education, holding press conferences, making well-publicized addresses to community and academic leaders, and seizing other opportunities to mount the "bully pulpit."

Though these alternatives cannot guarantee success, they do offer advantages. If they don't work, focused changes like these are more easily undone than a massive restructuring. The results of targeted remedies can be more readily measured, and there are fewer unintended consequences.

3. *Restructuring will dominate the academic landscape, interrupt current operations, and drive out other worthwhile initiatives.* To paraphrase Chairman Mao, restructuring is not a dinner party. Because the careers, the personal agendas, and often the identities of public and academic leaders are at risk in this process, reorganization dominates the waking hours and creates sleepless nights for the leaders involved. Moreover, the sheer work required to discuss, decide on, and implement new policies, protocols, and management systems and to communicate with all the players can be exhausting. As a consequence, not much else gets done, or done well. An additional cost of restructuring is the opportunity cost of other worthwhile activities that must be forgone or minimized to get the tasks of reorganization accomplished. Thus a whole range of ongoing activities, from curriculum development to program review, will be done less well, and new initiatives, say, the installation of a telecommunications system or the development of a new

quality assurance program, are apt to be put on the back burner in the face of the insistent demands of restructuring.

4. *Higher, not lower, costs are likely, at least in the short run.* If an important goal of restructuring is to reduce cost, decision makers might be better advised simply to reduce funding. Howard Bowen's famous revenue theory of cost (1977) holds that higher education institutions will spend all the money they get, and hence the best way to reduce cost is to provide less money. Without discipline, restructuring will most often run up higher bills than whatever system preceded it. At least temporarily, there will be duplicative personnel costs. The outgoing employees will have rights to severance and notice provisions, and in any event some overlap in the changing of the guard is desirable. Reorganization often requires expensive new technical systems to assist in managing the new enterprise, or at the very least, existing accounting and communication systems may need to be modified to meet new demands. Unexpected new costs crop up. In Minnesota, for example, merger included transfer of technical college employees from local school districts to state service. The resulting salary differential, estimated at $26 million, came as a surprise to merger proponents. This cost was only partially offset by a 20 percent reduction in the size of the central staff.

5. *Lessons from corporate restructuring and private college mergers apply only partially in the public sector.* It is important that board members who also serve as corporate executives realize that because power is so dispersed in public higher education, the path to restructuring will be quite different from that in the corporate setting. The legislature, the traditions of faculty independence, and the political clout of unions representing faculty and other staff combine to stymie the kind of direct, top-down restructuring that prevails in for-profit organizations. Corporations enjoy much greater freedom in buying out redundant executives, for example, than colleges and universities, whose practices are open to public scrutiny and subject to state regulation.

Even mergers and acquisitions in the independent higher education sector differ from those on the public side. Certainly the absence of legislative participation is critical, as is the greater likelihood that employees will not be collectively organized. But the most striking difference is that restructuring involving two or more private colleges or universities is always a voluntary action of their respective boards, whereas restructuring on the public side is most often foisted on the institutions by governors or legislators. As Martin and Samels (1994) point out in their excellent study based largely on mergers of independent institutions, restructuring may produce a good deal of anxiety on the part of faculty, students, and alumni. But these combinations are free-will acts of the trustees intended to contribute to what Martin and Samels call the "mutual growth" of the partners (p. 5). On the public side, at least initially, boards and executives are more apt to see themselves as the victim of change rather than its master.

6.   *There is no "one size fits all" model for a restructured system; each must be uniquely designed.* The most obvious reason why each restructuring process and system must be uniquely tailored to its state context is that each state differs in resources, political history and values, public policy goals, and institutional strengths. A highly centralized system may make sense in a state that traditionally looks to strong bureaucracies to oversee public services. Another state's traditions of local control may encourage a restructuring effort that includes powerful local boards. Moreover, the times are changing. The current widespread interest in reforming, reinventing, and downsizing all government activities is affecting the shape of restructuring across the nation. This impulse to redefine government's role and reduce its scope will play out differently in the states.

The nation offers many examples of mature, stable, and effective systems—Wisconsin's and North Carolina's come to mind. These establishments did not begin as the well-functioning networks they are today; they developed over time. It is instructive to study the stages in their evolution and the qualities of their leaders in order to understand the process of restructuring, but their current pattern should not be the template for structure elsewhere.

7.   *Dramatic results from restructuring may be a long time coming.* Once the organizational chart has been redrawn, the more profound reforms or other changes that restructuring was supposed to achieve will occur only over time. The stubborn barriers to change that predated restructuring will still be operating. Moreover, the

process of installing new managers and a new management system itself is time-consuming. New bargaining unit agreements may need to be negotiated and technical systems implemented. All of this takes much more time than is usually anticipated. If the restructuring process managed to alienate substantial numbers of people, or a few key people, they will not aid in a rapid transformation. Even skilled new leaders will need time to learn the political and organizational territory and to establish sufficient confidence and trust in their staff in order to move forward successfully with major changes.

A review of the cases in this book indicates that North Dakota produced widespread alterations in fairly short order in part because the capable staff who planned restructuring remained in place to assist the new executive in carrying it out. In other instances, the supposed benefits of restructuring came slowly or not at all.

8. *Governance restructuring can bring about positive change over the long run.* In light of all this, policy makers may ask if restructuring is worth the effort. Such skepticism is healthy. Yet there are instances in which changing the way all or a large part of a state's public higher education system is governed is both inevitable and sensible. Where a reduction in resources or population dictates a permanent downsizing of the higher education establishment or where an existing system has become irredeemably dysfunctional in its essential management and advocacy tasks and its ability to respond to public expectations, restructuring is worth serious consideration. By bringing in new leaders with broader authority, restructuring can bring about changes that the prior regime would have resisted or lacked the power to enforce. Large-scale organizational change can reduce barriers to institutional cooperation that no amount of goodwill could have achieved. Carefully planned and executed by capable leaders, governance restructuring can help establish educational reforms and management improvements that would be stoutly resisted as long as old governance patterns and relationships remained in place.

The overriding point is that *governance reorganization is a radical treatment.* Policy makers should listen to Edmund Burke's advice in "Reflections on the Revolution in France" (1790): "It is with infinite caution that any man ought to venture upon pulling down an edifice which has answered in any tolerable degree [its intended social purposes]." But once restructuring has been decided on, there are a number of practical steps leaders can take to help ensure its success. These are the topic to which we turn next.

Lessons for Executives

Having been fired, libeled, investigated for a fraud he did not commit, and tortured, an energetic and courageous public servant wryly observed that nothing is more dangerous or uncertain than the attempt to bring about a new order of things. Physical torture aside, what applied to Niccolò Machiavelli in sixteenth-century Florence may well describe the condition of leaders in late-twentieth-century America who have accepted the task of bringing about complex change. Those who accept the challenge of restructuring higher education find that these jobs are personally taxing, turnover is high, and the probabilities tilt toward failure. The constraints are familiar—lack of resources, interest group politics, decentralized authority—and amply documented by Warren Bennis (1989), among others. So what does it take to succeed in restructuring public higher education?

This section focuses on the actions of executives in bringing about such change. It argues that successful leaders will take advantage of crisis but cautiously analyze their situation before developing a vision for the new order. Leaders play different roles in different organizational positions. They have to elicit very broad-based participation in the change yet assemble a close-knit team to carry it out. Most important, leaders must take the time to create an organizational climate that supports innovation.

1. *Crisis creates opportunity.* A crisis is essential to every significant restructuring. There is nothing like a sharp, well-publicized plunge in state revenues or a voter rejection of a tax increase to unite public opinion around the need for change, to establish a widespread sense of urgency, and to heighten the collective energy level. The sudden drop in the price of crude oil galvanized Alaskans as few other public events could. The swift onslaught of economic recession in the Northeast precipitated the restructur-

ing movement in Massachusetts, although there had been dissatisfaction with the status quo for years. An immediate crisis dislodges the keystone, usually the financial keystone, of the old structure and creates an appetite for change. In other words, crisis creates the opportunity and the necessity for leadership.

But a crisis that garners broad public awareness of the need for restructuring need not be sudden. The steady, gradual erosion of the population and the economy of North Dakota created the context for regent action, although the voters' refusal to endorse a tax increase triggered restructuring itself. In Maryland, public complaints about the "mess in Baltimore" had simmered for years. It took the momentum created by an energetic governor, not a new crisis, to initiate that state's profound restructuring. One of the axioms of change is that demographic instability—depopulation or shifts in population from the countryside to the cities—will create instability in the state's higher education structure (McGuinness, 1994, p. 7), and in its political life generally. This was certainly the case in Minnesota, where the gradual shift in population from the farms and small towns to the Twin Cities played a role in a merger that could balance the competition between urban and rural interests. Even in Minnesota, however, the recession of the early 1990s whetted legislative interest in change. With population shifts and economic downturns a sure part of the nation's future, we can be confident that instability and interest in restructuring higher education will be part of the future as well.

2. *Analysis, principles, and vision must come together.* If crisis creates the opportunity for change, the response of leaders to that crisis will determine if the change results in improvement. Panicked or rigid reactions guarantee failure. As the stories of restructuring in Alaska, Maryland, and Massachusetts illustrate, once momentum for whole change builds, it is very difficult to control. Thus it is all the more important that a cool analysis of the desired results be performed very early in the process.

Thinking about the new structure should yield a set of operating guidelines or principles that will shape the new system and help decide basic structural choices. North Dakota, for example, consciously subscribed to the principles of total quality improvement (TQI) in its effort to reinvest in higher education. Whatever

238 Restructuring Higher Education

reservations may have existed about TQI in the minds of academics, there was no doubt that the board and the chancellor were committed to them. Merger in Minnesota included a commitment to decentralized decision making that led to the downsizing of the central staff by 20 percent and the attempt to regionalize service delivery in ways that treated institutions as customers. The belief in the need for strong executive authority drove both Massachusetts and Maryland to create leadership positions reporting directly to the governor. Lack of publicly acknowledged organizational principles means that either inherited beliefs will operate or decisions will be made without much consistency. The oscillation from one view to another that characterized much of the merger planning in Alaska may be explained by the lack of clearly stated principles for organizational reform. The presence of such principles does not guarantee success. The principles may not fit the situation or may be poorly implemented. But the absence of operating principles makes failure more likely.

Vision, which at best is an elegantly simple, easily communicated, and inspirational message expressing the value of the change, should come only after attentive listening to the stated needs of stakeholders. The importance of a strong vision statement is emphasized in textbooks on change, but in higher education, this need is seldom satisfied. Vision can be a critical tool in mobilizing the people who are asked to make these difficult changes and in communicating to the larger public. Examples of vision statements include the Minnesota commitment to creating a system "relevant to students' futures" and North Dakota's "one-university system" to serve the state. In practice, the pressure to act on so many fronts during the restructuring process meant that neither of these vision statements was sold forcefully enough to become persuasive. It is generally true that leaders in restructuring have not had or devoted the resources necessary to convince members of the public that the change will improve their lives.

3. *Leaders must take on different roles.* The quality of leadership demanded by restructuring is different from that necessary during so-called normal times, although change is now so often the order of the day that it largely defines normality. Those whose fortune it is to lead in these high-pressure environments should heed James

Macgregor Burns's admonition that "the effectiveness of leaders must be judged not by their press clippings but by actual social change measured . . . by the satisfaction of human needs and expectations" (1978, p. 3). The acid test at the very end, after all the passion expended on the change has been spent, is simply, Are our fellow citizens really better off? (Kotter, 1990, p. 5).

Restructuring is more apt to be successful, that is, to leave the citizens better off, if its leaders—governors, legislators, board members, and executives—take responsibility to act only within firm boundaries. Governors and key legislators may need to initiate the change and give it basic direction, but they should soon relinquish control to a board of talented laypersons. This self-discipline is necessary because the political process through which political innovators must operate will inevitably distort their original intentions. The tortured path of the higher education reform bill in the 1988 Maryland legislature illustrates this point all too well. The periodic and ultimately ineffectual intrusions by the Alaska legislature probably damaged premerger planning. By contrast, the effectiveness of the North Dakota regents in planning and then overseeing the implementation of restructuring is a tribute both to that board and to the good sense of the legislature.

Boards that have been content to preside over a stable structure in which crisis and change are exceptions must reorient themselves if they are to lead in restructuring. This will be especially challenging if that restructuring diminishes their authority or alters their responsibility in a major way. Richard Novak's recommendations in Chapter Two will be useful to board members who must become more active in defining the shape of higher education in their state. In some instances, the board itself may need to be the architect of change; in others, it may rely on staff or a commission of distinguished citizens to present options. Boards may assist their replacements in learning their new role and should continue to look after the interests of the units they oversee up to the point at which they lose authority.

The executive who is charged by the board with carrying out the restructuring should see the task as a project to be accomplished within a fixed period of time, after which that leader will most likely leave. This sense of a well-defined mission to be concluded within a finite period of time may apply these days to campus and system leaders generally, but during restructuring, the term of office is apt to be both shorter and more intense. As the Minnesota experience revealed, restructuring stirs up strong negative human emotions among the people whose lives and careers are about to be altered. The wise and skillful leader can manage these passions, but only to a degree. The board must recognize that its executive will need a very specific charge, strong support in implementing that charge, and then a means of graceful exit once the job is done.

There is no shortage of views regarding the most effective style of leadership in higher education. Fisher (1984) argues for a charismatic leader who heightens his or her stature and effectiveness by maintaining distance from constituents. Green (1988) makes the case for a more comprehensive leadership style that includes a generous dose of managerial skill in order to survive in these times of tight economy. Chapter Six, focused on the human side of restructuring, underscores the need for leaders who are themselves mature, centered, and understanding of human behavior and emotion.

The fact that restructuring fails more often because of human foible than some technical lapse supports this last view. It is true that effective leaders must display many skills, but if the task is restructuring, the most effective leaders seem to be those who are masters of collaboration. As Chrislip and Larson put it in *Collaborative Leadership* (1994, p. xx), "Leaders who are most effective in addressing public issues are not the ones who know the most about the issues. Rather, they are the ones who have the credibility to get their right people together to create visions, solve problems, and reach agreements about implementable actions."

4.   *Constituent participation is essential.* Participation in the restructuring process should include as many people as possible, both from within the higher education community and from the mass of citizens who support this enterprise. As the Minnesota experience indicates, people want to be involved in planning and implementing the changes that will affect their working lives and are more apt to be constructive when they are fully engaged in that process. It was widely rumored in Massachusetts that key elements of the 1980 restructuring were hashed out on a junket to Ireland by three powerful politicians (Hogarty, 1988, p. 15). The instability of that reorganization was due in part to the secrecy that sur-

rounded its creation. As one observer of the Minnesota scene put it, "Don't copy the secrecy of the Manhattan Project unless you want an explosion!"

If it makes sense to include as many people in the change process as possible, it is also necessary to identify the key stakeholders and manage their relationships with the process. Key stakeholders are those who, by virtue of their power, position, visibility, talent, or unique knowledge, need to have and know that they have a voice in the decision making. Individuals in this category in virtually every state would include the governor; legislative leaders (especially the chairs of higher education and finance committees); representatives of the business and, often, the labor community; special interest group leaders such as representatives of minority advocacy groups, newspaper publishers, editors, and leaders in the electronic media; and prominent citizens. All members of the academic community qualify as stakeholders, and special attention must be paid to board members, chancellors, presidents, system and campus leaders, faculty and student leaders, bargaining unit heads, and others who influence opinion, such as alumni and donors. Collectively, the stakeholder pool should represent individuals who lead, speak for, or influence every citizen in the state and sometimes bordering states as well.

The audience is massive, and each individual stakeholder or group will have a different role in the process. Leaders of the restructuring, usually the executive, his or her staff, and board members, must carefully gauge the degree of influence and therefore the kind of communication that is appropriate for various sectors of the audience. For example, some stakeholders need merely be kept abreast of progress through formal communication such as newsletters and group meetings. Others who have the capacity to exert veto authority over key decisions merit the personal touch. This group must be brought to have faith in the direction of restructuring and the competence of its leaders. There is a fine art to assuring powerful state figures that the change process will lead to worthwhile results without inviting them to make decisions. This role may fall to the executive, but widely respected board members are often the best ambassadors for the change.

The days when the academic mystique afforded protection from public scrutiny are long gone. In most of the states examined in this book, restructuring occurred because the public, or large and influential segments of it, was unhappy with the costs, the results, or the management of this public enterprise. Taxpayers in North Dakota refused to pay more for this and other public goods. Scandals involving college presidents and highly visible political bickering among the regents in Massachusetts provided Governor Weld with much of the fuel he needed to initiate restructuring. In many states, the relatively benign interest in reinventing government, including public higher education, is yielding to a trenchant desire to downsize either the system itself or the amount of public support it receives.

This marked decline in the public's faith in the management of higher education means that leaders must engage in a serious public communication program as part of restructuring itself. A simple message that explains how the change will leave citizens generally and those who attend a college or university better off should be the core of the communication effort. None of the states studied for this book succeeded in this task, which meant that the public's skepticism grew as critical voices defined the character of the change. At the time of this writing, the merger debate in Minnesota focuses on its cost, as no one has argued persuasively for its benefit. To a large extent, the remarkable achievements of the North Dakota regents and their staff have gone unrecognized and may be unrewarded by the general public. The vehicles for effective communication to the public, from toll-free numbers to electronic town meetings to old-fashioned speeches in local high school gyms and college assembly halls, are readily available. Leaders of the next wave of restructuring would be well advised to use them.

5. *A restructuring team is indispensable.* Anyone who has read this far will realize that restructuring is a team sport. To carry out the bureaucratic changes alone requires a group of competent professionals. But to bring about the educational and administrative reform that is often an expected part of restructuring demands a team that shares the vision and is prepared for long hours and personal sacrifice. Restructuring in North Dakota worked well in large measure because the chancellor selected to implement the change inherited a senior staff that understood the tenets of the national

educational reform movement and was committed to its implementation. For all the confusion surrounding the staffing process in Minnesota, the interim chancellor there had the pick of talented administrators from three mature systems. By all accounts, the plan to reduce the core administration by 20 percent will not diminish the effectiveness of this group. Yet excessive downsizing can be debilitating. Too few people in the central office in Massachusetts has meant that the new system is unable to accomplish many of its basic goals.

Assembling the team to lead in restructuring differs from staffing the senior administration in a more static environment. As suggested earlier, because there is a high turnover rate in the position of leader of the new scheme, it is important that the senior staff be selected with an eye to their ability to serve for a number of years. The senior staff, or some of them, will likely be asked to remain to continue implementing the change after the leader has moved along. Because the staff are being asked to lead in implementing a change, not merely to manage the status quo, their qualifications should include imagination, toughness, and political savvy. Finally, they need to be able to function as a team that will be loyal to all of its members and the boss. This does not mean that strong personalities should apply elsewhere but rather that someone, either a chief of staff or the executive, must be able to orchestrate the various talents into an effective whole.

Selection of senior staff should follow a clear depiction of the specific agenda to be carried out. In all probability, for example, the financial officer will be asked to lead a downsizing of the financial and facilities management area and at the same time to implement a new electronic communications or accounting setup to accommodate the new system. In this situation, someone familiar with current systems but unable to envision new and less costly alternatives will not do.

Two functions often assigned lesser status in conventional environments merit greater prominence during restructuring. These are the lobbyist and the public communication expert. Whether the impetus for restructuring came from the statehouse or not, the process will be highly politicized. Advocates on all sides will attempt to use their political connections to achieve advantage. Being without a knowledgeable and respected lobbyist in these conditions is like going into battle blindfolded. The need to persuade the public at large of the benefits of the change requires more than a system press officer or publications staff. Since part of the restructuring process should be a systematic public communication campaign, competent leadership, probably with a political background, is very important.

6.   *Leaders must develop specific organizational virtues.* This section began with a reference to Machiavelli, that brilliant, much maligned public servant whose bequest to the world of public management and affairs was that we should see things as they are and not as we would like them to be. It is fitting that this chapter should close by introducing empirical research that finds that reinvention works best and lasts longest in organizations characterized by the communal virtues of honesty, trust, rigor, and faith. Paul Light, a former Washington staffer turned professor at the Hubert Humphrey Institute, a public policy think tank in Minnesota, has discovered an alarming failure rate among innovations in the public sector. As part of his research for a project called Reinventing Government Revisited, Light found that *at least* 50 percent of award-winning projects that were heralded in a given year either were never fully implemented or were discarded over the course of the next four or five years (Light, 1994).

The causes of failure will not surprise readers of this book. Leadership instability, public expectations for immediate results, failure to plan carefully, and lack of resources are among them. Light argues that what separates successful from failed innovations is not the merit of the original idea for change or reform—there are plenty of good ideas, he says—but rather the conditions of the organizational soil into which the idea is placed. Organizations that display certain virtues are hospitable to reinvention, innovation, and reform. In other words, the soil is more important than the seed.

Organizations that breed successful change are honest in their self-appraisals. They are unflinching in accepting responsibility for their mistakes and learn from them. These organizations take a rigorous look at what their clients, customers, and stakeholders say about their performance. This willingness to look outward in a regular and systematic way is accompanied by a readiness to adjust in response to the messages received from external groups. Internally, these enterprises that nourish positive change are characterized by a high level of trust. There is broad understanding that only the timid never err, that mistakes are to be expected and should be accepted for the lessons they offer. Finally, faith that actions taken today will yield results tomorrow or next week or next year permeates agencies that are congenial to new ideas.

Light's work focuses on nonacademic enterprises—the administration of a modern public zoo, for example, and the government of a large suburb. These organizations may not be a great deal less complex than systems of higher education. Other commentators on leadership and organizational behavior, the widely read Steven Covey (1989) among them, have drawn attention to the effectiveness of moral, principle-centered leadership, to use Covey's term, in bringing about change. What is remarkable about Light's findings, however, is that they grow out of a hard-nosed examination of successes and failures in specific agencies.

The lesson that restructuring is more apt to be successful where these virtues exist in the central administration is confirmed by the experiences presented in this book. By all accounts, the reform effort in North Dakota, the most successful example of restructuring described here, was characterized by these virtues. But the reason for emphasizing the importance of these virtues is to suggest that along with all the other skills necessary to successful restructuring—political insight, a bent for cool analysis and planning in the midst of crisis, the capacity to envision change and communicate its value to vastly different audiences—the leaders of change need to create an organization around them that displays the basic human virtues of honesty, rigor, trust, and faith.

References

Bennis, W. *Why Leaders Can't Lead: The Unconscious Conspiracy Continues.* San Francisco: Jossey-Bass, 1989.

Bowen, H. R. *Investment in Learning: The Individual and Social Value of American Higher Education.* San Francisco: Jossey-Bass, 1977.

Burns, J. M. *Leadership.* New York: HarperCollins, 1978.

Chrislip, D., and Larson, C. *Collaborative Leadership: How Citizens and Civic Leaders Can Make a Difference.* San Francisco: Jossey-Bass, 1994.

Covey, S. *The Seven Habits of Highly Effective People: Powerful Lessons for Personal Change.* New York: Simon & Schuster, 1989.

Fisher, S. *The Power of the Presidency.* New York: American Council on Education, 1984.

Green, M. F. *Leaders for a New Era: Strategies for Higher Education.* New York: American Council on Education, 1988.

Hammer, M., and Champy, J. *Reengineering the Corporation: A Manifesto for Business Revolution.* New York: HarperCollins, 1993.

Hogarty, R. "The Search for a Massachusetts Chancellor: Autonomy and Politics in Higher Education." *New England Journal of Public Policy,* 1988, *4*(2), 7–38.

Kotter, J. *A Force for Change: How Leadership Differs from Management.* New York: Free Press, 1990.

Light, P. "Reinventing Government Revisited." Speech to the Minnesota Citizens League, Aug. 10, 1994.

McGuinness, A. C., Jr. "The Changing Structure of State Higher Education Leadership." In A. C. McGuinness Jr., R. Epper, and S. Arredondo (eds.), *State Postsecondary Education Structures Handbook: State Coordinating and Governing Boards.* Denver, Colo.: Education Commission of the States, 1994.

Martin, J., Samels, J., and Associates. *Merging Colleges for Mutual Growth: A New Strategy for Academic Managers.* Baltimore, Md.: Johns Hopkins University Press, 1994.

Index

P

Pan American University, 36

Pandora, 198

Participation, in restructuring, 240–242

Peabody Institute, 162, 176

Pennsylvania, consolidation in, 24–25, 38

Perpich, R., 136

Peters, T., 6, 15

Petronius Arbiter, 198

Pew Charitable Trusts, 11

Pew Higher Education Research Program, 11, 15, 30, 49

Pew Higher Education Roundtable, 29

Phoenix, University of, 8

Planning retreats, for one-university system, 57, 70

Policy makers, lessons for, 230–236

Politics: in Alaska, 115–116, 118, 125, 127, 128; destabilizing, 7–8; in Maryland, 158–160, 173–175, 192–197; and multicampus systems, 207–210; and public stewardship, 99

Power, redistribution of, 194–195, 196–197

President's Commission on Higher Education, 20, 49

Prince Georges Community College, 162, 176

Productivity, learning, 11–12

Proprietary schools, competition from, 8

Puerto Rico, decentralization in, 31

Q

Quality. *See* Total quality movement

Quayle, D., 7

R

Redford, E. S., 194, 199

Reform: failure of, 12–14; restructuring role in, 187; status of, 10–12; support for, 69

Restructuring: aftermath of, 157–199; alternatives to, 40–42, 231–232; analysis of, 16–50; anti-authoritarian trend in, 9–10; case studies of, 51–199; concept of, 18–19; context for, 1–50; corporate, 6, 33–34, 35, 233–234; and costs, 124–125, 233; domination by, 232–233; and failure of reform, 3–15; and fiscal crisis, 101, 111–113, 236–237; human side of, 132–156; institutional, 29–30; lessons of, 201–246; as means, not end, 231; with multi-campus systems, 203–229; participation in, 240–242; and politics, 74–102; positive change from, 235–236; pressures for, 4–8; and reinventing government, 6–7, 29, 91, 204–205, 244; successful, 53–73; team for, 242–244; theories on, 194–197; time needed for, 234–235; unique design for, 234; as way of life, 103–131

Richardson, J., 55, 56–57

Robertson, P., 91, 92, 95

Robinson, E., 72, 73

Rogers, B., 113–114, 131

Rourke, E., 89

Rowinski, L., 105, 130

S

St. John's College, 162, 176

Saint Mary's College: funding for, 183, 185; governance of, 162, 171, 174, 176, 177; independence of, 10, 34, 161, 167, 188, 191, 198

St. Mary's Seminary and University, 176

Salisbury State University, 162, 176, 183

Samels, J. E., 37, 49, 234, 246

Saxon, D., 84, 88–89

Schaefer, W. D., 157, 160, 165, 172, 178, 180, 184, 188, 193, 197

Schick, E. B., 21, 22, 23, 24, 32, 41, 49, 204, 229